IELTS 应试指南

陈卫东　编著

北京语言文化大学出版社

（京）新登字 157 号

图书在版编目（CIP）数据

IELTS 应试指南/陈卫东编著.
-北京：北京语言文化大学出版社，2000
ISBN 7-5619-0880-6
Ⅰ.I…
Ⅱ.陈…
Ⅲ.英语-水平考试-自学参考资料
Ⅳ.H310.41
中国版本图书馆 CIP 数据核字（2000）第 41852 号

责任印制：乔学军
责任校对：苏 琰
出版发行：北京语言文化大学出版社
（北京海淀区学院路 15 号 邮政编码 100083）
印 刷：北京北林印刷厂
经 销：全国新华书店
版 次：2000 年第 10 月第 1 版 2000 年 10 月第 1 次印刷
开 本：787 毫米×1092 毫米 1/16 印张：17
字 数：271 千字 印数：1-20000
书 号：ISBN 7-5619-0880-6/H·0066
定 价：26.00 元

出　版　说　明

自IELTS考试在我国实施以来，北京语言文化大学一直在举办IELTS应试培训，至今已有十多年的历史，并出版了一套《IELTS考试技能训练教程》，包括听力、阅读、口语、写作四本。这套教程的作者都曾专赴英国进行IELTS考试培训进修，是中英IELTS合作项目组的成员，十多年来一直从事IELTS考试培训教学。因此，这套教程以其针对性强、实用性强等特点深受广大IELTS考生的欢迎。

近年来，随着加拿大、新西兰、澳大利亚等国相继将IELTS考试成绩作为衡量非英语国家留学生及移民英语水平的标准，IELTS考生，尤其是准备申请移民的IELTS考生人数激增。为了满足不同英语基础及不同目的的IELTS考生的需求，我们对《IELTS考试技能训练教程》进行了修订，并新增了几个IELTS考试用书的品种，供读者根据自己的实际情况选用。这次新增的品种包括：

《IELTS应试指南》

《IELTS阅读模拟试题集(General Training)》

《IELTS听力模拟试题集》

《IELTS词汇学习手册》

其中前三册仍由《IELTS考试技能训练教程》的作者编写；《IELTS词汇学习手册》由具有丰富词典编纂经验及英语教学经验的史宝辉教授编写。书中内容经过反复筛选、精心推敲，以确保其既涵盖IELTS考试的重点，又针对IELTS考生的难点。相信我们重新修订的《IELTS考试技能训练教程》和新增加的几本IELTS考试用书一定能帮助您高效、有的放矢地备考IELTS，并使您的IELTS考试成绩有一个新的飞跃。

北京语言文化大学出版社

前　言

《IELTS 考试技能训练教程·阅读》出版已两年多了，在这两年里，我继续从事 IELTS 的考试培训，自然也要关注该考试的各种发展、变化。北京语言文化大学出国人员培训部的雅思课程按考试的几个分项设听、说、读、写几门课，课程的设置、教学内容得到了学员的认同。但常有其他不能参加我部培训班的人询问：是否有综合教材。

我和几位同事先后共出版了六七本教材，都是多年教学的经验积累，但基本上内容专一，每人仅关注几个分项考试中的某一项。我先后参加过三次考试，又多年负责整个培训项目，自然不仅关注阅读，也注重其他三个部分。经过反复考虑，又在教研室和出版社的游说下，终于下决心写一本综合性的教材。

此教材分五个部分，分别介绍了考试的综合情况和听、说、读、写几个分项部分。各部分均有练习题，其中一部分设有题解。

在教学中常被学生问到"应试技巧"及如何提高某项能力，已尽我所能在书中有所表述，但仍感到离考生及学员的期望甚远，主要因为对语言学习有些很不"入时"的看法。

许多读者都知道，有些英语学习方法颇受学生的关注，其热烈程度不亚于一些经实践证明根本无效的健身、减肥方法。这些方法之所以有轰动效应，主要是由于不客观的宣传和盲目轻信所致。语言学习是来不得虚伪的，没有捷径，如果那个老师说他有什么灵丹妙药，最好别信。

IELTS 是一个注重能力的考试，只会出现英语不错的人因不熟悉考试形式而考不好，绝不会出现水平不高的人因掌握了一些"窍门"而取得好成绩。因此建议读者从个人实际水平出发，设立能够达到的目标，通过多做练习、了解题型特点来向自己的目标努力。

这也就是我的观点不"入时"之处，也许读者会有完全不同的看法。无论如何，大家提高英语水平，在考试中取得好成绩一直是我们的希望。

陈卫东

2000 年 7 月

目　录

第一章 IELTS 考试简介

一、报名

随着 IELTS(雅思)考试的社会需求的增加,在我国的一些大城市相继出现了雅思考试的报名点(见附录 2)。由于雅思考试的听、读试卷由人工阅判(TOEFL等考试是由机器阅卷),又有一对一的口试和四百词左右的作文,每次考试所能接纳的考生有限。考生在决定何时参加考试后应尽快与报名点联系,以免因报名额满而影响考试计划。很多考生因一个报名点的名额已满而不得不到另一个城市报名,也有一些考生不得不推延考试时间。报名时,应出示身份证(或护照)原件,交 1150 元报名费,按考点规定的时间及时将填好的报名表和三张证件照片交回到报名点。报名表须由考生本人填写。

二、考试

考试各部分的顺序及时间请见图 1。

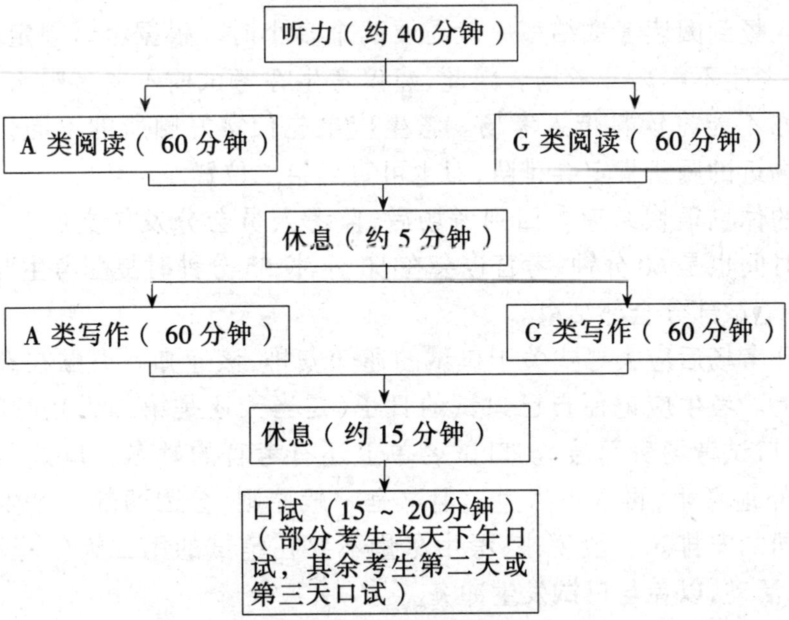

图 1　考试流程

考生在考试当天须携带身份证原件、准考证、报名费收据、数根 HB 铅笔和一块橡皮，在规定的时间之前到考场门外等候。然后由考官唱名，考生逐个验证入场。入场后考生可依次找到自己的座位。考场大多是语言实验室，均使用有线耳机。桌上有一张印有考生姓名（拼音）、考号、生日和类别（Academic 类还是 General Training 类）的纸条。待全体考生就座后，主考官会做一番介绍，之后发答题卡和听力考试的试题本（booklet for the listening test）。

答题卡的正面用来答听力题，背面用来答阅读题。在答题卡的正面应填写考生姓名（拼音）和考号，并用铅笔将考试年、月、日和表示 Version number 的长方形小框涂黑。Version number 是每套题的编号，考官会告诉考生当天使用的听力题的编号是多少。之后开始听力考试。听力考试结束后由监考人员收走听力试题本，然后发阅读试题本。考生须在答题卡背面填写 Version number，标明类别，然后开始阅读考试。

特别值得一提的是，有试题内容的听力磁带约为 30 分钟，做题时先将答案写在试题本上。磁带上的试题内容放完后，考生有 10 分钟的时间将答案眷写到答题卡上。阅读考试的答题则应直接写在答题卡上。阅读考试的时间为 60 分钟，考生不再有额外的时间眷写答案。在做阅读题时，可以用笔在试题本上划线或做标记，这一点与 TOEFL 考试不同（TOEFL 考试不允许在试题本上做标记）。考官会在阅读考试进行到 50 分钟和 55 分钟时提醒考生时间。

阅读考试结束后由监考人员将试题和答题卡收走。清点无误后全体考生退场，有五分钟的休息时间。

从等候入场到阅读考试结束一般需要两个多小时。根据考试规定，在这段考试时间内，考生不得离开考场。因此，建议考生在考试前不要多喝水，以免有“急”。考生亦不能将饮料带入考场。考生应事先侦察好厕所的不同位置。休息期间离考场近的厕所肯定会排队，考生可直奔第二位置。

五分钟的休息很快结束。回到考场后，监考人员会分发作文题和作文纸。作文考试的时间也是 60 分钟，考官也会在 50 分钟、55 分钟时提醒考生时间。60 分钟后收卷，笔试部分全部结束。

考生离开考场后应去寻找关于口试的通知安排，该通知一般贴在离考场不远的布告栏上。考生应记住自己口试的日子（是当天还是第二天）、时间（几点几分）、地点（口试考场房间号）。口试名单上还有考官的姓名。口试顺序的安排一般是先外地考生，再本市考生。但这是一般原则，会因两部分考生的比例不同而有不同的安排。一般说来，考生尽量不要在笔试的第二天（一般是星期日）安排其他活动，以免与口试发生冲突。

口试时一定要提前半小时左右在考场附近等候，因为前面的考生可能会迟到，也可能会因笔试考得不理想而放弃口试。如果出现这种情况，后面的考生能够及时补上，避免考场出现空档，节省了大家的时间，特别是节省了考官的时间，这对让考官有个好心情也许会有点帮助。

三、考试成绩

考试结束后四周左右，考生可持身份证原件到考点领取成绩。去领成绩之前最好先打电话询问，以确定成绩是否已到。考点只回答成绩是否已到，不回答具体得分。考生亦可通过考点的网页了解成绩单是否已到考点。考生也可以在报名或考试时留下写好地址、贴足邮票的信封，由考点工作人员将成绩单寄出。

每位考生只能收到一份成绩单，收到后一定要妥善保存。考试报名费包含由英国使馆文化处将三份成绩单寄往用分单位的费用。各用分单位（如大学或移民局）只认可由英国使馆文化处寄出的成绩单。由考生陈述的分数或由考生寄出的成绩单复印件不被视为有效的成绩证明。

英国使馆文化处会在考试后两年内应考生的要求寄出成绩单（超出三份后考生需交纳费用，每份 50 元）。两年之后考生的成绩将不被认为是考生当前英语水平的反映。换言之，英国使馆文化处认为考试成绩的有效期为两年，两年之后则失效，也就不会再出具考生的成绩证明。但考试成绩的有效期更取决于用分单位的规定。比如英国的大学一般认为考试成绩有效期为一年。雅思考试被越来越多的部门接受，考生如欲了解成绩的有效期，应向用分单位询问。

四、分数的换算

雅思考试分听、读、写、说四个部分，成绩用 band（段）表示，每部分的满分为 9 段。（为更加符合汉语的用法，下文中将用“分”取代“段”。）总分是四部分成绩的平均。听力和阅读可以有 0.5 分，如 5.5 分、6.5 分等。写作和口试只有整数分。计算总分的方法是四个部分的成绩相加除以 4，如遇小数则或舍或入（0.5 除外）。小数为 0.25、0.375、0.75、0.875 时向上进一个分数段。例如：$(6+6+6+7)\div 4=6.25$，总成绩为 6.5 分；$(5.5+6+6+7)\div 4=6.125$，总成绩为 6 分。

听力和阅读考试均为 40 道题（也有个别试卷多一两题或少一两题）。分数的算法并不是 40（题）÷ 9（段）= 4.4（每一段的跨度），而是用一套很独特的方法来计算。

每一套听力或阅读题在正式投入使用之前均已在某一群体中进行过试测。北京语言文化大学出国人员培训部的公派出国培训生就曾经被剑桥大学用来试测雅思试题。试测结果不仅是对试题进行修正的依据，也是每套题的分数换算依据。换言之，每套题根据试测的结果有自己的正确题数与分数段之间的换算表，而没有一个统一的换算公式。换算方法大致体现以下两个原则：

1. 分数高到一定程度或低于一定程度时，分数段之间的差异不再具有明显意义。例如8段和9段之间,2段和3段之间。前两个分数段均已大幅度超出用分单位所规定的分数。以到英国或澳大利亚读研究生为例,大多数学校要求总分6.5。后两个分数段离任何用分单位所规定的起点都相差甚远。因此,这两种情况每个分数段之间的跨度也就是一两道题。

2. 最具有表明考生英语水平与实际生活、学习所要求的英语水平之间的差异的分数段应有较好的区分度。换言之,在5段到7段之间,每一段的跨度几乎是上述4.4跨度的两倍。图2大致表明正确题数与分段数之间的关系。

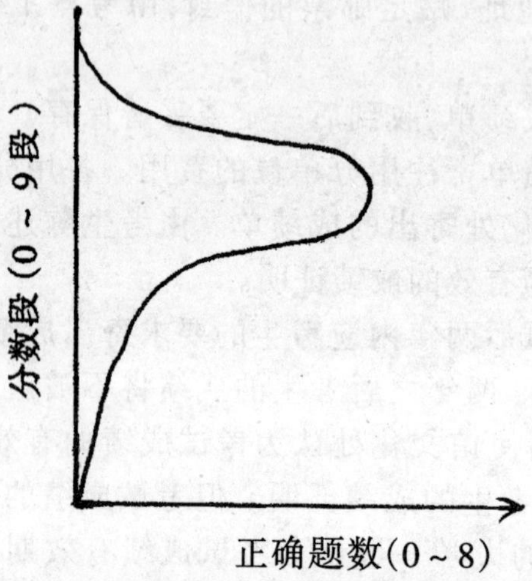

图2　正确题数与分数段换算示意

由于有这样一种评分思想,对大多数具备一定实力的考生来说,如果想在听力和阅读上提高一段,就要多做对七八道题。这样一个台阶的升幅是相当大的,迈上一个台阶实在不容易。

根据这样的评分思想,每套题有自己的分数换算表,用调节此换算表来调节由于试卷难易不等而造成的成绩不等的幅度。以下是较有意义的分数段与正确题数的换算方法,此方法适用于一般难度的试题,对于高于或低于一般难度的题,此表有相应的变化。

	5段	6段	7段
听力	18~24	25~31	32+
A类阅读	18~24	25~31	32+
G类阅读	22~28	29~35	36+

表1　5段、6段和7段所需要的正确题数

说明:不知出于何种原因,剑桥大学考试中心从未将较细致的正确题数与分数段之间的换算方式公布于众。表 1 的内容是基于我部十多年的培训经验,特别是基于对考生水平及考生的雅思考试成绩的分析而作出的,未必十分精确,但基本反映实际评分标准。

听力和阅读考试均设有标准答案。评判时考官仅需客观地在考生的答案和标准答案之间做对比,相同则为正确,不同则为错误。这种评判方法称为客观评判,分数段可以定得较细致,因此有 0.5 段。而口试和作文则要求考官根据主观印象去评分,这样的评判方法称为主观评判。主观评判会因考官之间的看法不同而给予同一份作文或同一考生的口试不同的分数。因此,主观评判的线条较粗,只设整数分数段。如果考官训练有素,掌握相对统一的标准,这种只设整数分数段的做法应较好地避免同样水平的考生得到不同分数的现象。

五、考官

雅思考试的考官(examiners)均为母语为英语、有海外英语教学经验的人。如果这样的人想成为雅思考官,他们首先要向英国使馆文化处申请,然后自学一套由剑桥大学考试中心提供的培训教材,再参加一次考官考试,如通过就可以获得雅思考官的证书,“持证上岗”。他们虽然都经过了选拔、培训、考试,但在实际工作中难免会有差异,个别考生的成绩可能会受到这种差异的影响。例如,有 80 多名经我国教育部门严格选拔参加出国培训的大学教师和科技人员,他们在英语水平(均达到 EPT 考试 110 分)、脱产培训时间(四个月)等多方面情况相近,英语水平近似,因公派出国需要在脱产培训结束时参加雅思考试。当时有四名雅思考试的考官对他们进行口试,每位考官考 20 人左右。他们中 20%左右的人未能达到所要求的平均分数段而不得不再次参加脱产培训。这批“二进宫”的考生几乎全都被同一考官口试。有很充分的理由认为,这位考官在执行口试标准时明显“严”于其他三位考官。这个例子说明,在掌握评判尺度时,考官之间有时会有很大的差别。

主观评判虽没有标准答案,但每位考官手里都有一份 band description。这是一份用文字来描述每个分数段的考生所应具备的能力和做出的表现。那么 band description 是如何定义每个分数段的呢?大家可记住一点:在口试中,只要不出现“交流中断”(communication breakdown),6 段基本上有保证。“交流中断”指口试中的双方听不懂对方或考生答非所问。作文的情况也类似,只要文章完整,论点、论据清楚,字数不明显少于要求,即可得 6 段。

六、能力与应试技巧

近年来一直在英语教学中占主流地位的交际教学法(communicative approach)也一直在影响着语言测试。这种理论认为语言是用来交流的,只要完成了交流的任务,语言这一交流工具所应发挥的作用就得到了发挥。出于这种思想,口语中语音、语调的缺陷,作文中的拼写错误及不伤大雅的语法错误都不对评判造成实质性影响。当然这是相对于考生的综合能力而言。也就是说,如果一个考生可以用英文去"侃"某个题目,如大城市交通阻塞的原因、解决问题的出路等,他在语音、语调、语法等方面的不完善不会影响他的得分。同样,一个考生的作文如果论点清楚,论据有力,有一定的思想深度,那么个别的拼写错误和语法、用词方面的不当也不会影响他的得分。因此,考生在准备考试时,应分清主次,把时间和精力放在主要问题上,如口语的连贯表达,写作中对论点、论据的陈述等,而不必在拼写或是讲英音还是讲美音这样的支节问题上浪费时间。

一般来说,能力考试是无法突击准备的。短期的应试培训班的作用只能是让考生熟悉题型,了解自己的能力,做到知己知彼。任何高于这一点的目标都很难达到。几乎所有的应试培训班都打出"传授应试技巧"的旗号。但是,在考生做过几套模拟试题、了解了题型特点之后,这些培训班还有多少敢拿到桌面上来的"技术"可以向学员传授?我部有十多年雅思应试培训的历史,在方法、教材等方面均有一定的积累,而对这个问题却从不敢夸口。原因很简单,雅思考试是能力考试,而能力的提高是一个缓慢、甚至是痛苦的过程。许多所谓的技巧均以能力为前提。举个简单的例子:大名鼎鼎的马俊仁教练应有很多奇招,否则马家军的女弟子们怎么会跑出那么出色的成绩?但是这些招只有在诸如王军霞那样的人身上才能得以发挥,随便在街上拉一个年龄、身高、体重都相同的姑娘,让马教练耳语几句,就能跑出好成绩吗?当然不能。王军霞等人达到能够使用马教练的"招"的水平之前所付出的艰辛常人难以想像。英语也是这样。以提高阅读速度为例,许多学员都希望他们的老师能传授给他们一些"招"。但细想一下,影响阅读速度的因素很多,如词汇量、语法知识、文章的难度(是原文还是经过改写的)、题材是否熟悉、体裁如何(是新闻,还是小说或科技文章等)、个人的知识面等等。既然有这么多的因素在发挥不同程度的作用,哪个老师又能有奇招呢?再比如,许多阅读课本都有一定的篇幅讲不同的阅读技巧,比如"How to guess the meaning of a new word from the context"(如何根据上下文猜某个生词的意思)。这真的是一个老师可以向学生传授的"招"吗?如果能看懂上下文,只是某句中有个别生词,那么不用老师教,学生也会去猜。而且如果这个学生再熟悉一点构词法的原理,猜出这个词的大概意思是有可能的。但设想一下,如果文章是一篇英国的某个外科大夫发表在《脑外科学报》上的论文,即使是让那些编写上述阅读教材的老师们去现身说法,猜句中的某个生词的意思,恐怕也是强人所难。因此,还是那句老话:熟能生巧。这一点不仅适用于阅读,也适用于听、说、写。

第二章 听力考试

一、听力考试简介

雅思的听力考试分为四个部分(sections),第一部分是一篇对话。第四部分是一篇有一定长度的报告,主题可以是某个历史人物,或以社会、环保、健康为主题,长度为四至五分钟,分两部分播放,中间有用来检查前四五题和预览后四五题的时间。第二、三部分可能都是对话,也可能一篇是对话,另一篇是独白。如果是独白,它所谈论的内容更贴近生活,长度也较第四部分稍短。

这四部分的题数基本相等,即每部分有十道题左右。前三部分之间没有明显的难度、长度差异,第四部分最长、最难。每一道题的分量相同,每道题非对即错,不会因为答对一半而得 0.5 分,部分答对统统被视为错。

雅思的听力考试非常独特,完全不同于广大考生熟悉的诸如 TOEFL 或四、六级考试中的听力部分。其最独特之处在于,考生要边听、边看、边写。这个特点使得很多听力水平较高、能在其他听力考试中取得出色成绩的人感到不适应,因而无法获得好成绩。对于广大考生来说,解决这一问题需要两方面的能力:一是综合的听力,这种能力是长时间注意听力培养,特别是在大量地做了不同类型的高级听力练习之后的积累。这种能力不是靠上几十学时的强化班就能获得的。所谓高级听力练习,主要是指诸如原文广播(正常语速)那样难度的材料,而不是美国之音 special English 的难度。另一方面就是耳、眼、手共用的能力。这种能力是可以在短期内获得较大幅度提高的,但前提是考生已具备第一种能力。

雅思听力考试到底有什么样的特点,考生可以通过做一两套模拟题就了解得很透彻。接下来就是总结经验,摸索规律,做大量听、看、写同时进行的练习。目前,市场上除有限的几本雅思考试辅导材料外,与雅思听力考试在难度和题型上近似的材料几乎没有。因此,要做大量的练习有难度,因为所有能买到的听力模拟题加起来不过就只有 20 小时左右的内容,这使得准备这个考试更难。

雅思考试的听力部分,从十多年前开始设计一直到今天,都体现了一个要求:边听边做笔记。这个要求来自对考生将来出国后所实际面临的语言环境的分析。首先,考生到英国(或其他英语国家)所要听的内容常常是有上下文,有相当长度的内容,而不是没有上下文的单句或是只有一来一往的对话(这种形式的听力练习较为考生熟悉)。另外,雅思考试的大部分考生是留学类考生,(在我国近几年中有大量的移民类考生,但就全球来讲,General Training 的考生只占很小的比例),听课、做笔记是在英语国家学习的最常见的形式之一,在语言水平考试中自然要体现考生将来在这方面的需要。根据这两个特点,考生可以自己选一些有长度、有难度的材料来练习,最常见的就是新闻广播,重点练习记笔记。

设计雅思考试的最核心的几位英国人曾与我国教育部在"全国公共英语等级考试"项目中有过密切的合作,在这个简称为 PETS 的考试中,多处体现着雅思考试的思想。PETS 四级和五级的听力材料可用来做雅思听力考试的"热身"练习。

雅思考试的特点之一是题型、题数不固定,用哪类题型主要取决于原材料的特点。所谓题数,并不是指总题数,而是指听力或阅读考试中各部分中题数的分布。由于这两个特点,考生不得不花时间去听或读 directions(指令)。因此,考生应尽早地明确 task,即在答题时要选择字母还是在卷面上填写数字、人名或是其他内容。这是考生要注意的第一个方面。

另一个值得注意的方面就是要充分利用放试题录音的空白时间。在开始播放与答题有关的录音内容之前或播放完这些内容之后,根据指令,考生有 30 到 60 秒的时间预览问题,检查答案。要充分利用这段时间认真阅读试卷上的文字,根据文字内容推测 1)录音内容的大概范畴;2)答题的形式(填空、选择等)。在这两方面获得的信息量直接与答题正确率有关。

填空题有几种情况:1)填写数字(电话号码、人数、产量等);2)填写年、月、日、星期;3)填写人名、地名;4)填写关键词。

数字一直是很多考生的弱点,除了多练没有更好的"招"。根据个人经验,人脑内似乎有一个语言转换开关。具有一定英语水平的人,这个开关的转换可能在瞬间完成,具体的例子就是英汉互译。但就数字来说,这个开关就不是那么瞬时,而是有一定的惯性。如果一直在用中文思考时突然听到一串英文的数字,这个反应时间比听到一句话的反应要慢。如果这是个普遍现象,那就应该在正式考试之前突击几分钟数字听力练习。在雅思考试中,凡是答案为电话号码的题,在原文(即录音)中总是要重复一遍的,但其他的数字是不会重复的。

在碰到与日期有关的问题时,一定要用简写形式来记录,也不妨用中文。例如,将听到的 September 写成 9,将听到的 Wednesday 写成三,如果花时间去拼写这两个单词,可能会因脑和手被占用而听不到其他一些关键内容。

答案涉及人名、地名时有两种情况。一种是试题设计者认为考生可能会遇到拼写困难,会在录音中逐字母拼写一个单词,如澳洲城市 Brisbane,录音会再将该词的八个字母念一遍。这种根据字母来听写单词的形式很少见于雅思考试以外的练习,考生需要一定时间来熟悉这种形式。另一种则是常见的人名(如 John, Susan, Peter, Maria)或地名(如 London, Australia)。这样的词在录音中既不会像读电话号码那样再重复一遍,也不会读这些词的拼写。遇到这样的题可采取上述对付月份、星期的做法。

普通单词的填空也要先用省略的方法做,待录音内容结束后,再根据略填的信息完整地拼写该单词。

二、听力模拟试题一

INTERNATIONAL ENGLISH LANGUAGE TESTING SYSTEM

PRACTICE TEST (Version One)

LISTENING

TIME: 30 MINUTES
NUMBER OF QUESTIONS: 40

Instructions

You will hear a number of different recordings and you will have to answer questions on what you hear.

There will be time for you to read the instructions and questions, and you will have a chance to check your work.
All recordings will be played **ONCE** only.

The test is in four sections. Write all your answers in the listening question booklet.

At the end of the real test you will be given ten minutes to transfer your answers to an answer sheet.

Now turn to Section 1.

Section 1 *Questions 1 – 11*

Questions 1 – 4

Listen to the conversation between Lily and her friend. Circle the letter that answers the following questions.

Example:

Why is Lily going to buy a compact disc?

A. She enjoys listening to music.

C. She collects albums of a particular star.

Ⓑ She is going to give it to her brother.

D. She needs it for the coming new term.

1. What kind of music does Lily's brother like?

A. Classical. C. Opera.

B. Musical. D. Pop.

2. What kind of music does Lily like?

A. Classical. C. Opera.

B. Musical. D. Pop.

3. What has Lily decided to buy for her brother?

A. Romeo and Juliet. C. Carmen.

B. Oklahoma. D. West Side Story.

4. How much is Lily going to pay?

A. 24 dollars. C. 15 dollars.

B. 18 dollars. D. 9 dollars.

Questions 5 – 8

Fill in the blanks with ***NO MORE THAN THREE WORDS OR A NUMBER*** *for each answer.*

The College Badminton Club

Accepts both Students and ...(5)... .

Membership Fees: ...(6)... per college term.

Beginners' level meets on Thursday;

Intermediate level meets on ...(7)...;

Advanced level meets on Monday.

All meetings are at ...(8)... o'clock.

Membership fees cover equipment, court, drinks.

Registration will close soon!

Questions 9 – 11

Fill in the form with ***NO MORE THAN THREE WORDS OR A NUMBER*** *for each answer.*

Registration Form for the College Badminton Club

Last Name:	...(9)...	First Name:	...Lily...
Address:	22...(10)...Avenue, Old Town		
Home Phone:	2252355		
Level:	...(11)...		

Section 2 *Questions 12 – 19*

Fill in the blanks in the sentences below with **NO MORE THAN THREE WORDS** *for each answer.*

12. Australians consume ____________ tons of aspirin each year.

13. Aspirin has side effects but they are usually ____________.

14. Aspirin is the only drug that works for people suffering from ____________.

15. Aspirin was first sold in Germany in the year ____________.

16. Aspirin became available in Australia in the year ____________.

17. Aspirin relieves pain by slowing down the formation of certain ____________.

18. Aspirin is irritating to the ____________.

19. One way of taking aspirin is to ____________ the tablets and swallow them with water.

Section 3 *Questions 20 – 30*

Questions 20 – 22

Fill in the missing information about Mrs. Smith's children, using ***NO MORE THAN THREE WORDS OR A NUMBER*** *for each answer.*

Number of children	(20)
Age	(21)
Sex	(22)

Questions 23 – 24

Answer the questions using ***NO MORE THAN THREE WORDS OR A NUMBER*** *for each answer.*

23. How many bedrooms does Mrs. Smith want? ______________

24. How long does Mrs. Smith plan to stay in the city? ______________

Questions 25 – 29

Fill in the missing information about the flat the manager is telling Mrs. Smith about, using ***NO MORE THAN THREE WORDS OR A NUMBER*** *for each answer.*

Number of bedrooms	(25)
Monthly rent	(26)
In case of breaking anything	(27)
Rent includes	(28)
Rent does not includes	(29)

Question 30

Circle the letter that correctly indicates the location of the building that Mrs. Smith will visit.

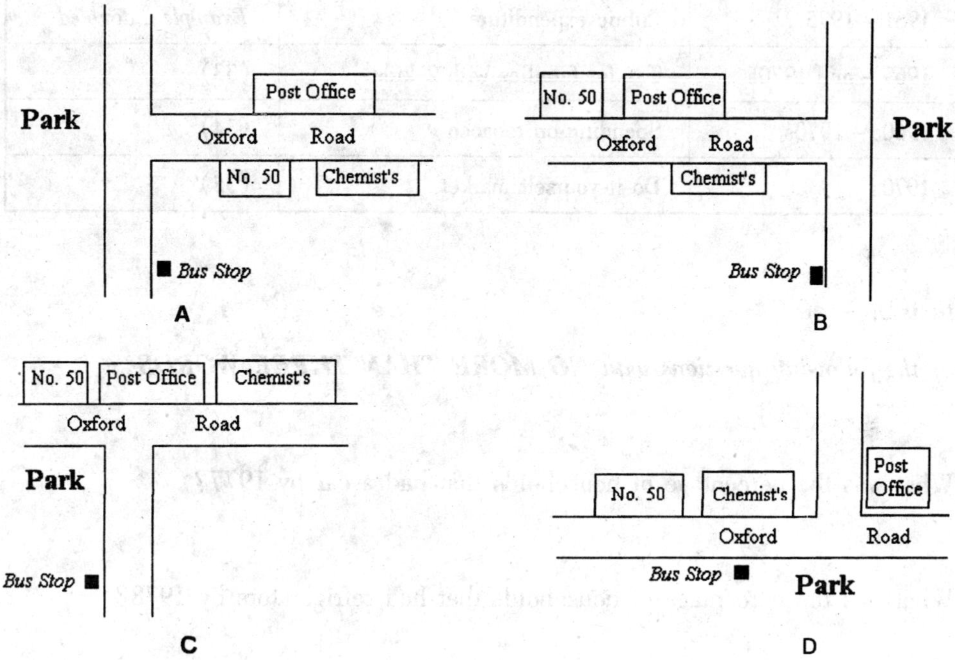

Section 4 *Questions 31 – 40*

Questions 31 – 32

Indicate the other two of the three changes since 1951, using **NO MORE THAN THREE WORDS** *for each answer.*

Young people could afford radios and	*Example*: *cars*, *houses*
Woman had more opportunities for	(31)
People had more time for	(32)

Questions 33 – 35

Indicate the changes during the following periods, using ***NO MORE THAN THREE WORDS*** *for each answer.*

1961 – 1975	Public expenditure	*Example: doubled*
1969 – mid 1970s	Tax for families with 2 kids	(33)
1960s – 1970s	Spending on tobacco	(34)
1970s	Do-it-yourself market	(35)

Questions 36 – 40

Answer the following questions with ***NO MORE THAN THREE WORDS.***

36. What was the percentage of households that had a car by 1977?

37. What was the percentage of households that had refrigerators by 1978?

38. What was the percentage of women who went to hospital to give births in 1977?

39. By 1978, the British people ate more chickens but what did they eat less?

40. When was colour television introduced to British households?

三、听力模拟试题二

INTERNATIONAL ENGLISH LANGUAGE TESTING SYSTEM

PRACTICE TEST (Version Two)

LISTENING

TIME: 30 MINUTES
NUMBER OF QUESTIONS: 40

Instructions

You will hear a number of different recordings and you will have to answer questions on what you hear.

There will be time for you to read the instructions and questions, and you will have a chance to check your work.
All recordings will be played **ONCE** only.

The test is in four sections. Write all your answers in the listening question booklet.

At the end of the real test you will be given ten minutes to transfer your answers to an answer sheet.

Now turn to Section 1.

Section 1 *Questions 1 – 11*

Questions 1 – 5

Listen to the conversation between Jean and a man who works at a sports centre. Fill in the blanks with ***NO MORE THAN THREE WORDS OR LETTERS.***

Sports Smart Swimming Pool

Example:

Opening time: Mon. Tue. Wed. Fri.: from 9 am to *9 pm.*

Thur.: from (1)______ to 9 pm

Sat. Sun.: from 9 am to (2)______

Cost: two dollars per person

(3)______ dollars for students

one dollar for old persons

Introductory session: (4)______ dollars

Normal session: one dollar

Season ticket: (5)______ dollars (valid for three months)

Questions 6 – 10

Circle the correct letter.

6. What is the time for Jean's introductory session?

A. Wednesday 4:30 pm.   B. Wednesday 7:00 pm.

C. Thursday 6:45 pm.   D. Thursday 7:15 pm.

7. What is Jean's family name?

A. K-U-R-A-C-H-E-K.   B. K-A-C-H-U-R-E-K.

C. K-E-C-H-A-R-U-K.   D. K-U-C-H-A-R-E-K.

8. Which map correctly indicates the location of Sports Smart Center.

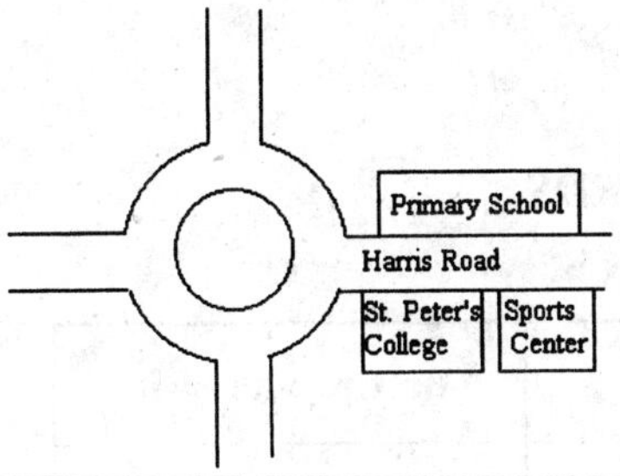

A

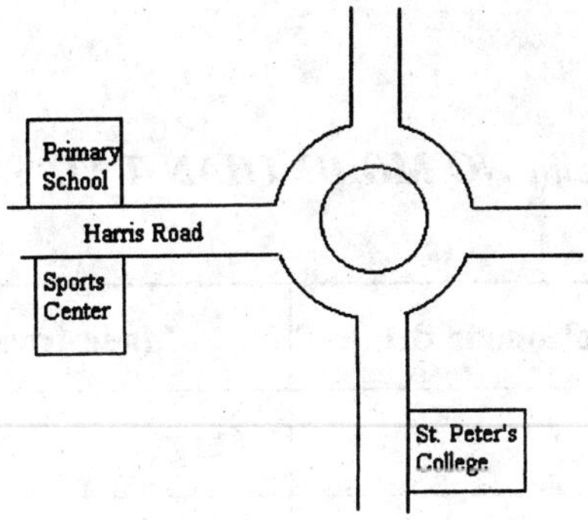

B

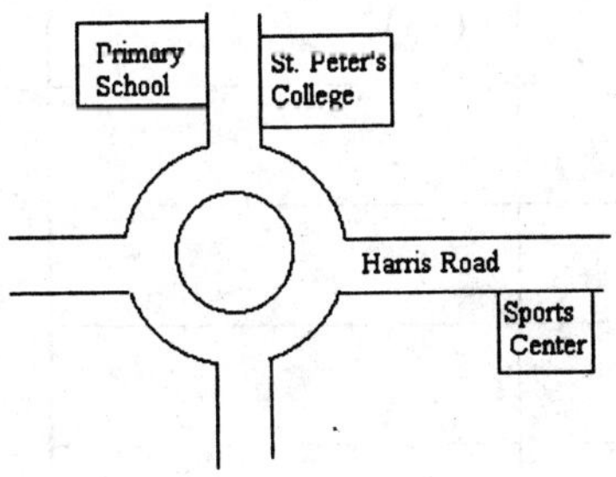

C

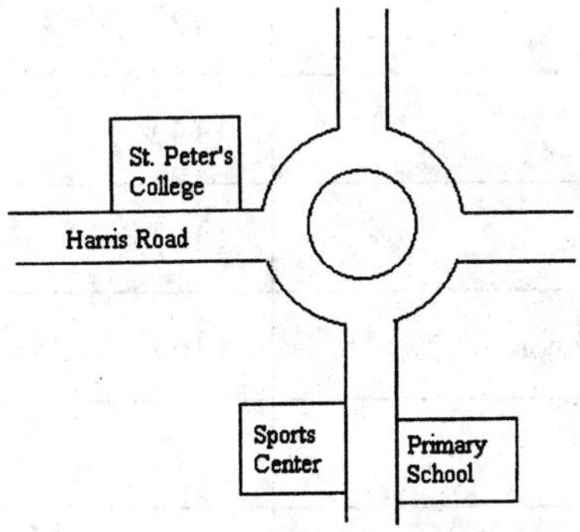

D

9. What should Jean wear when she goes for the introductory session?

A. Shorts, loose T-shirt, black sports shoes.

B. Tight trousers, T-shirt, comfortable sports shoes.

C. Tracksuit trousers, loose T-shirt, white sports shoes.

D. Loose trousers, tight T-shirt, hard sole shoes.

10. What should Jean bring when she goes for the introductory session?

A. Money, student card, photo.

B. Money, photo.

C. Money, student card.

D. Student card, photo.

Section 2 *Questions 11 – 21*

Questions 11 – 21

Fill in the blanks with ***NO MORE THAN TWO WORDS.***

Types of alcoholic drinks	**Made from**	**Best produced in**
Red wine	(11)	*e.g. France, Italy*
White wine	*e.g. white grapes*	*e.g. France, Italy*
Sherry	(12)	(13)
Beer	(14)	
English ale	(15)	
Japanese beer	(16)	
Vodka	(17)	(18)
Rum	(19)	
Cider	(20)	(21)

Section 3 *Questions 22 – 30*

Questions 22 – 30

Indicate if Dr. Simon would agree with the following statements by writing **YES** *or* **NO**.

If it is a job you don't want, reject it.	*e.g.* *YES*
The importance of an interview depends on the importance of the job on offer.	(22)
Try to please the interviewer.	(23)
Talking with somebody sitting next to you on an airplane can be real fun.	(24)
It is important to control the interview.	(25)
Feel free to interrupt the interviewer.	(26)
If you don't agree with the interviewer, don't show it.	(27)
You can change your mind during the interview.	(28)
Arrive on time for an interview.	(29)
After the interview, write to the interviewer to express thanks.	(30)

Section 4 *Questions 31 – 40*

Questions 31 – 35

Complete the table below with numbers to indicate how many hours people worked in the corresponding period of time.

Time	Number of working hours each week
Before the industrial revolution	(31)
1850	(32)
1966	(33)
1979	(34)
1981	(35)

Questions 36 – 40

*Decide if the lecturer supports the following statements or not. Write **YES** if she supports the statement. If she does not, write **NO**.*

36. Many experts feel that the growth of leisure is a curse. ______
37. The issue of increased leisure does not affect university students. ______
38. Uses of leisure are private matters rather than public issues. ______
39. Scientists should study urgent problems instead of wasting time on the issue of leisure. ______
40. Schools should educate children for leisure. ______

四、听力模拟试题三

INTERNATIONAL ENGLISH LANGUAGE TESTING SYSTEM

PRACTICE TEST（Version Three）

LISTENING

TIME：30 MINUTES
NUMBER OF QUESTIONS：40

Instructions

You will hear a number of different recordings and you will have to answer questions on what you hear.

There will be time for you to read the instructions and questions, and you will have a chance to check your work.
All recordings will be played **ONCE** only.

The test is in four sections. Write all your answers in the listening question booklet.

At the end of the real test you will be given ten minutes to transfer your answers to an answer sheet.

Now turn to Section 1.

Section 1 *Questions 1 – 10*

Questions 1 – 5

Tick (√) the relevant boxes.

Title	Author	In stock	To be ordered	Not available
e.g. Language Acquisition	Armstrong	√		
(1) Learner Difference	Dickinson			
(2) Language and Mind	Wallace			
(3) Language Testing	Robinson			
(4) Speaking Activities	Johnson			
(5) Language Games for Teachers	Strong			

Questions 6 – 9

Fill in the gaps.

Purchasing Slip

Customer's Last Name: (6) ________ Initial: E

Profession: (7) ________

Address: Miller's Hall, Richmond College, (8) ________

Method of Payment: (9) ________

Credit Card Number: 9498, 0019, 1323, 5157 Expire Date: October 2001

Question 10

Circle the letter that correctly indicates the location of the bookstore.

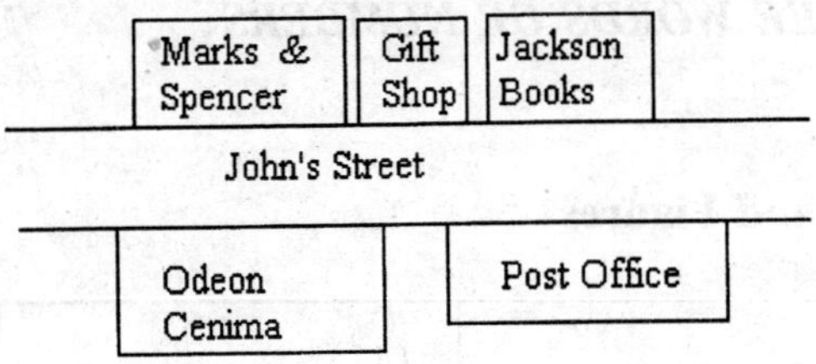

A

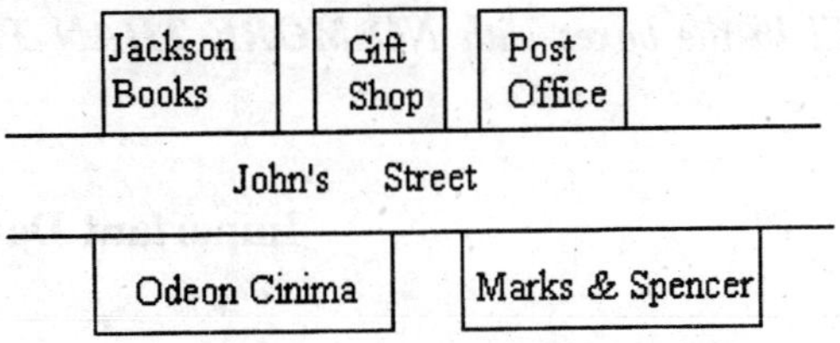

B

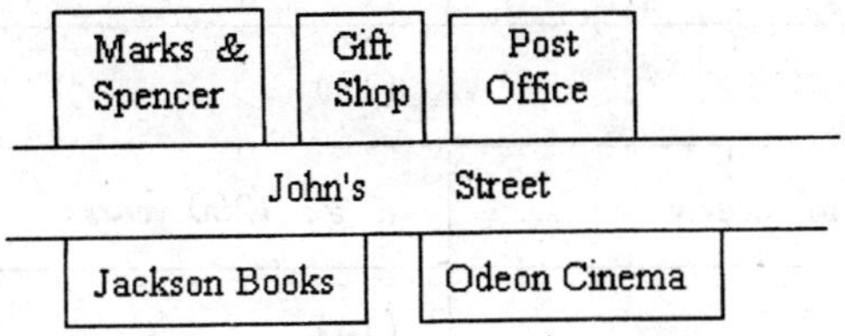

C

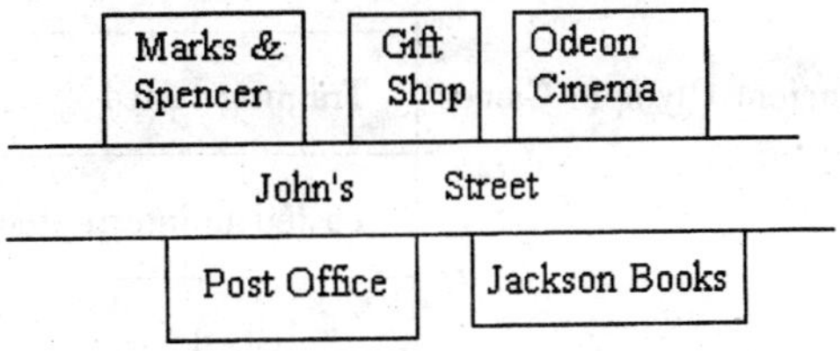

D

Section 2 *Questions 11 – 20*

Questions 11 – 17

Fill in the boxes with ***NO MORE THAN THREE WORDS OR NUMBERS.***

Important Dates and Figures

Ancient Olympic Games	Frequency of the Games	(11)
	Started	(12)
	Training lasted	(13)
	Lasted uninterruptedly for nearly	*e.g. 1200 years*
	Abolished	(14)
Modern Olympic Games	Started again	(15)
	First Olympic Games held outside Greece	*e.g. (in) 1908*
	The Munich Games with 120 countries	(16)
	The marathon race started	(17)

Questions 18 – 20

Fill in the boxes with ***NO MORE THAN THREE WORDS.***

Other Important Details

Ancient Olympic Games	Not allowed to watch the games	(18)
	Field events included	(19)
	Day four	*e.g. a holy day*
	Day six	(20)

Section 3 *Questions 21 – 30*

Questions 21 – 30

Fill in the boxes with ***NO MORE THAN THREE WORDS OR NUMBERS.***

Most of the time the man feels	*e.g. tense / nervy*
Doctor's comment on patient's conditions	(21)
Number of cigarettes patient smokes daily	(22)
Numbers of times patient's tried to quit smoking	(23)
For breakfast, patient eats	(24)
Place where patient has lunch	(25)
Time when patient has dinner	(26)
Doctor's recommendation for breakfast	(27)
Doctor's recommendation for dinner	(28)
Doctor's recommendation for eating manners	(29)
Time when patient feels tense	(30)

Section 4 *Questions 31 – 40*

Questions 31 – 35

Fill in the blanks in the table below to indicate the Recommended Daily Allowance (RDA) needed by each age group. One has been done as an example.

Age groups	RDA
Adult men	(31)
Adult women	(32)
Children 1 – 3 years old	(33)
Children 4 – 6 years old	*e.g.: 30*
Girls 11 – 18 years old	(34)
Boys 15 years and older	(35)

Questions 36 – 40

Answer the following questions with ***NO MORE THAN THREE WORDS OR NUMBERS.***

36. How many types of amino acids are there that combine to form proteins?

37. How many type of amino acids can not be synthesized in human body?

38. Give an example of something that contains high-quality protein.

39. What complements the limiting amino acid in beans?

40. What is the percentage of protein found in cooked rice?

五、听力模拟试题四

INTERNATIONAL ENGLISH LANGUAGE TESTING SYSTEM

PRACTICE TEST (Version Four)

LISTENING

TIME: 30 MINUTES
NUMBER OF QUESTIONS: 40

Instructions

You will hear a number of different recordings and you will have to answer questions on what you hear.

There will be time for you to read the instructions and questions, and you will have a chance to check your work.
All recordings will be played **ONCE** only.

The test is in four sections. Write all your answers in the listening question booklet.

At the end of the real test you will be given ten minutes to transfer your answers to an answer sheet.

Now turn to Section 1.

Section 1 *Questions 1 – 11*

Questions 1 – 5

Fill in the boxes using ***NO MORE THAN THREE WORDS*** *.*

	First job	Second job	Current employer	Marital status	Number of children
Philip	researcher	(1)	*e.g.* *Sydney University*	(2)	no
Janet	(3)	artist	(4)	married	(5)

Questions 6 – 11

Fill in the boxes using ***NO MORE THAN THREE WORDS*** *.*

	Working in	Current job	Married to / Dating
Alison	(6)	(7)	John
John	(8)	(9)	Alison
Helen	Somali	(10)	(11)

Section 2 *Questions 12 – 20*

Questions 12 – 20

Fill in the blanks in the sentences below using ***NO MORE THAN THREE WORDS*** *for each answer.*

12. Many people who suffer from insomnia rely on ______________.

13. It is wrong to believe that ______________ hours of sleep is necessary.

14. Dr. Jones thinks that tiredness is caused by ______________ rather than by lack of sleep.

15. The normal range of sleeping time is between 4.5 hours and ______________ hours.

16. Insomnia can also be caused by physical problems such as ______________.

17. If you've had a bad night's sleep, don't ______________ later the next morning.

18. When you go to bed, don't plan your next day's activities. You may become too ______________.

19. If you can't sleep, do something, but make sure it is ______________.

20. Exercise is a great sleep ______________.

Section 3 *Questions 21 – 30*

Questions 21 – 30

Fill in the boxes with ***NO MORE THAN THREE WORDS OR NUMBERS.***

Mr. Bradley	A light / heavy / chain smoker?	*Example*: *heavy*
	How many cigarettes each day?	(21)
	Also smokes pipe / cigar?	(22)
	Number of times attempts to quit smoking?	(23)
Mrs. Bradley	A light / heavy / chain smoker?	(24)
	How many ciqarettes each day?	(25)
	Started smoking at the age of	*Example*: *17*
	How many cigarettes a day when first started?	(26)
	Reason for the first attempt to quit smoking?	*Example*: *save money*
	Reason for the second attempt to quit smoking?	(27)
	Reason for no more attempts to quit smoking?	(28)
	Usually smokes more when	(29)
	Never smokes when	*Example*: *doing housework*
	Always has one cigarette when	(30)

Section 4 *Questions 31 – 40*

Questions 31 – 35

Fill in the blanks in the sentences with ***NO MORE THAN THREE WORDS.***

31. Alcohol is not a ______________.

32. Safe drinking limit per day is ______________ pure alcohol.

33. To be sober, the blood-alcohol level should be below ______________.

34. The blood-alcohol level of most drunk drivers reaches ______________.

35. ______________ percent of alcohol drunk goes directly from stomach into the bloodstream.

Questions 36 – 40

Fill in the blanks in the summary below with ***NO MORE THAN THREE WORDS.***

To reduce the effect of alcohol on our body, it is better to drink with food in the stomach. Typically, (36) ____________ slows absorption. Also, it is not good time to drink when we are (37) ____________ upset or lonely. Alcohol is like many other drugs in that (38) ____________ is related to result, that is, you get what you want to get. (39) ____________ indicated alcohol abuse happens to children aged 12 – 17. We should share the available (40) ____________ on matters like when and how much to drink.

六、答 案

听力模拟试题一

1. C	2. B	3. B	4. A	5. staff
6. $ 20	7. Tuesday	8. four	9. Shevsky	10. Gordon
11. intermediate	12. 1500	13. mild	14. arthritis	15. 1899
16. 1921	17. acids	18. stomach(lining)	19. chew / crush	20. two
21. 9, 5	22. male	23. Three.	24. One year.	25. two
26. £495	27. leave a note	28. gas	29. electricity and water	
30. B	31. paid jobs	32. holidays / hobbies	33. increased	
34. fell / decreased / dropped		35. expanded	36. 57	37. 90
38. 98	39. Fresh fish.	40. Late 1960s.		

听力模拟试题二

1. 4 pm	2. 7 pm	3. 1.25	4. 5	5. 20
6. D	7. D	8. B	9. C	10. A
11. dark grapes	12. grapes	13. Spain, Portugal	14. barley	15. barley
16. rice	17. potatoes	18. Russia	19. sugar cane	20. apples
21. southern England	22. YES	23. NO	24. YES	25. NO
26. YES	27. NO	28. YES	29. NO	30. YES
31. 72	32. 60	33. 48	34. 44	35. 39
36. YES	37. NO	38. NO	39. NO	40. YES

听力模拟试题三

1. In stock	2. To be ordered	3. To be ordered	4. Not available	5. Not available
6. Jordan	7. student	8. New Town	9. Credit card / Master Express	

10. A 11. every 4 years 12. 776 B.C. 13. 10 months 14. 394 A.D.

15. 1896 16. 1972 17. 1896 18. married woman

19. discus, javelin 20. last day 21. nothing wrong / very fit 22. 40 – 50

23. several 24. cereal / bacon / egg / bread / tomato / toast / marmalade 25. pub

26. 8 27. eat less 28. soup / salad / fruit 29. more leisurely 30. after dinner

31. 56 grams 32. 44 grams 33. 23 grams 34. 46 grams 35. 56 grams

36. 22 37. 8 or 9 38. meat / milk / egg 39. rice 40. 2

听力模拟试题四

1. teacher 2. separated 3. photographic reporter 4. a design company

5. 2 6. London 7. accountant 8. Oxford 9. civil servant

10. teacher 11. a French scientist 12. sleeping pills 13. 8

14. stress 15. 9 16. itching / ache / arthritis / heart problems

17. stay in bed 18. anxious / stimulated 19. something dull

20. inducer 21. 20 or more 22. cigar 23. 0 24. light

25. less than 10 26. 2 or 3 27. expecting / pregnant

28. her husband smokes 29. watching TV / reading / in company 30. after a meal

31. stimulant 32. 1.5 ounces 33. 0.05% 34. 0.2% 35. 20

36. protein / fatty product 37. physically or emotionally

38. expectation 39. Surveys / Studies 40. knowledge

七、录音文本

听力模拟试题一

Instructions:

You'll have a number of different recordings and you'll have to answer questions on what you hear. There will be time for you to read the instructions and the questions and you'll have a chance to check your work. All the recordings will be played once only. The test is in four sections.

Now turn to Section 1.

Section 1

You'll hear Lily talking to a friend at the college. They are going to the campus music shop. First, look at the example and questions 1 – 4. For each of the questions, four alternatives are given. Decide which of the alternatives, A, B, C or D best fits what you hear on the tape and circle the appropriate letter. First, listen to the example.

M: Where are we going, Lily?

W: To the music store.

M: What are you going to buy?

W: A compact disc. It's my brother's birthday the day after tomorrow.

Lily is looking for a disc as a birthday present for her brother. So in the example, B has been circled.

Now we shall begin. You should answer the questions as you listen because you'll not hear the recordings the second time. First you'll have another chance to look at questions 1 – 4.

Now listen carefully and answer the questions as you are instructed to do so.

M: Where are we going, Lily?

W: To the music store.

M: What are you going to buy?

W: A compact disc. It's my brother's birthday the day after tomorrow.

M: What kind of music does your brother like?

W: Opera.

M: That's quite unusual. How old is your brother?

W: 17. Yes, kids of his age are more into pop music.

M: Here we are. Now, classic, folk, heavy metal, jazz, pop, opera. That's the section you need. Opera.

W: OK. Come on. But they are all too expensive.

M: Does your brother have favourite singers?

W: Honestly, I don't know. I know he likes *Carmen*.

M: Here is one, *Carmen*, conducted by Rubinsky.

W: Yes, but it is 18 dollars, a bit too expensive.

M: How about this one, by John Miller?

W: Well, I don't know. Maybe I should give him something slightly different. Last year he got a *Madam Butterfly* from me. I'll see if there is anything else.

M: What about musicals? That's also a sort of opera.

W: Yes. In fact, I have recently become fond of musicals.

M: Oh, have you? Which ones do you like?

W: *West Side Story*.

M: What is it about?

W: It's a contemporary version of *Romeo and Juliet*, with a New York setting.

M: Oh, that one. That's very old, isn't it?

W: Yes, I know. I got to know it from my drama teacher, Mrs Jones. She showed excerpts of it during class. I really enjoyed it.

M: OK. Here is your favourite musical, *West Side Story*.

W: Thanks. It's 15 dollars. Well, maybe I'll buy it for myself. Yes, I want it for myself.

M: What about your brother?

W: I'll buy him another musical and I can later borrow it from him.

M: That's a good idea. You have anything in your mind?

W: No.

M: Look. This one is on sale. *Oklahoma*. Only 9 dollars.

W: What's it about?

M: It's a love story. On a farm, I think.

W: Sounds a bell. OK. I'll buy the two.

M: Right. While you are queuing, I'll look around and we can meet outside.

W: OK.

Lily and her friend look around in the college. It's the first day of the term and various college clubs are registering new members. As you listen to the recording, complete the summary of Lily's conversation with the club representatives. Write the missing words in the advertisement for the badminton club. First, you'll have some time to look at questions 5–8.

New you'll hear the conversation. Listen carefully and answer questions 5 – 8.

W: Oh, look. The Badminton Club. I love badminton. Let's go and check it out.

M1: Badminton? You are not serious.

W: Yes. Come on. ... Hi. Could you tell me something about your club?

M2: Sure. It's a really active club. It's got about forty members.

W: That's quite a lot. Can anyone from the college join?

M2: Oh, yeah. The club is for all the students and staff of the college .

W: And is it free?

M2: You are joking. Nothing is free nowadays. Well, we charge 20 dollars per term. So 40 dollars per year. That's to cover the cost of equipment.

W: So I don't have to bring my own racket.

M2: Oh, no. It's all provided. We provide tea or coffee, too.

W: That's good. When do you meet?

M2: Well, depends on your level. Beginners are on Thursdays. Intermediate on Tuesdays and advanced on Mondays. Starting at four until whenever people feel like it.

W: Well, four o'clock should be alright for me, really.

M2: And once a month we organise a kind of social activities. Maybe a picnic, a dinner, a bus trip, or something like that.

W: It sounds great.

M1: I'll join on the bus trips as long as I don't have to play badminton.

M2: Sure. You are welcome to come along.

W: Do you have any tournament?

M2: Yes, we have regular tournament within the club, against other clubs in the area.

W: It's a long time since I played a tournament.

M2: But they are not compulsory. It's up to you. So what do you think?

W: I'd love to join. What do I do?

Lily registers as a new member of the college badminton club. As you listen to the recording, fill in the gaps 9 – 11 *on the registration form for the badminton club.*

M2: Well, we just have to get a few details from you and then you can pay the joining fee and you are a member. Do you have money with you today?

W: Yes.

M2: Now let's see. First, what's your name?

W: Lily Shevski. That's S-H-E-V-S-K-I.

M2: And your address?

W: 22 Gordon Avenue. G-O-R-D-O-N. Old Town.

M2: G-O-R-D-O-N. You are on a phone?

W: Yes. 2252355.

M2: Right. What level would you say you are?

W: Well, I'm not sure. I guess... well, I am not a beginner. I mean I have been playing for a few years. But I'm not that good.

M2: OK. Why don't I put you down to the intermediate group and then you can move on to advanced when you feel comfortable with that. That's what I divide you in.

W: That sounds alright.

M2: OK, Lily, welcome to the club.

W: Thanks.

That's the end of Section 1. You now have half a minute to check your answers.

Now turn to Section 2.

Section 2

You'll now hear an excerpt from a radio program called Health Time. As you listen to the talk, answer questions 12 – 19. First, you have some time to look at the questions.

Now you'll hear the excerpt.

Good morning everyone. In today's *Health Time*, I am going to tell you something about a drug that you probably already know a lot — aspirin. Aspirin is the most popular drug in the world today. Many people take aspirin when they have a headache. It is effective in relieving other pains too.

Australians this year will swallow 1,500 tons of aspirin, one of the safest and most effective drugs invented by man. The most popular medicine in the world today, it is an effective pain reliever. Its bad effects are relatively mild, and it is cheap.

For millions of people suffering from arthritis, it is the only thing that works. Aspirin, in short, is truly the 20th-century wonder drug. It is also the second largest suicide drug and is the leading cause of poisoning among children. It has side effects that, although relatively mild, are largely unrecognized among users.

Although aspirin was first sold by a German company in 1899, it has been around much longer than that. Hippocrates, in ancient Greece, understood the medical value of the leaves and tree bark which today are known to contain salicylates, the chemical in aspirin. During the 19th century, there was a great deal of experimentation in Europe with this chemical, and it led to the introduction of aspirin. By 1921, aspirin tablets were available in Australia.

A small quantity of aspirin, normally two 30 mg tablets, relieves pain and inflammation. It also reduces fever by interfering with some of the body's reactions. Specifically, aspirin seems to slow down the formation of the acids involved in pain and the chemical reactions that cause fever. The chemistry of these acids is not fully understood but the slowing effect of aspirin is well known.

Aspirin is very irritating to the stomach lining and many aspirin takers complain about upset stomach. There is a right way and a wrong way to take aspirin. The best way is to chew the tablets before swallowing them with water, but few people can stand the bitter taste. Some people suggest crushing the tablets in milk or orange juice and drinking that. Most people simply swallow the tablets with water....

That's the end of Section 2. You now have half a minute to check your answers.

Now turn to Section 3.

Section 3

You'll now hear a telephone conversation between Mrs. Smith and the manager of a building. As you listen to the conversation, answer questions 20 – 30. *First, you'll have some time to look at questions* 20 – 30.

Now Listen to the conversation and answer questions 20 – 30.

(*Phone bell rings.*)

M: Good morning. 233-5767

W: Good morning. I got your phone number from the newspaper. I understand you have flats to let.

M: Yes, we do.

W: Good. I am looking for a place to stay. My husband got a job in this city and we moved here about ten days ago. We are now staying in a hotel, and ...

M: You would like to move out as soon as possible.

W: Yes, exactly.

M: Well, we have flats of different sizes, and there are a number of vacancies now.

W: We have two boys, one 9 years old, the other 5. Do you have three-bedroom flats?

M: Yes, we do. How long do you want it for?

W: We hope to stay here for... I don't know. It depends on my husband's job. I would say a year.

M: I'm asking because rents depend on the length of stay. If you are staying longer than 6 months, you have some kind of reduction.

W: That's good. How much is the rent?

M: Depending on the size. Ranging from £600 to £720 each month.

W: Oh, that is a bit expensive.

M: Considering the area and the neighbourhood, it is not too bad.

W: Do you have anything within £500?

M: Yes, we do. In fact, there is a family of four that just left. They stayed here for 18 months and their kids are of similar age to yours except that they are two girls.

W: Does it have three bedrooms?

M: No. There are two. It is very difficult to find a three-bedroom flat at that price in this area.

W: Yes, I know. Believe me, I have been looking for over a week. The few three-bedroom flats that I have found are either extremely expensive or the owner won't allow children as tenants.

M: I know that it is smaller than you wanted but it is one of the nicest flats in the building.

W: OK. Could you tell me more about it?

M: Certainly. The master bedroom is quite spacious. Maybe you could let the children share the larger room, and you and your husband could use the smaller one.

W: I suppose that I could do that.

M: And the owner allows two children in this flat complex but no pets, please.

W: Aren't you the owner?

M: No. I am the manager. I live here, too, on the first floor of this building.

W: Oh. That's nice. Then if anything gets broken...

M: Just leave a note on my door.

W: You said that the rent is within £500 but how much exactly is it a month?

M: £495.

W: Does that include any of the utilities?

M: Yes. It includes gas. Your furnace and stove are gas, so, as you can imagine, your other utilities, electricity and water, are quite inexpensive.

W: This sounds better and better. But before I sign a lease I would like for my husband to see it.

M: Why not stop by with him this evening?

W: How late are you open? He doesn't get off work until five.

M: Come by at six. I will still be in the office. I am sure that you are eager to move from the hotel, and if we get the paper worked out of the way tonight, you can move in tomorrow.

W: Oh, that would be wonderful.

M: Could you tell me your name, please?

W: Mr. and Mrs. Smith. Could you tell me where exactly you are?

M: Of course. Do you know the area well?

W: I don't think so.

M: Well, have you got a map?

W: Yes.

M: We are in Regent's Park area.

W: Yes, I know. That's the area I am interested in.

M: Can you find the park on the map?

W: Yes.

M: We are very close to the west end of the park, on Oxford Road.

W: Yes, I got that.

M: Where are you staying now?

W: Carlton Hotel.

M: Carlton Hotel, let me see. Yes, you take Bus No. 15 northbound and get off at the Regent's Park.

W: Yes.

M: Walk further down the road and turn left at the T-junction. Walk for about 300 yards and you'll see a chemist's shop. Cross the road from there and walk further down for 50 yards. That's where we are.

W: What is your address?

M: No. 50 Oxford Road. You'll first come across a post office. We are the next building, a five-story brownish building.

W: 50 Oxford Road, next to a post office. Lovely. I think I can find it.

M: You have our phone number. Call me if you have problems.

W: Great. I'll see you at six.

M: See you. Bye.

That is the end of Section 3. You now have half a minute to check your answers.

Now turn to Section 4.

Section 4

The following is a lecture about the changes that took place between 1950 and 1980. Listen to the lecture and answer questions 31 – 40. First you'll have some time to look at questions 31 – 35.

Now listen carefully to the first part of the lecture and answer questions 31 – 35.

Good morning. In today's lecture, I'll be mainly looking at the period between 1950 and 1980. We'll be discussing the social changes which have taken place over this period of time and the influence which education has had on these changes.

First, let's look at the living standards since the 1950s.

Despite the economic gloom of the 1970s, material prosperity has increased greatly since 1950. Growing unemployment and dependency on cash benefits existed alongside a booming leisure industry, increased choice in consumption and more company perks.

Sue Toland, of the Central Statistical Office, has written a survey of changes in living standards since the 1950s. She concludes that three changes since 1951 are particularly significant. Opportunities open to young people have broadened, with more opting for higher education and earning enough to buy their own radios, cars and, later, their own houses. Women, particularly mothers, became more likely in the 1970s to have paid jobs, increasing the number of families with more than one earner. And people work fewer hours and with longer holidays creating more opportunity for hobbies.

Public expenditure doubled between 1961 and 1975, although there was a startling reversal of the fortunes of the family in favour of single people. Between 1961 and 1969, single non-pensioner households paid proportionately more income tax than households with two adults and two children. Between 1969 and the mid-1970s, the trend was reversed; over the whole period, households with two children and two adults were subjected to the greatest increase, from 9 to 20 per cent, in direct taxation.

The rise in incomes and the fall in the real cost of consumer durables created substantial changes in spending patterns. The proportion spent on food, clothing and footwear fell, whereas housing took a larger slice during the 1960s and 1970s. Spending on alcohol rose, while tobacco fell. As the ownership of motor cars progressed from luxury to the commonplace in the 1950s and 1960s, spending on transport and vehicles rose before levelling off in the late 1970s.

In 1951, a majority of households lived in rented accommodation; by 1978, more than half of all households were owner-occupiers. The number of people inside each dwelling fell, partly because during the 1960s more and more young married couples were able to afford their own homes, and more single people moved away from their parents. The do-it-yourself market, boosted by the growth of leisure time, expanded enormously during the 1970s and the average full-time manual work hours fell from 48 hours weekly in 1951 to 44 in 1978.

Now you have some time to check your answers to questions 31 – 35.

Now you have some time to look at questions 36 – 40.

Listen carefully to the second part of the lecture and answer questions 36 – 40.

The increased use of motor cars and cycles was at least partly due to the cuts in public transport — the railway network was reduced by about 20 per cent between 1963 and 1967. In the early 1950s, public road and railway transport accounted for about two thirds of all passenger journeys. By contrast, distances travelled by private vehicles increased threefold between 1951 and 1961 and had doubled again by 1977 when about 57 per cent of all households had the use of a car.

The widespread use of other consumer goods which were rare in the early 1950s, such as vacuum cleaners and washing machines, meant that people did not have to spend so much time on routine housekeeping tasks. Only about 8 per cent of households possessed a refrigerator in 1956, compared with 90 per cent in 1978.

During this period, people also benefited greatly from the public health and education services, with an increasing proportion of children making use of the education system, both before and after compulsory school years. About 11 per cent of three and four year olds had some kind of formal education in 1951, compared with 37 per cent in 1977. At the other end of the age range, about 10 per cent of 17 and 18 year olds were continuing their education in the late 1950s, compared with 25 per cent in 1977.

The national health service largely succeeded in at least one of its aims — to ensure that all first babies were born in hospital. By 1977, 98 per cent of all births did occur in hospital. The average length of stay in a hospital bed fell, while the number of patients rose. Waiting lists for treatment increased from 604,000 in 1966 to 715,000 in 1977. Fewer people suffered strokes during the 1970s, but more had cancer, particularly in the lung, and heart disease.

People's eating habits changed as their working habits altered; fewer undertook heavy manual work and more took up sedentary employment, so they needed to expend less energy. Even so, people ate too much, and the richer they were, the greater was the excess.

Some large households and pensioners, by contrast, did not get enough vitamins, protein or iron. The increasing number of married women who worked led to more consumption of convenience foods.

By 1978, Britain was consuming eight times as many chickens as in 1957 but was eating less fresh fish. And people spent more proportionately on alcohol, even though it became proportionately cheaper.

The biggest change in leisure activities was brought about by the television set, a relative rarity in the early 1950s but an item in most homes by the end of 1970s. Colour television was introduced on a commercial scale in the late 1960s, and by 1976 over half of those households with a TV had a colour set. Television caused a severe drop in the popularity of the cinema. People became able to record sound and vision.

Some expansion was less reassuring. In 1977, 25 million prescriptions for tranquillisers were issued, an increase of nine million from the previous decade. It seems that all this affluence and leisure cannot be said to have improved the nation's frame of mind.

That is the end of Section 4. You now have half a minute to check your answers.

The test is nearly over. You now have one more minute to check all your answers.

Now you have 10 minutes to transfer all your answers to the answer sheet. In the real test, you'll be told to stop writing and hand in your question booklet at the end of the ten minutes.

听力模拟试题二

Instructions:

You'll have a number of different recordings and you'll have to answer questions on what you hear. There will be time for you to read the instructions and the questions and you'll have a chance to check your work. All the recordings will be played once only. The test is in four sections.

Now turn to Section 1.

Section 1

You'll listen to a telephone conversation between a woman called Jean and a staff member of a sports centre. First, listen to the example.

(*Phone bell rings.*)

M: Hello, Sports Smart.

W: Hello, is that the sports centre?

M: Yes.

W: I'm quite new to the area and I would like to have some information about facilities at the centre.

M: Well, at the moment, I'm afraid it's mainly swimming. The sports hall for the time being is closed for renovation. The basketball and volleyball grounds are also closed. So that's not available either. There's however a new fitness centre with weights and so on.

W: Oh, right. Fine. I am quite happy if I could use the pool and the fitness centre. What time is the pool open?

M: Well, the pool is open everyday from 9 am to 9 in the evening with the exception of Thursday.

The man says the pool is open from 9 am to 9 in the evening, except on Thursday. Therefore, the blank in the example is filled with 9 pm. Now we shall begin. You should answer the questions as you listen because you'll not hear the recordings the second time. First, you'll have some time to look at questions 1 – 5.

The conversation will now begin. Listen carefully and fill in the answers to questions 1 – 5.

(*Phone bell rings.*)

M: Hello, Sports Smart.

W: Hello, is that the sports centre?

M: Yes.

W: I'm quite new to the area and I would like to have some information about facilities at the centre.

M: Well, at the moment, I'm afraid it's mainly swimming. The sports hall for the time being is closed for renovation. The basketball and volleyball grounds are also closed. So that's not available either. There's however a new fitness centre with weights and so on.

W: Oh, right. Fine. I am quite happy if I could use the pool and the fitness centre. What time is the pool open?

M: Well, the pool is open everyday from 9 am to 9 in the evening with the exception of Thursday when it's closed from 9 am to 3 pm to the public because we have a school's day. It is open from 4 to 9.

W: OK.

M: And Saturday and Sunday we close two hours earlier.

W: Alright. And how much is it please?

M: Two dollars per session with concession to students and OAPs. Students are one dollar twenty-five and pensioners are one dollar.

W: Oh, well, I'm a student. Could I ask about the fitness centre, please?

M: Yeah.

W: I've never used one before, so I'll probably need some help at the beginning.

M: Yes, indeed. Beginners do need training sessions and you're allocated to your own instructor and the session will cost you 5 dollars.

W: 5 dollars?

M: Yes, I'm afraid so. But it is worth it — much safer. You are taught how to use the weights, and most important, how not to strain yourself.
W: Oh, yeah.
M: Once you've had that introductory session, it'll cost a dollar a session or a season ticket for 20 dollars.
W: Right. And how long does that last?
M: That'll last for 3 months.
W: Hm. Yeah. That's fine. Perhaps I could call back to book a session when I am more organised.
M: Yes, certainly.
W: Well, thank you for your help. Bye, now.
M: Bye.

The customer rings back to book her introductory session at the fitness centre. As you listen to the recording, circle one letter for each of the questions. First, you'll have some time to look at questions 6 – 10.

Now you'll hear the conversation. Listen carefully and answer questions 6 – 10.

(*Phone bell rings.*)
M: Hello, Sports Smart.
W: I'm... Hello. I'd like to book an introductory session in the weight training centre please.
M: Oh, yes. Sure. When would you like?
W: Well, is Wednesday afternoon possible at about 4:30?
M: One moment, please. I'll check. Er... sorry, no, ... there's no free staff at that time.
W: Oh, dear. What about Thursday?
M: Er, I'll check that one for you. Is evening alright with you?
W: OK. Fine. Er, ... can you tell me the exact time please?
M: A quarter past seven.
W: Yeah. I could make that. So that's Thursday, the 27th, a quarter to seven.
M: No, no, no. That's a quarter past seven. 7:15.
W: Oh, sorry.
M: What's the name, please?
W: Ah, yes. It's Jean Kucharek.
M: Ah, I'll have to ask you to spell that.
W: OK. That's K-U-C-H-A-R-E-K.
M: Good. I've got it.
W: And, how do I get to the centre, please.
M: Well, how well do you know the area?
W: I've just started at St. Peter's College.

M: That's fine. That's very close. Let me think. If you go out of the college, do you know the roundabout at the end of the road?

W: Er, yes. I do.

M: Well, turn left into Harris Road. You've got that?

W: Yeah.

M: Harris Road.

W: Yes.

M: Go down there. The centre is about half way down on the left. In fact, it's exactly opposite to the primary school.

W: OK. Yes, I think I know it actually. That' lovely. There ought to be no problem. Could I ask just one more question? What is the best to wear for these weight sessions?

M: Well, our advice is that you wear something loose. Tracksuit trousers for example, not shorts. A loose T-shirt. Also, please wear soft, white sole sports shoes, not the black ones, please.

W: Oh, alright.

M: Er, the room has a special floor and we can't risk having black marks on it.

W: Right. Yeah. I understand, fine.

M: Did you say you are a student?

W: Yes. At St. Peter's College.

W: Well, there is concession for students, so maybe you should bring your Student Union card. And a photo so that you can have your card.

W: Alright. I'll do that. OK. Thanks very much for your help. Bye.

M: Bye.

That's the end of Section 1. *You now have half a minute to check your answers.*

Now turn to Section 2.

Section 2

The following is a talk about different types of alcoholic drinks. Listen to the talk and answer questions 11 – 21. *First you'll have some time to look at questions* 11 – 21.

Now listen carefully to the talk and answer questions 11 – 21.

Early in the development of agriculture men discovered how to make alcoholic drinks from grapes and corn. The ancient Egyptians drank both wine and beer, and the Greeks carried on a lively trade in wine throughout the Mediterranean. The vines of grapes are all of a single species, *Vitis vinifera*, although there are hundreds of varieties adapted to different soils and climates.

Wine is the fermented juice of fresh grapes. The juice of the wine grape contains sugar, and growths of yeast form on the outside of the grape skins. In wine-making, the grapes are crushed in a wine press and the yeast converts the sugar to alcohol, when there is no air present, by a process called fermentation. Red wine is made from dark grapes, and white wine from white grapes or from dark grapes whose skins have been removed from the wine press at an early stage.

The most famous wine-growing countries are France and Italy. Wine was made in England in the Middle Ages, but the climate is not really suitable for grapevines. Wines must be drunk quickly once they are opened, otherwise bacteria will use the air to convert the alcohol to vinegar. The bacteria are killed by a higher alcohol content than is found in wine and that is why sherry and port, the specialties of Spain and Portugal, are fortified by the addition of spirits to make them last longer.

Beer is made from sprouting barley grains which is fermented with yeast to produce alcohol; hops are added for flavour. The best beer is brewed in Germany and I am sure everybody who drinks beer can name a few German beers. Ale, the most common drink in England in the Middle Ages, was also made from barley, but without hops; the ale of today is merely a type of beer. In Japan beer is made from rice.

Spirits have a higher alcoholic content than beer and wine and are made by distillation from a base of grain or some other vegetable. Gin and vodka can be distilled from a variety of ingredients, including potatoes. The best vodka is, of course, produced in Russia; gin is flavoured with juniper berries. Scotch whisky is obtained from a base of fermented barley, and brandy from the distillation of wine. Rum is derived from sugar cane by fermentation of molasses, a by-product in refining sugar. Cider is made from apples and the cider made in southern England is very famous. South American Indians make alcoholic drinks from cactus leaves and the shoots of certain palm trees.

That is the end of Section 2. You now have half a minute to check your answers.

Now turn to Section 3.

Section 3

You'll now hear part of a radio program, a conversation between the presenter and a guest speaker. As you listen to the conversation, answer questions 22 – 30. First, you'll have some time to look at questions 22 – 30.

Now listen to the conversation and answer questions 22 – 30.

W: Good morning and welcome to this session of career time. Last time we had Dr. Jerrold Simon, psychologist and career development specialist at the London School of Economics. Dr. Simon talked about things to pay attention to when doing job-hunting. That was a well received talk and we had a number of calls concerning job interviews. Today we are very happy to have Dr. Simon again who is going to answer some of these questions. Now Dr. Simon.

M: Thanks, Susan. Yes, last time a lot of things were said about writing an impressive CV. And this time we'll mainly be talking about job interviews. Susan, what kind of questions have you received from the listeners?

W: I think they fall into different categories. Let's look at the first category. A number of listener would like to know more about the purpose of an interview, which I think was touched upon in our last session. To come to the point, the listeners would like to know if the aim of interviewing is to obtain a job offer, or there is something else in it.

M: I think about half of it is for obtaining a job offer but the real aim of an interview is to obtain the job *you want*. *That* often means rejecting job offers you don't want! Incompetent job-seekers, however, become so used to accommodating employers' expectations that they often easily qualify for jobs they don't want. So, before you do back-flips for an employer, be sure you want the job.

W: Dr. Simon, I think this depends on individual cases. Some people need a job more badly than others.

M: Yes, that's true. And if it is a really important interview, it often means an equally important position or high salary, etc. Not many people who are interviewed for a manager's position are happy to become a receptionist.

W: That's true. Another question is whether the job-hunters should try to please the interviewer.

M: No, definitely not. Try to please yourself. Giving answers that you think will suit a potential employer, losing touch with your own feelings in order to get in touch with some other person's feelings, and, in general, practising an policy of appeasement are certain to get you nowhere. Of course, don't be hostile — nobody wants to hire someone disagreeable. But there is plainly a middle ground between being too ingratiating and being hostile. An effective interview, whether you are offered the job or not, is like an exciting encounter in conversation with your seatmate on an airplane.

W: Does that mean be yourself?

M: Exactly.

W: How about trying to control the interview?

M: Nobody controls an interview — neither you nor the interviewer — although one or both parties often try. Then it becomes a phony exchange between two human beings; no business is likely to be transacted. When somebody tries to control us, we resent it. When we try to control somebody, she resents us. Remember, you can't control what an employer thinks of you, just as she can't control what you think of her. So hang loose when interviewing: Never dominate the interview. Compulsive behavior turns off your authenticity.

W: What about politeness? For example, can I interrupt the interviewer?

M: Although an interview is an opportunity that calls for some appropriateness, for example you don't argue with the interviewer, sensible interruptions are certainly necessary. Study the style of an effective conversationalist: She interrupts and is interrupted! An exciting conversation always makes us feel free, free to interrupt, to disagree, to agree enthusiastically. We feel comfortable with people who allow us to be natural. So, when interviewing, half the responsibility lies with you. Do you seem uptight? Try being yourself for a change. Employers will either like or dislike you, but at least you'll have made *an impression*. Leaving an employer indifferent is the worst impression you can make. And the way to make an effective impression is to feel free to be yourself, which frees your interviewer to be *herself*!

W: One caller said his interview went wrong because he disagreed with the interviewer and would like to tell people to learn from his lessons and not to show disagreement.

M: This is another silly myth. If you don't disagree at times, you become, in effect, a "yes" woman. Don't be afraid to disagree with your interviewer—in an agreeable way, of course. And don't hesitate to change your mind. The worst that could happen would be that the interviewer says to herself, "There's a person with an open mind!" The conventional wisdom says "be yourself," true enough. But how many people can be themselves if they don't feel free to disagree?

W: Thanks, Dr. Simon. That covers nearly all the questions we've had. However, since job interviews are so important that the result can sometimes change our life, why don't you say a few more words about it?

M: Yes, I do have some comments to say. First, be sure to call the day before to confirm it. Meantime, prepare yourself. Research the company and the job by reading books and business journals in the library. Secondly, on the big day, arrive 15 minutes early. Act calm, even though you're trembling inside at 6.5 on the Richter scale. At every chance, let your interviewer see that your personal skills and qualifications relate to the job at hand. If it's a sales position, for example, go all out to show how articulate and persuasive you are. Afterwards, follow through with a brief thank-you note. This is a fine opportunity to restate your qualifications and add any important points you didn't get a chance to bring up during the interview.

W: Thanks, Dr. Simon. We really appreciate your advice and hope that our listeners find them useful too.

That is the end of Section 3. You now have half a minute to check your answers.

Now turn to Section 4.

Section 4

The following is a lecture about leisure. Listen to the lecture and answer questions 31 – 40. First you'll have some time to look at questions 31 – 35.

Now listen carefully to the first part of the lecture and answer questions 31 – 35.

Today, we'll be looking at the evolution of leisure, people's need to work and their workload. We'll be also looking into the issue that when people have more leisure, what they will do about it and what the educational institutions should do to prepare people for the increased leisure time.

We'll start from a retrospective point of view. Before the industrial revolution, that is about 240 years ago, in manufacturing, 12 hours work between 6:00 am and 6:00 pm, six days a week, was customary. I am sure people at that time would also like to work for fewer hours but because of the low productivity at that time, it was necessary to work 12 hours so as to earn enough to feed the family. You probably would think that reducing working hours was a natural trend since the industrial revolution. However, during the first half of the nineteenth century, some employers, notably in textiles, tried to lengthen the working week instead of shortening it, but with little success of course, and since 1850 the trend has been progressively downwards. Between 1850 and 1966 the normal working week was cut by a third, from 60 to 48 hours.

This trend continued after 1966. By the late 1970s, average hours worked by manual employees were 44 hours each week. Overtime became part of the "normal" working week during this period. Actual working time did not decline at the rate achieved from 1850 to 1939, but there was a substantial increase of wages which was equivalent to a half of the rise in workers' standards of living. But it would be wrong to infer that the historical trend towards shorter hours has ground to a permanent halt. Unlike wage increases, gains in leisure time have been achieved in short episodes: 1871 to 1874, 1919 to 1920, and 1946 to 1949. Between these falls, weekly hours of work have settled on medium-term plateaux. Trade unions have consistently demanded shorter hours and higher pay, but employers have more strongly resisted the unions' demand for reduced working hours. They have never relished the prospect of machines standing idle, or paying overtime premiums. Breakthroughs have been won only when growing prosperity and low unemployment have accentuated trade unions' bargaining power, and when labour has been troubled by fears of impending unemployment. This combination of circumstances has occurred only occasionally. Is it likely to be repeated sometime in the future? Many commentators predict another erosion of the working week, maybe more dramatic than any of its predecessors, sometime during the early 21st century.

When Britain's engineering workers negotiated a 39-hour working week in 1981, the trade union movement hailed it as a breakthrough towards the 35 hour week sometime during the next decade. One argument currently used to support claims for shorter working hours is that machines are progressively replacing workers. The silicon chip is seen as accelerating this trend. Unemployment is a prevalent fear. As has been said earlier, we need to consider the place of education in an era of unemployment. To many observers the only relevant question is when, not whether, the working week will fall from its present plateau and continue the long-term historical slide.

Now you have some time to check your answers to questions 31 – 35.

Now you have some time to look at questions 36 – 40.

Listen carefully to the second part of the lecture and answer questions 36 – 40.

Another way of viewing the "decline of work" is to proclaim a "growth of leisure". Some experts say that the next generation, those in school and college at the moment, will enjoy considerably more leisure than their parents. Will such a growth of leisure be a blessing or a curse? Many writers contend that more leisure will create problems unless we prepare and plan appropriately. Preparing for leisure, according to one school of thought, must include education for leisure, and our schools must recognize the major role that leisure will play in their present and future pupils' lives. Rather than preparing our pupils for the labour market, it is argued that schooling must concentrate more on learning to play.

This is the contemporary issue that will be examined in the later part of this lecture series. Is a "leisure explosion" probable? If so, is it a problem? Should education for leisure be accorded greater priority? These are issues on which the "experts" disagree. This lecture, therefore, is not offering an agreed body of knowledge. It tries to present the relevant evidence, the different sides of the arguments, and invites you to draw your own conclusions.

You may feel that you are not suffering any leisure problem, particularly as a university student, or you may believe that uses of leisure are private matters rather than public issues. In either event, you may feel that social scientists could be better occupied, that there are more urgent problems for investigation, and that students should be taught something really useful. After reading some of the books on the list that I will give you soon, you may notice how much your opinions change. Denying the existence of any leisure problem that demands solutions from educators, the recreation professions or government bodies is a perfectly respectable point of view. If correct, it is a view that needs to be argued forcefully. Simply dismiss the study of leisure as a joke, and the laugh could be on you. Before long you are likely to find the recreation professions spending more of your money, and the schools educating your children for leisure.

That is the end of Section 4. You now have half a minute to check your answers.

The test is nearly over. You now have one more minute to check all your answers.

Now you have 10 minutes to transfer all your answers to the answer sheet. In the real test, you'll be told to stop writing and hand in your question booklet at the end of the ten minutes.

听力模拟试题三

Instructions:

You'll hear a number of different recordings and you'll have to answer questions on what you hear. There will be time for you to read the instructions and the questions and you'll have a chance to check your work. All recordings will be played once only. The test is in four sections.

Now turn to Section 1.

Section 1

You'll hear a man telephoning a bookstore. He wants to buy some books for his work. First, look at the example and questions 1 – 5. For each of the questions, you need to decide if the bookstore has the relevant book or not. First , listen to the example.

(*Phone bell rings.*)

W: Good morning, Jackson Book Centre.

M: Good morning. I wonder if you could help me. Er... I've been given your name by my tutor. I'm working on language teaching and I need a number of specialist books on that.

W: Language books, did you say?

M: Yes, books on language teaching.

W: Oh, yes. We do specialise in education books. OK. I think you can give the titles you need and we'll see if we have them.

M: Sure, yes. OK. The first one is Arlington, no, Armstrong, *Language Acquisition*.

W: Right, let me see. Right. That's in stock. No problem.

The sales woman says they have the book Language Acquisition. So the column "In stock" has been ticked. Decide what the sales woman says about each book for questions 1 – 5 *and tick in the corresponding columns.*

Now we shall begin. You should answer the questions as you listen because you'll not hear the recordings the second time. First you'll have another chance to look at questions 1 – 5.

Now listen carefully and answer questions 1 – 5.

(*Phone bell rings.*)

W: Good morning, Jackson Book Centre.

M: Good morning. I wonder if you could help me. Er... I've been given your name by my tutor. I'm working on language teaching and I need a number of specialist books on that.

W: Language books, did you say?

M: Yes, books on language teaching.

W: Oh, yes. We do specialise in education books. OK. I think you can give the titles you need and we'll see if we have them.

M: Sure, yes. OK. The first one is Arlington, no, Armstrong, *Language Acquisition*.

W: Right, let me see. Right. That's in stock. No problem.

M: And Dickinson, *Learner Difference*.

W: No problem with that one either. We had a lot of requests for that recently.

M: OK. Lovely. The most important one is, er... Wallace, and that's *Language and Mind*.

W: *Language and Mind*. I'll just check that one on the computer. Sorry. Couldn't find it. When was it published?

M: It's quite old, I'm afraid. Er... 1982.

W: OK. That's fine, then. Er, I'll look into another index. I'll get a colleague to do it. Meanwhile, let's try the next one.

M: What about Robinson's *Language Testing*?

W: Fine, yes. But I'll have to order it. We don't often get ask for that one.

M: Try the *Language Games*, by Johnson. Sorry, no. Wait a moment. That's not *Language Games*. It's *Speaking Activities*.

W: Right. Well, I had someone asking Johnson last week. So I happened to know. I'm afraid it's out of print.

M: Oh, god. I was worried about that. Oh, well, what can I do?...

W: My colleague just told me that we can order *Language and Mind* for you but it might take a while.

M: That's OK. No problem. I'll wait. And what about *Language Games for Teachers*?

W: Who is it by?

M: Strong, Benjamin Strong.

W: Hm. Let me see. No longer available, I'm afraid. And we can't even order it.

M: OK, er..., thanks very much.

Now look at questions 6 – 10. The sales woman and the customer continue to talk about the price of one of the books and payment for the order. As you listen, answer questions 6 – 10. First, you'll have some time to read questions 6 – 10.

Now you'll hear the conversation. Listen carefully and answer questions 6 – 10.

W: Now, then, it seems that *Language and Mind* is hard back. I'm afraid it's quite expensive.

M: How much is it?

W: £19.75

M: Oh, gosh. I thought it was going to be expensive. Is there no chance for a paper back? Usually, you know, they are about 10 pounds cheaper.

W: No, I'm sorry. It's all we've got.

M: Oh. Right. If you keep that for me, that'll be fine.

W: OK.

M: OK. That's fine. Look, I won't be able to come to town for a couple of weeks. And I... er... I really do need the Dickinson and Armstrong. So is there any chance you could send them to me?

W: Of course. That's no problem. How do you want to pay?

M: Well, is credit card OK?

W: Fine.

M: I've got Master Express.

W: Fine. That's OK. I'll just take the details. Master Express. Surname and initials?

M: Jordan.

W: J-O-R-D-O-N.

M: No, no. That's J-O-R-D-A-N. Edward.

W: Initial E.

M: Yeah.

W: OK. Number?

M: 9498, 0019, 1323, 5157.

W: Expire date, please?

M: OK. It's October, 2001.

W: Right. October, 2001. Fine. And address?

M: Richmond College. Do you know that? Miller's Hall, Richmond College, New Town.

W: Lovely. OK. I'll get those off to you. By the way, because you are a college student, you don't pay post and packing.

M: That's very good. I'll come to your shop within the next couple of weeks, you know, to get the rest of the books on my list. I know where you are.

W: We have recently moved. Don't know if you know that.

M: No, I don't. Yeah. I think you need to tell me where you are now.

W: OK. Do you know the central area?

M: Yes?

W: The Odeon Cinema.

M: Yeah.

W: Well, it's near there. On the other side of the road. Directly opposite the main post office, very close to the Marks and Spencer. You know, on John's Street.

M: OK, I know where that is. Next to the Marks and Spencer.

W: Well, not immediately next. There is a gift shop in between.

M: OK, I've got it. Lovely. Now, thanks very much for your help.

W: I'll send the books off to you the first thing tomorrow and they should be with you in a couple of days.

M: Lovely. Bye now.

W: Bye.

That's the end of Section 1. You'll have half a minute to check your answers.

Now turn to Section 2.

Section 2

You'll hear a talk about the Olympic Games. As you listen to the talk, answer questions 11 – 20. *First, you'll have some time to look at the questions.*

Now listen to the talk and answer questions 11 – 20.

Good morning. Today I would like to talk about the history of the Olympic Games.

In ancient Greece athletic festivals were very important and had strong religious associations. The Olympian athletic festival, held every four years in honour of Zeus, eventually lost its local character, became first a national event, and then, after the rules against foreign competitors had been waived, international. No one knows exactly how far back the Olympic Games go, but some official records date from 776 B.C.

The Games took place in August on the plain by Mount Olympus. Many thousands of spectators gathered from all parts of Greece, but no married women were admitted even as a spectator. Slaves, women and dishonoured persons were not allowed to compete. The exact sequence of events is uncertain, but events included boys' gymnastics, horse-racing, field events, such as discus and javelin throwing, and the very important foot races. There was also boxing and wrestling and special tests of varied ability such as the pentathlon, the winner of which excelled in running, jumping, discus and javelin throwing and wrestling. The evening of the third day was devoted to sacrificial offerings to the heroes of the day, and the fourth day, that of the full moon, was set aside as a holy day.

On the sixth and last day, all the victors were crowned with holy garlands of wild olive from a sacred wood. So great was the honour that the winner of the foot race gave his name to the year of his victory. Although Olympic winners received no prize money, they were, in fact, richly rewarded by their state authorities. The public honour also made the strict discipline of the ten-month training period worthwhile. In spite of the lengthy training, however runners were known to drop dead from strain at the winning post. How their results compared with modern standards, we unfortunately have no means of telling.

After an uninterrupted history of almost 1,200 years, the Games were abolished in A.D. 394, the Christian era, because of their pagan origin. It was over 1,500 years before there was another such international athletics gathering. The Greek institution was revived in 1896 and the first small meeting took place in Athens. After the 1908 London Olympics, which was the first one held outside Greece, success was re-established and nations sent their best representatives. In time of peace, the Games have taken place ever since at four-yearly intervals. In Munich in 1972 competitors from more than 120 countries were watched by huge crowds.

Nowadays, the Games are held in different countries in turn. The host country provides vast facilities, including a stadium, swimming pools and living accommodation, but competing countries pay their own athletes' expenses. Athletic contests are still the main feature, but now many more sports are represented, women compete, the ancient pentathlon, for example, has been modified into a more comprehensive test, and the marathon races, initiated in 1896, are now a celebrated event.

The Olympic starts with the arrival in the stadium of a torch, lighted on Mount Olympus by the sun's rays. It is carried by a succession of runners to the stadium. The torch symbolizes the continuation of the ancient Greek athletic ideals, and it burns throughout the Games until the closing ceremony. The well-known Olympic flag, however, is a modern conception: the five interlocking rings symbolize the uniting of all five continents participating in the Games.

That's the end of Section 2. You now have half a minute to check your answers.

Now turn to Section 3.

Section 3

You'll now hear a dialogue between a doctor and her patient. As you listen to the dialogue, answer questions 21 – 30. *First, you'll have some time to look at the questions.*

Now listen to the dialogue and answer questions 21 – 30.

W: Well, Mr. Thomson, the first and important thing I have to tell you is that ... mm ... there is really nothing seriously wrong with you ... physically, that is. My er ... my very thorough re-examination and the analyst's report show that basically you are very fit. Yes ... very fit...

M: So ... Why is it, doctor, that I'm always so nervy ... tense ... ready to jump on anybody — my wife, children, colleagues?

W: I think ... erm ... I think your condition has a lot to do with er... what shall we call it? — Way of life? Habits?

M: Way of life? Habits?

W: Yes. Now tell me, Mr. Thomson, ... you smoke, don't you?

M: Yes, I'm afraid ... I'm afraid I do, doctor.

W: And er... rather heavily, I imagine.

M: Well, yes. I smoke — what ... about forty ... fifty a day, I suppose.

W: You should do your best to stop, you know.

M: Yes ... I see. But er ... well ... it won't be the first time. I've tried to give up smoking several times but it's ... it's no good.

W: You see ... fifty a day is overdoing it. You must admit. You must cut it down at least that. Oh yes. I know that when you're feeling tense you ... you probably feel that a cigarette relaxes you. But in the long run ... I do advise you to make ... to make a real effort.

M: Of course. But ... well, it's easy to say "give it up" or "cut it down" ... but ... oh, you know, ...

W: Well, in my opinion you have no choice. Either you make a real effort or ... or there's no real chance of your feeling better. You see ... well, obviously I could prescribe some kind of tranquilliser ... but would that help? I'd prefer — and I'm quite sure you'll agree — I'd prefer to see you really back to normal ... not just seemingly so. And that's my reason for asking you several more questions about ... about your other habits.

M: Right.

W: Your eating habits for example. What do you eat normally... during a normal day?

M: Yes, well ...yes, I'd say I'm a good eater. Now let's see, up at eight in the morning and my wife has a good breakfast ready.

W: A good breakfast?

M: The usual. A cereal followed by bacon and eggs with fried bread and perhaps a tomato or two. Then toast and marmalade ... all washed down with a couple of cups of tea. I er ... yes ... I really enjoy my breakfast.

W: Er ... yes ... I can see you do, but I'd advise you to eat rather less. We'll come to that later. Go on.

M: Then lunch ... no, first brunch. A cup of coffee and a bun at eleven. Lunch has to be quick because there's so much to do in the office about that time. So I have a pint and a sandwich in the pub. All very hurried.

W: Try to be in less of a hurry.

M: But I make up for it in the evening. I get home at about seven. Dinner's round about eight. Er ... yes ... my wife's an excellent cook ... excellent. It's usually some meat dish ... and we like spaghetti as a first course. Spaghetti, a meat dish, cheese, a sweet. But er ... but then ... at the end of the day shall we say ... then..., well, then I begin to feel on edge again. Most evenings after dinner we read or watch TV ... but I ... I get this terrible feeling of tension.

W: Well ... I'm sorry to have to say this because you obviously enjoy your food ... but ... er ... I really do recommend that you ... that you eat less and, secondly, that you eat more healthily. Instead of having that enormous breakfast for example ... er ... well ... try to be content with a fruit juice and some cereal.

M: I see, but er...

W: Elevenses ... right ... well, that's all right. But lunch should be more leisurely. Remember your health is at stake, not your job. As for dinner ... er ... I'd advise you to eat a soup perhaps... with a salad ... a salad followed by some fruit.

M: But my wife's cooking...

W: ... is superb, granted, and she probably enjoys preparing delicious meals for you. If you like ... well ... er I'll have a word with your wife...

M: No ... that won't be necessary ... erm. Thanks just the same, doctor, but no...

W: And on that subject, Mr. Thomson ... erm ... er ... just one other thing ... er... I'm sure this won't embarrass you. You say you feel tense in the evenings after dinner. Might I ask ... please forgive this question but it's necessary... Might I ask about your relationship — your sexual relationship, that is — with your wife?

M: Well ... erm ... er ... you see ... er...

That is the end of Section 3. You now have half a minute to check your answers.

Now turn to Section 4.

Section 4

The following is a lecture about protein. Listen to the lecture and answer questions 31 – 40. First you'll have some time to look at questions 31 – 35.

Now listen carefully to the first part of the lecture and answer questions 31 – 35.

Good morning. Today we'll be looking at what protein is and how the human body must receive the protein it needs.

Protein has assumed an almost religious importance in the diet of this country. Some people still believe that eating protein makes you stronger and that strenuous exercise requires eating extra protein, though those notions were disproved long ago. Protein's primary function in the body is the creation and repair of tissue — from skin, muscles and bones to hair and finger nails. The amount of protein you need, therefore, depends more on your size and age than on your activity.

An average man's Recommended Daily Allowance, or RDA, for protein is 56 grams, a woman's is 44 grams. Controlled studies have shown that men eating only 30 to 35 grams of protein a day lost no body protein. That amount would be provided by as little as four ounces of Swiss cheese, tuna or similar protein-rich food.

The RDA for children is proportionally more for their weight than the RDA for adults because children are growing. The RDA for children under four years is 23 gram, about half that for an adult woman. Of course, that is an average. You can't expect a three-month old baby to have the same amount of protein as a three-year-old child. For children between four and six, the RDA is 30 grams, nearly half the amount for an adult man. Children from seven to ten should have an averaged RDA of 34 grams, whether they are boys or girls. When children further grow, there seems to be different needs in quantity for boys and girls. For kids from 11 to 14, girls generally need a little more than boys, approximately 46 grams for girls and 44 grams for boys. Girls' needs for protein remain more or less the same as they grow but for boys from 15 onwards, they need the same amount of protein as adult men, that is, 56 grams.

Now you have some time to check your answers to questions 31 – 35.

Now you have some time to look at questions 36 – 40.

Listen carefully to the second part of the lecture and answer questions 36 – 40.

The RDAs for protein, as for other nutrients, are set high to allow for the range of individual needs and for a margin of safety against deficiency. The RDAs also allow for the different absorption rates of animal and plant protein. Besides eating enough protein, you have to eat enough high-quality protein.

The quality of a protein is determined by its amino acids. Proteins are large molecules composed of various combinations of 22 smaller compounds called amino acids. The human body, if it has enough raw material, can synthesize most of those amino acids. But eight or nine — called the essential amino acids — cannot be synthesized. They must be supplied in food, and they are needed in certain proportions.

Other animals produce proteins whose amino acids are in roughly the same proportion as those required by humans, so protein from animal flesh, milk, and eggs is called complete, or high-quality protein. Wheat germ, dried yeast, and soybeans approach animal protein in quality. But most plant proteins are low in one or more essential amino acids; the deficient, or limiting amino acid varies from plant to plant.

The body doesn't care where its amino acids come from, and few vegetarians eat just one plant food. Most of them eat some animal protein, and most animal protein is complete. Animal protein also improves the quality of plant protein when the two are eaten together, an effect known as protein complementation. Thus, the limiting amino acids in macaroni, shredded wheat, or rye bread are filled in when those foods are eaten as macaroni and cheese, shredded wheat and milk, or an egg-salad sandwich on rye.

It's also possible to improve the quality of plant protein by combining foods with different limiting amino acids. And because the limiting amino acids of similar plant foods tend to be similar, you don't have to memorize an amino-acid table to complement plant protein. Beans and rice, for example, are a food combination in almost every part of the world. The limiting amino acid of the beans, called methionine, is supplied by the rice, and the limiting amino acid of the rice, called lysine, is supplied by the beans. I think it is safe to say that grains, such as rice, oats, wheat, and corn complement with beans and peas. Other plant proteins don't complement the protein in grains and beans quite as well but are still useful as protein sources.

Protein malnutrition usually occurs only when you don't get enough food to eat. The person most vulnerable is the young child eating a monotonous all-plant diet. Plant foods are generally bulky and have a low protein content. Cooked rice, for example, is only about 2 percent protein. It's therefore sometimes hard for small children to eat enough to meet their protein needs. Even a small amount of animal protein, such as milk, can significantly improve the quality of protein a child eats. Fortified soy milk can also be useful in helping a child get enough high-quality protein.

That is the end of Section 4. You now have half a minute to check your answers.

The test is nearly over. You now have one more minute to check all your answers.

Now you have 10 minutes to transfer all your answers to the answer sheet. In the real test, you'll be told to stop writing and hand in your question booklet at the end of the ten minutes.

听力模拟试题四

Instructions:

You'll have a number of different recordings and you'll have to answer questions on what you hear.

There will be time for you to read the instructions and the questions and you'll have a chance to check your work. All the recordings will be played once only. The test is in four sections.

Now turn to Section 1.

Section 1

You'll hear a conversation between Janet and Philip who bump into each other in another country. First, look at the example and questions 1 – 5. For each of the questions, fill in the boxes with no more than three words or letters. First, listen to the example.

W: Hey! Philip! I can hardly believe it!

M: Janet ... Janet Adams! Well, I'll be blowed!

W: It must be all of ... how many years?

M: Six ... no ... seven. Would you believe it! And here we are in Sydney. What a coincidence!

W: What're you doing here? On holiday?

M: No. I work here now. I teach at Sydney University.

Philip is teaching at Sydney University. Therefore his current employer is Sydney University. Now we shall begin. You should answer the questions as you listen because you'll not hear the recordings a second time. First you'll have another chance to look at questions 1 – 5.

Now listen carefully and answer questions 1 – 5.

W: Hey! Philip! I can hardly believe it!

M: Janet ... Janet Adams! Well, I'll be blowed!

W: It must be all of ... how many years?

M: Six ... no ... seven. Would you believe it! And here we are in Sydney. What a coincidence!

W: What're you doing here? On holiday?

M: No. I work here now. I teach at Sydney University. What about you?

W: Oh, I'm on holiday.

M: So you're just over for the...

W: ... for three days ... that's it. Came over on the boat this morning. It's an excursion. Everybody in the party came over. It's a package holiday... but ... well, you know, these organised holidays, you know what they're like. Everybody doing everything together ... all at the same time. You sometimes need to lose the others for a bit. Tell me, Philip, when did you come to Australia?

M: I've been here for two years. Got an offer in 1995 and came over the following year.

W: Doing the same job ever since?

M: No. My first job was a research position in a company. This is my second.

W: You married?

M: Well, yes and no. I was married but it didn't last long. Her name is Susan. She is Australian. We are separated.

W: No kids?

M: No, fortunately. What about you? You haven't said anything about yourself.

W: Do you remember Jack?

M: How could I forget him? The life and soul of our class. What about him?

W: We got married.

M: Really? Congratulations! Where is he now?

W: He said he wanted to send some postcards and is now in that post office.

M: Are you still in photography?

W: No. I worked for a magazine as a photographic reporter. Did not last long. Had to travel a lot. I was pregnant. So I had to find a different job. Call me artist if you want. I am working for a design company. Trendy stuff, fashion, jewelry.

M: Good money, er?

W: Not too bad.

M: How old is your child?

W: I got a pair of twin girls.

M: Oh, Janet. You are wonderful. How old are they?

W: Three.

M: Are they with you?

W: No. My mother is looking after them.

M: Well, well, great. Are you sure you didn't lose Jack?

W: He can't get rid of me. I'm sure he'll be here in a minute.

Janet and Philip continue their conversation. As you listen to the second part of the conversation, fill in boxes 6 – 11. First, you'll have some time to look at questions 6 – 11.

Now you'll hear the second part of the conversation. Listen carefully and answer questions 6 – 11.

W: Well, Philip, don't you want to ask about Alison?

M: OK. What about her?

W: She is now in London, working for a computer company. She studied for a year at London School of Economics and got a master degree, accounting. She's doing very well. Philip, you've got to tell me what happened? Everyone said you and Alison were a perfect match.

M: That was how we felt at the beginning. It didn't work out. Very complicated. If you really want to know, I'll tell you later. Is she married?

W: No, but I heard that she's been dating John.

M: Which John?

W: The leader of our team, remember?

M: You mean the research project we did before we graduated?

W: Yes.

M: But he was courting Helen.

W: Yes. Helen got a job right after graduation, in Somali, working for the United Nations, as an assistant project manager. She asked John if he wanted to be there for two years, but John got a good offer studying geology, oh, no, I think it was remote sensing, at Cambridge, so he didn't go to Somali.

M: What is John doing now?

W: He is now a civil servant, working in Oxford for the Ministry of Environment.

M: Yes, that's like him. Of course he didn't want to go to Africa. He is too good for that.

W: Are you jealous?

M: I never like him. How about Helen? Is she still in Somali.

W: Yes, I think so. Helen is very unusual. She had an accident, car crash. Stayed in hospital for three months.

M: In Somali?

W: No, in Manchester, when she went back for holiday.

M: And she went back to Somali.

W: Yes, she did. She is not working for the UN anymore. She's now doing voluntary work, teaching English. And she is married to a French scientist working there.

M: You are still your old self. Very popular. Everyone wants to share secrets with you.

W: Not you, Philip.

M: No. I sort of shut myself. I knew Alison and I had problems so the best thing to do is go abroad. You keep in touch with many people, don't you?

W: In fact, you were the only one that vanished. Before Helen went back to Africa, we had a big party. More than a dozen turned up. Alison was there too. Pity you were not there.

M: Next time you have a party, tell me.

M2: Hey, Janet. I was looking for you.

W: See who I've been talking with.

M2: Oh, my god. Philip. How on earth...

M: Hi, Jack. What a surprise.

M2: We knew you were in Australia. Fancy meeting you in Sydney. I thought you were in the jungles, catching crocodiles...

That's the end of Section 1. You'll have half a minute to check your answers.

Now turn to Section 2.

Section 2

You'll now hear an excerpt from a radio program called Health Time. As you listen to the talk, answer questions 12 – 20. *First, you have some time to look at the questions.*

Now listen to the excerpt and answer questions 12 – 20.

M: This is *Health Time*, Radio Four. Good morning. Today we have invited Dr. Jones, who is an expert in sleep related problems, to tell us something about what we should do about a common problem that many of us sometimes suffer — insomnia, that is, the difficulty we experience when it is time for us to sleep. Now, Dr. Jones.

W: Thanks, David. Well, millions of people are plagued by difficulty in falling asleep — and staying asleep. Many of us have formed the bad habit of relying on sleeping pills. We all know this does us no good in the long run but the problem is what else can we do apart from taking the pills that we hate. Well, here are some medically proven ways to get a better night's sleep without dangerous or habit-forming drugs.

Many of us still believe that in order to be healthy we must have eight hours of sleep a night; or that if we sleep poorly over a period of time, we'll get lines in our faces, bags under our eyes, a worn look, and worst of all, be unable to perform our daily tasks sufficiently.

Well, how much of this belief is true? Not very much of it. You may look awful to yourself, but except for the first hour or so in the morning when you probably will be puffy-eyed due to depletion of a certain hormone that's the result of lack of sleep, you'll soon look like your usual self and perform normally. If you do feel worn, the cause is stress, not lack of sleep. Also, there is no set number of hours you must sleep to maintain good health. Some people get along beautifully on four and a half hours, others sleep nine hours. Anywhere within that range is normal.

So, no big worries. But what causes insomnia?

Recent studies of patients at sleep clinics have revealed significant facts about the causes of insomnia as well as ways to deal with it. It's no surprise that stress and depression over family, health, job, or other problems are linked to insomnia. Also, insomnia may be caused by physical illness: itching, aches, arthritis, and heart problems that involve shortness of breath or difficulty in breathing.

In order to overcome insomnia, many of us turn to drugs — both over-the-counter drugs and prescription drugs. What can I say about these drugs? Well, remember this: "No pill will produce normal sleep." You reach no proper levels of sleep through a pill; you're merely sedated.

What can you do if you suffer from insomnia? Two things: you can eat certain foods that will help you fall asleep and stay asleep, and you can do certain things that are sleep-inducing. Here are some do's and don'ts Dr. Milner has worked out after years of research. I'll give you the don'ts first.

If you've had a bad night's sleep, don't stay in bed later the next morning.

Second, don't go to bed earlier the next night. Stick to your usual bedtime and rising pattern.

Another thing that you shouldn't be doing is nap during the day. Naps cut down on night sleep-time.

Furthermore, never lie awake in bed for more than 30 minutes. By lying in bed sleepless you form an association between your bed and sleeplessness, thus reinforcing your poor sleeping pattern.

Finally, when you retire for the night, don't lie there rehashing the mistakes of the day. Nor is this the time to plan your next day's activities — you may become too anxious or over stimulated.

Now what can you do to have a good sleep?

First, when you get out of bed after half an hour of sleeplessness, do something, but make sure it's something dull. Read a book that doesn't interest you much. Never watch TV or listen to the radio.

Or, you can try sitting still in a chair in a darkened room — you'll be surprised how fast you'll get sleepy.

Of course, get as much exercise as possible, preferably early in the day. Exercise is a great sleep inducer.

Also, develop a bedtime routine: closing up the house and turning out the lights in a certain way, bathing, plumping up the pillows. Sleep studies show that doing things in sequence — in a way that tends to calm and soothe — can help you achieve a good sleep pattern.

M: Thank you very much, Dr. Jones. Now it is question and answer time. We already have someone waiting on the line. Yes, Mrs. Renshaw, is it? What is your question...

That is the end of Section 2. You now have half a minute to check your answers.

Now turn to Section 3.

Section 3

You'll hear an interview outside a tobacco shop between a man and a woman whose name is Mrs. Bradley. The man asks Mrs. Bradley questions about her and her husband's smoking habit. First, you'll have some time to look at the examples and questions 21 – 30.

The conversation will now begin. Listen carefully and fill in the answers to questions 21 – 30.

M: Excuse me, madam.

W: Yes?

M: I wonder whether you'd help us. We're doing a survey on smokers' habits. Would you and... ?

W: Well... I'm in a bit of a hurry actually.

M: It'll only take a few minutes. We'd very much appreciate your help.

W: Well, all right. I can spare that, I suppose.

M: Thank you. You are a smoker ... of course?

W: Yes, I'm afraid I am. My husband is too. As you can see ... I've just bought the week's ration.

M: Would you describe yourself as being a heavy smoker?

W: Heavy ... no. I wouldn't call three packets of twenty a week heavy smoking. That's not even ten a day. No ... a light smoker. My husband... he's different...

M: Yes?

W: I get in twice as many a week for him. He smokes twenty or more a day.

M: You wouldn't describe him as a chain-smoker... ?

W: No, he's not as bad as that.

M: Right. Thank you, Mrs. ...?

W: Bradley. Doris Bradley.

M: Mrs. Bradley, you and your husband smoke cigarettes I see. What about cigars ... a pipe ... Does your husband?

W: Oh he's never smoked a pipe. He's the restless, nervy type. I always associate pipe-smoking with people of another kind ... the calm contented type. As for cigars I suppose he only smokes a few in a year — normally during Christmas time, especially after his Christmas dinner. Of course I only smoke cigarettes.

M: Right. Now let's keep to you, Mrs. Bradley. When and why — if that's not asking too much — did you begin to smoke? Can you remember?

W: Yes, I remember very well. I'm thirty-two now ... so I must have been ... er ... yes ... seventeen ... when I had my first cigarette. It was at a party and — you know — at that age you want to do everything your friends do. So when my boyfriend — not my husband — when he offered me a cigarette I accepted it. I remember feeling awfully grown-up about it. Then I started smoking... let's see now ... just two or three a day ... and I gradually increased.

M: I see. That's very clear. Now ... might I ask if you have ever tried to give up smoking?

W: Yes — twice. The first time about six months before getting married. Oh, that was because I was saving up and... yes ... I used to smoke more in those days. Sometimes thirty a day. So I decided to give it up — but only succeeded, I'm afraid, in cutting it down. I still smoked a little...

M: And the second time?

W: Oh the second time I did manage to give up completely for a while. I was expecting and the doctor advised me not to smoke at all. I went for about seven or eight months ... without a single cigarette.

M: Then you took it up again.

W: Yes ... a couple of weeks after the baby was born. It was all right then because the baby was being bottle-fed anyway.

M: Good. That's interesting. So if you'd been breast-feeding you would have gone for longer without smoking?

W: Definitely. It's what the doctors advise, though not all mothers do as their doctors say.

M: Well, Mrs. Bradley, you tried twice to quit but both attempts failed. Have you thought about giving a third try?

W: Yes, I have, but, you know ... this is really because of my husband. He's a heavy smoker and it has never occurred to him that he should stop smoking. If he is like that, there's no chance that I can succeed. So I don't even bother to try.

M: Now, Mrs. Bradley, when do you smoke most?

W: Erm ... when I'm sitting watching TV or ... or ... reading a book ... but especially when I'm with ... when I'm in company. Yes... that's it ... when I'm with friends. I never smoke when I'm doing the housework ... never. There's always too much to do.

M: Do you ever smoke at mealtimes?

W: I always have one cigarette after a meal, never on an empty stomach, which reminds me — I must be going. My husband will be waiting for his lunch, and Keith ... he's my son...

M: Just one more question and that'll be all.

W: Well, if you insist.

M: How would you describe the effect that smoking has on you?

W: What do you mean?

M: Well ... does smoking — for example — make you excitable ... keep you awake...?

W: Oh no — quite the contrary. As I told you before I smoke most at times when I'm most relaxed. Though quite honestly I... I don't really know whether I smoke because I'm relaxed or ... er... you know ... in order to relax. Now I really must be ... Please excuse me. I see you're... you're carrying a tape-recorder. This won't be on the radio, will it?

M: No, Mrs. Bradley ... I'm afraid not. But we do thank you all the same.

W: Right. Goodbye.

M: Goodbye, Mrs. Bradley.

That is the end of Section 3. *You now have half a minute to check your answers.*

Now turn to Section 4.

Section 4

The following is a lecture about alcoholic drinking. Listen to the lecture and answer questions 31 – 40. *First you'll have some time to look at questions* 31 – 35.

Now listen carefully to the first part of the lecture and answer questions 31 – 35.

I have devoted most of my professional life to the problems of alcohol. Alcohol is a drug and alcohol abuse is the most serious drug problem this nation faces. Nonetheless, I believe firmly that alcohol can do more good than harm. For there is a safe way to drink.

Pharmacologically, alcohol is an anesthetic, not a stimulant. That is to say, it slows down the body whereas a stimulant speeds it up. In moderate amounts, it appears to stimulate because it inhibits those brain centers which restrict "less civilized" outbursts, as well as those which make us aware of exhaustion. Then we feel physically abler and emotionally freer. But with increasing doses, alcohol puts to sleep the brain centers which affect judgment, knowledge and social controls. Sufficient dosage can put us to sleep for keeps by anesthetizing those centers which control breathing and heartbeat.

An essential point is that there is a known, safe level of drinking. My colleagues and I found that researchers all over the world were independently using the same level to define safe or moderate drinking: one and half ounces of pure alcohol per day — the equivalent of three one-ounce drinks of 100-proof whiskey (which is 50-percent alcohol), four eight-ounce glasses of beer, or half a bottle of wine.

This limit, of course, is only a statistical average. For some people, even one drop of alcohol is too much. Nor do our findings permit saving up one day's ration in order to drink more the next day. At no time should any individual wishing to remain within the safe-limits consume more than one and half ounces of pure alcohol in a single day.

Studies show that the driver who has consumed an amount of alcohol within this limit is no more likely to have an automobile accident than the driver who does not take any alcohol. But beyond this limit, when the blood-alcohol level, that is, the concentration of alcohol in the blood, begins to creep over the 0.05 percent "sober" level, the risk of a traffic accident jumps enormously. By the time the blood-alcohol level reaches 0.2 percent, the level of most drunk drivers who are arrested, the risk of an accident is 100 times that of the non-drinking driver.

The manner of drinking is also crucial. One should always sip slowly. Alcohol is a highly unusual foodstuff in that at least 20 percent of it is absorbed directly from the stomach into the bloodstream without going through any digestive processes. Therefore, gulping alcohol produces a sudden, marked rise in the alcohol level in the blood and hence in the brain. Once alcohol is in the bloodstream, nothing, with the exception of a kidney-dialysis machine, can clear it from the blood more quickly than the body's own steady metabolic rate of three quarters of an ounce of pure alcohol per hour.

Now you have some time to check your answers to questions 31 – 35.

Now you have some time to look at questions 36 – 40.

Listen carefully to the second part of the lecture and answer questions 36 – 40.

Another rule of safe drinking is that food in the stomach, preferably protein or fatty products, effectively delays alcohol's invasion of our systems. Food covers the stomach wall, making capillaries less accessible. It also sponges up the alcohol and carries it gradually through the digestive process, slowing absorption and allowing the metabolism and brain to adapt. So, as any experienced drinker knows, the same dose taken with food in the stomach will provide a more pleasant outcome than alcohol on an empty stomach.

A number of other factors also influence our response to a drink. It's best not to take alcohol when physically or emotionally upset, lonely or in need of solace. It is true that alcohol's anesthetic effect will dull the pain of loneliness. But alcohol is no substitute for another person. In other words, do not drink alone.

Regardless of where and how you drink, what you expect from alcohol is what you get. As with almost all drugs, expectation is strongly related to outcome. If you're part of a group that wants to act drunk, even with small doses, you'll feel drunk.

Alcoholism is a social problem in this country and we feel guilty about alcohol. If we can be more open to the problem, I think we could do more for people with alcohol problems. We might also do more for our children. Surveys completed in 1995 show that children in this country between the ages of 12 and 17 are already manifesting severe alcohol abuse; in fact, five percent of these "kids" get drunk at least once a week.

Indeed, always to focus on alcohol in the context of alcoholism is, I think, to miss the point. If you are preoccupied with alcohol, if you or others in your environment are discomfited by this preoccupation, if alcohol interferes with your ability to function in other necessary ways, then you have an alcohol problem.

Our country is very concerned these days with safety and health. We have to remind ourselves that anything that affects human beings has a potential for harm. In too great a quantity, even oxygen and water, those essentials of life, can harm or kill. So life is a risk, and I suspect the only sure way to be safe from disease and dying is to be dead.

But there are safe limits that people can use in making their decisions about risk-taking, such as choosing to drink or not to drink or how much to drink. We ought to share with young and old alike the best available knowledge on such subjects. And then let each individual make up his or her own mind.

That is the end of Section 4. *You now have half a minute to check your answers.*

The test is nearly over. You now have one more minute to check all your answers.

Now you have 10 *minutes to transfer all your answers to the answer sheet. In the real test, you'll be told to stop writing and hand in your question booklet at the end of the ten minutes.*

第三章　口语考试

一、口语考试简介

口语考试称为 interview，分五个阶段或部分：1）个人情况介绍；2）深谈某一话题；3）角色扮演；4）憧憬未来；5）结束。以下是各部分的形式、内容及注意事项。

（一）个人情况介绍

考生走进口试考场后，考官首先会请考生就座，介绍自己，讲一两句寒暄、安慰的话，然后开始口试。考官首先会请考生做一点自我介绍。考生应先介绍自己的姓名、年龄、婚姻状况（如已婚，提一下配偶的职业或工作单位；如有孩子，提一下孩子的性别、年龄、是上幼儿园还是上小学）。然后用两三句话介绍自己的工作。比如：

例 1：

My name is Wang Tong. I am 28. I am single. Now I work for a Chinese computer company. My responsibility is to develop software according to customers' needs.

例 2：

My name is Li Hui. I have an English name, Grace. I am 32. I am married. My husband is a university teacher, teaching chemistry. We have a 5-year-old son. He'll go to primary school next year, which is going to be a big change for him, and for me and my husband, too. I work in a pharmaceutical company. It is a joint-venture company. I am the manager of the sales department.

培训班有可能把考生变得像出自同一个模子，教材亦是如此。希望考生们能在“套路”上稍做变化，以使自己不同于其他考生。这一点不仅适用于口语考试，也适用于写作考试。但基本的模式不应有太大的变化，因为这些模式符合两方的习惯。例如，在做自我介绍时先说出生年、月、日，再说小学、中学、大学……，就不符合西方的模式。

在介绍完自己的姓名、年龄、婚姻状况和工作后，考生即可停止，等待考官的下一个问题。

在这部分有以下几点值得注意：

1. 与婚姻有关的表达方法。

I am married. 我已婚。

I've married for two years. 我结婚两年了。

I got married last year. 我于去年结婚。

I am married to an army officer. 我嫁(娶)了一个军官。

I am divorced. 我离婚了。

I got divorced last year. 我去年离了婚。

marry 一词用法比较灵活，考生应注意准确使用。

2. 自己及配偶的工作单位的英文名称应该记住。机构特点、隶属关系等具有“中国特色”的单位可能会引起考官的兴趣，但有时因情况特殊，无法用三言两语说清。遇有这种情况，不妨说点谎话。比如，可以把经贸委与经贸部统称为 Ministry of Trade，因为考官如果问起两者之间在作用、结构等方面的差别，考生回答时可能会有困难。再如，可把中医说成西医，以避免用英文叙述中医理论与实践(诸如经络学说、滋阴壮阳等等)。

3. 为口试的第二部分做一定的铺垫。如果自己的工作、家庭等有进一步发挥的余地，可稍加渲染，使其成为第二部分的话题。但要小心，不要作茧自缚。说自己喜欢足球或音乐就比较危险，因为英语口语不出色的话，最好还是不要和英国人侃足球。侃音乐也少不了要提到作曲家的名字和曲目名。用英语表达这些内容未必是我们的长处。这只是两个简单的例子，考生可以认真地设计一番，把自己的情况勾画出来，看看哪些是安全的枝叉，可以继续延伸，哪些是危险的枝叉，不能去碰。

(二) 深谈某话题

在前一段对话的基础上，考官会自然地接过一个话题，让考生较详细地描述某事物或发表对某事的看法。比如让考生比较家乡和另一城市的区别，或让考生谈对城市交通现状和未来的看法。

这部分是整个口试最重要的部分，考生的口试成绩主要看他在这一部分的表现。无论考生做怎样的准备，考生的实力终将在这部分中暴露。训练有素的考官可以轻易地识破那些试图掩盖实际能力的招术，如果考官发现考生是出自他不喜欢的门派就更惨了(有些考官对某些培训点传授的招术很不以为然)。那么考生在口试的这部分中除了“被人鱼肉”就束手无策了吗？其实未必。以下是一些“招”，未必灵验，但不会起负作用。

1. 持真诚的态度。既然来参加考试，每个考生都想取得好成绩，但要靠真才实学，不要把考场看成是一个战场，那些玩弄心理战的做法不会见效。例如，某培训点告诉考生，应设法拉近考生和考官之间的距离，做法之一就是问“Have we met before?”如果某考官碰到不止一名考生提这样的问题，他很容易就知道这是考生用的“招”。凡是用此招的考生，必然不会有好结果。这是个真实的故事，希望考生引以为诫。一些培训点利用考生急功近利的心态，不负责任地传授一些拙劣的招数，以换取考生对教学效果的承认。希望考生端正心态，以一种真诚的态度对待口试。

2. 认真对付新话题。一般来说，第二部分的话题是第一部分对话的自然的延伸，但在以下几种情况下，考官会给考生提出新的话题：1)考生出色地完成了第一个话题；2)考生不具备谈论第一个话题的能力；3)考官发现考生事先做了准备。遇到新话题，首先要认真地去“侃”，让考官感到你的真诚。有一位考生口语非常出色，多次因公出国，去过澳洲。考官恰好也是澳洲人，话题自然是考生对澳洲的看法、印象。在很投机地聊了一阵之后，考官让考生进一步谈澳洲的某些事情。考生冒出一句：“I was in Australia for only two weeks. How could I know everything?”这两句话所传达的信息是“I don't want to talk about it”。这位本来可得9段的考生只得了6段，他分析自己口试得分如此之低的原因就是说了上述很不得体的话。

3. 充分认识到口试第二部分的重要性及考官的意图。这部分口试的目的很明确，就是要看考生是否有用英语发表长篇大论的能力。因此，考生要尽量地就考官指定的话题更深、更广地进行议论，以显示自己有这方面的能力，而不要戛然而止。例如，考官让考生比较成都与北京的同、异。考生说：“Well, there are too many people in Beijing and the traffic conditions are often in a mess. Chengdu is too hot in summer. In fact, I don't like either Beijing or Chengdu.”在没有进行充分的讨论的情况下就得出了结论，为这个话题画上了句号。在这种情况下，考官要么再给你一个修补的机会，或者给你一个新话题，要么就得出“He is not good enough to talk about this”的结论，结束这部分考试，进行下一部分。

(三) 角色扮演

在口试的第三部分中，考生需根据考官提供的一张指示卡(a cue card)提问。这部分口试的目的是看考生是否能用得体的句子结构来提问。

提示卡所描述的情景可大体分为两类：

1. “生人之间”的关系

在某个英语国家，考生由于初来乍到，有一些事情不明白(如某新生询问图书馆的各种使用情况)，考官是工作人员(秘书、接待员、活动的组织者、老师等)。考生要向考官打听提示卡上列出的若干项内容(如图书馆的营业时间、如何办证、借书期限及数量、逾期有何惩罚、还有哪些其他服务等)。与考官的关系可简单的称为“生人之间”的关系,这种关系决定了提问的方式和语气要客气。

提问前先根据口试是在上午还是在下午打个招呼:Good morning 或 Good afternoon。然后简单地介绍自己的情况,如:

I am a new student. I need some information about ...

I would like to know the details of .... Don't know if you could help me.

介绍部分仅需一两句话,不要啰嗦。然后就用正式、客气、礼貌的方式提问。如 Could you tell me when the library is open? 要注意变化提问方式,不能每句都以同样的词开始。随着交流的深入,两人之间的距离也在缩小。有这样一个转变的过程才显得自然,也更为得体。因此,“正式、客气、礼貌”更多地用于头一两个问题,以后的问题可以更加直接一些,例如:How much does it cost? 而不是 Would you mind telling me how much it costs? 也可以用陈述句的形式来表达询问:I would like to know if the library provides other services.

这部分特别要注意的是,不要把一个太大的问题交给考官,如:Could you tell me something about the conference? 而是要针对会议的时间、地点、与会人数、会务费、会议期间的交通、食宿等一项一项地问。

在结束这一部分时应对考官回答问题表示感谢,这也是考试内容。结束的方式有:

You've been very helpful. Thank you very much.

I have got all the information I need. Thanks.

I really appreciate your help.

That's lovely. I think I have got all the details. Thank you.

最后用 Good-bye 将球踢回给考官。

2. “熟人之间”的关系

你的某个同事或朋友要参加某项活动,或刚参加过某项活动,你出于好奇、关心或实际需要等原因,向他打听他的经历、感觉、计划、目的、印象等。这种关系可以简单地称为“熟人之间”的关系。这类提示卡出现的频率低于前一类,提问时不应用“客气、正式、礼貌”的方式,而是更随便一些。其实这两者的差别就在于前者用“Could you please ...?”“I wonder if you could ... .”“Would you mind ... ?”,后者直接用疑问代词或疑问副词开始的问句。例如,考官结束了一个你正想参加的活动(课程、旅游等),你需要了解一些这项活动情况:

Hi, John.(如考官是女性,随便选一个女性的名字。男性的名字也绝不止 John 一个,应尽量用别的名字,以避免与其他考生雷同)I am thinking of attending a computer skill course. Susan told me you just finished one. Maybe you could tell me something about it. For example, how much did it cost?

其他可能的问题有:How many people were there in your class? Did you have to do a lot of homework? How long was the course? 等等。

结束时可以说：Thanks. I'll think about it. My class will begin soon. I've got to go. I'll talk to you later.

在"角色扮演"部分里，考生还应注意以下几点。

1. 这部分的重要性远不如口试的第二部分，但考生常常在这部分的准备过程中花太多的精力。这也许和所谓"真题"有关。许多培训点在口语教学中均使用与"真题"很近似的提示卡，考生很容易将培训点提供的提示卡视为救命稻草，抓住不放，反复要求教员支"招"。其实，这部分只是根据考试要求走个过场。换言之，在这一部分的表现再出色，也不会给口试的成绩带来分量。主要原因有二：1)提示卡交代的情景缺乏深度，考生应完成的口语任务缺乏区分度；2)考题极易泄露，许多考生有备而来。虽然考生在这部分的出色表现也许不起什么作用，但表现欠佳却会带来负面影响。因此，适当地做一些准备是有必要的，但不必过多地纠缠。

2. 提示卡在简单地交代情景之后列出应该询问的六七个方面，原则上应全问到，但不必完全按提示卡上的顺序。考生亦可酌情增加一两个问题，但不要画蛇添足。比如在询问交通费、门票、会员费等与价格有关的事项时，可以加问学生是否有优惠(reduction 或 concession)。但这个"招"不能在所有与价格有关的方面都问。例如，学生团体的会员费或是学校专门为学生组织的活动就不会因为你是学生而有优惠。再比如，去参加一般 party 可以问是否能带自己的朋友，但导师请你吃饭就不应该问"Can I bring my friend?"

3. 口试应视为是一个自然的交流机会，即使这部分设定了一个"假定"的语言环境，交流时也要自然。有的考生喜欢在考官回答完每一个问题后都有一点 response。如："Oh, really?""That's great.""I see.""I like that." 如果做得过分，有太多的表演色彩，会让人觉得不自然，甚至不舒服。

4. 既然反复强调自然，就要做到考官在回答问题时与他有目光接触，让考官知道你在听。由于英语水平等原因，有的考生在提出问题之后马上去看提示卡，脑子里在准备下一个问题，根本没有在听考官的回答。这既说明这位考生的英语不好，也显得缺乏礼貌。因此，无论是在问，还是在听，都要有频繁的目光接触。

5. 许多培训点都在使用与"真题"极为近似的提示卡。在实际考试中如遇到熟悉的卡，千万不要喜形于色，否则考官会更换提示卡。拿到这样的卡后，也要"认真地"去看三四十秒，然后"底气不足"地问"Can I begin?"

6. 在设计提示卡时，作者已考虑到词汇问题，一般不会使用偏词、难词。但如果考生确有个别词不认识，应该在开始提问之前先解决生词的问题：

Excuse me. I don't know the meaning of ...

Could you tell me what ... means?

Before I start, could I ask you about the meaning of a word?

这样做非但不会使你显得“词汇有限”,反而证明你能够把断桥修好,对你获得更好的口试成绩有积极作用。采取回避的方法会有负作用。

7. 在问完了所有该问的问题之后,应及时做出表示,不要既不提问,也不结束。应果断地表达你不再有其他问题,希望结束这段对话。(见前文关于“生人之间”和“熟人之间”应如何收尾。)

(四) 憧憬未来

第三部分结束后,谈话从假定的、人工的语言环境回到现实。考官要问考生对自己不久的将来有何展望。如果是出国留学,考官会问到联系了哪些大学,为什么选择某所大学,预料在学习和生活方面会有何困难,毕业后有何打算,如回国能否有提升或更好的工作等。对出国移民的考生主要围绕将打算如何生存,会有哪方面的问题等。

计划留学的考生在回答这部分问题时可畅所欲言,如对学习和生活方面的问题有思想准备,学习结束后希望有一定的工作机会,最终要回中国发展等。这类考生的出国动机不会对考官造成威胁。出国留学是对西方教育制度信任、欣赏的表现,留学生所交的学费也是英国、澳大利亚大学的重要收入来源。一般来说,考官是欢迎考生去留学的。

计划移民的考生则不然。他们要向公民一样享受教育,医疗等方面的待遇,要参加就业市场的竞争。这可能会使某些考官感到一种威胁。因此,考生在谈话时要有所顾忌。例如:

I'll first find a job to earn some money. Then I'll study for an MBA degree. When I have a higher degree, I'll be able to find a job that pays a good salary. After working for one or two years, I'll start my own business.

这种愿望也许会使某个考官感到一个 Chinese invasion 正在到来。

在出国定居的道路上存在着许多未知因素。考生在语言、文化、就业等方面都会遇到困难。可就这些问题展开,表达一种忧虑、担心前途未卜的心情。比如:

I've been working for a number of years and have saved some money. I hope this money can last me for a year. When I arrive in Canada (or Australia), I'll first improve my English. If there is a job, I'll certainly take it. I know there will be problems, such as cultural shock, loneliness. It'll take some time for me to become settled. If I can afford it, I'll study for a higher degree. Now I have a bachelor's degree. If the worst comes to the worst, I mean if there's no job, no opportunities, I can always return to China and do the same job that I have been doing. ...

（五）结束

听完考生对未来的展望，考官会对考生说 Thank you. That's all for today's interview. I wish you a success in your immigration application. You may leave now.

考生应回答：

It was nice talking to you. Thank you for your time. Hope we can meet again. Bye.

口试结束时考生惟一要注意的事情就是要在离开考场之前说一两句表示感谢的话。

二、口试中的常见问题

1. 礼貌问题

雅思考试的口试一词是 interview，有访谈、面试等意思。在西方文化中，它常指求职时的面试，其重要性不言而喻。雅思考试的考生也无一例外地是因为要出国才来参加考试的。因此，考官一般认为这个考试对考生来说很重要。但由于客观条件的限制（如考生坐了一夜火车来参加考试，从火车站直奔考点，衬衫不净，还有点蓬头垢面），考官会觉得考生不重视这个 interview。有时因为口语水平、考试紧张、缺乏与"外宾"交往的经验等，不会说客套话，这也让考官感到不舒服。因此建议考生对自己的服饰、容貌稍加修理，要做到干净、利落。女考生一定要化妆。如果是冬天，进考场之前先脱掉大衣。进门后先打招呼，然后将大衣放在椅背上、书包放在椅旁的地上。考官自然会先请考生就坐，然后先介绍自己，再开始口试。

在口试的第三部分以及在全部口试结束时，考生应向考官致谢，道别（见前文）。

2. 时间观念问题

上午的笔试结束后，考生可在考试办公室附近查到自己的口试安排。考生不应迟到，这不言而喻。但如果前面的考生因故不参加口试或迟到，就会造成考场的空档。根据公布的口试安排，每位考生的口试时间是 20 分钟。在实际操作中，很多考生的口试时间仅需 15 分钟。因此，每位考生都应提前 25 分钟左右到考场外等候。

3. 主导考试问题

有的考生在口试中会滔滔不绝地说，目的就是想"主导"考试，以使考官没有发问的机会。这种意图很容易被考官识破，他自然会打断考生。另外，要想做到"反客为主"，考生自然要用许多不着边际的内容来填充时间。在一次模拟口试中，一位考生的发言中就有"I love my grandmother very much.""My wife is a beautiful woman"，事后问他为什么这么做，他答道："我说得多，考官不就没有机会问了嘛。"其实，这样做结果往往会弄巧成拙。

4. 背"套路"的问题

考生出于急功近利的需要，背了很多内容，其中一些内容是由培训点统一提供的。这种做法很快会被考官识破,考生也会因此而不得不回答更难的问题。有的考官甚至让考生向为他们提供过培训的培训点转达:“我们(考官)不喜欢他们(培训点)的做法”。可以想像这样的考生会得什么样的分数。

这种背套路的做法更多地被用在口试的第二部分,即深谈某一话题。其实,由于大多数考生日常的语言环境完全是中文,没有什么讲英文的机会,不靠背诵就永远达不到“侃”的水平。所以,背书是必不可少的,问题在于怎么背,背什么。

假设有一位考生,他的妻子在某国营单位任工程师,有一个三岁的女儿,考生本人毕业于中山大学,毕业后先后在上海若干家外企工作过,现在一家日本公司工作。针对这些情况,这位考生可就以下话题做准备:国营单位在工作量、工资、责任等方面与外企的不同;子女教育问题(这涉及到独生子女教育、素质教育、中小学减负等方面);广州与上海的区别(天气、文化、经济、居民的性格、思维方式等);日本公司与其他外企公司的区别等等。考生可将自己的情况分析一番,找出若干可能会被考官拿来当话题的方面,将每一个方面都列出至少五六条,先写好,再去背。一定要自己写,这样才不会与别人的雷同。

5. 不断升高的横杆。雅思考试的口试原则之一是尽量给考生更多的空间,让他们证明自己可以用英语做更难的事,此做法与跳高的搭杆不断升高类似。我曾经三次参加雅思考试,在第三次考试的口试中就碰到了这一不断升高的横杆。我在北京语言文化大学出国人员培训部工作。因此,话题自然地落到“人才外流”(brain drain)。在谈论完这个话题后,考官又让我描述修补自行车内胎的过程。之后,考官又让我发表对联合国的作用的看法。至此,考官才罢休,拿出口试第三部分用的提示卡。

其实,对大多数考生来说,口试的目标是5段或6段,达到这个目标根本用不着去调侃“补车胎”和“联合国”。随着整个社会的英语水平的提高,加上很多人渴望出国学习、生活,许多考生早就在注意口语能力的提高,达到5段或6段的考生大有人在。因此,考生不必担心可能会出现很难的口语题。这些题是给两类人准备的,一类是英语口语能力很强的人,另一类是那些背了些套路、被考官识破的人。

三、为口试做准备

(一) 常用的口试问题

What is the meaning of your given name?

Does your name affect your personality?

Tell me something about your hometown.

What are the differences in accent between your hometown and Beijing (or another city in China)?

What is the character of the people like in your hometown?
What is people's favourite food in the region where you live?
What will you do during the Spring Festival this year?
Are there any traditional festivals in your region?
Describe a typical Spring Festival for a Chinese family.
Tell me something about the Lantern Festival.
Describe your wedding.
How have weddings changed in recent years?
Tell me something about the Qingming Festival.
Describe a traditional wedding ceremony.
How do Chinese usually celebrate birthdays?
Are there any traditions concerning the birth of a baby?
How do you like Beijing (or another city in China)? Compare it to your hometown.
What place do you like best in Beijing (or another city in China)?
What places in Beijing (or another city in China) should a foreigner visit?
What places would you recommend a visitor to go to in your region(or hometown)?
Have recent changes created any problems in the place you live in?
What changes have you seen in the past few years in your town?
If you had the choice, where would you choose to live in China?
Which parts of China would you recommend a foreigner to visit?
Tell me something about your family.
Which is the worst place you've been to in China?
Who takes the greatest responsibility for bringing up your child in your family?
Which is the best place you've been to in China?
Who does most of the household chores in your family?
Are the traditional sexual roles within the family changing?
Why is the divorce rate increasing so rapidly? Is it a problem?
What is your opinion of the one-child policy?
How do you discipline your child?
Is it acceptable for couples to live together without marrying?
If you had the choice, would you have a son or a daughter?
Are you going to bring your child up any differently from the way your parents did?
What hopes do you have for your child?
Do women still have too heavy a burden in their day-to-day life?
Is the increasing influence of the West largely a positive or negative thing?

What, in your opinion, has been the greatest change in recent years?
What, in your opinion, has been the most problematic change in recent years?
If you are a lecturer what changes have you seen in education over the past few years?
Who should bear the responsibility for payment of tuition fees?
What can be done to improve education in rural areas?
Have recent changes affected your job in any way?
Do you agree with private education?
What can be done to close the gap between urban and rural areas?
If you had the power, what reforms would you carry out within education?
Describe a typical working day for you.
How do you see yourself in 10 years time?
If you had the opportunity to change your job, what would you do instead?
If you had 1 million yuan, what would you do with it?
If you could start your life again, would you do anything differently?
Do you have any ambitions?
Which country (or place) would you most like to visit?
What changes do you think China will see in the next few years?
Will any possible future changes affect your job in any way?
How do you think you will cope in Britain (or Canada, Australia)?
Does anything worry you about going to the UK (or Canada, Australia)?
Are you looking forward to anything in particular in Britain (or Canada, Australia)?
What are your plans on your return to China?
Did you ever attend an IELTS training session? What do you think of the training?
What do you do in your spare time?
What will you do if you fail the IELTS?

(二) 角色扮演的几个问题

1. 如可能,尽量不要用提示卡上的词提问,因为这些词一般较正式,而在日常口语中,人们用更加口语化的词汇。如:

过于正式: Who are the participants?

比较口语化: Who will be at the meeting?

过于正式: What about place of submission?

比较口语化: Where must I hand it in?

2. 注意前文提到的生、熟人之间的不同语气,同时应注意尽量用简洁的方法表达自己的意思。

3. 如有生词或其他不明白的地方，一定要在开始 role play 之前询问。

4. 如是生人之间的关系，考生常常要做自我介绍。切记介绍时不要啰嗦。如：

比较啰嗦：Good morning. I'm a newcomer here. I've just arrived from China. I'm going to study for a master's degree at this university. . . .

比较简练：Hello. I've just arrived in Britain and I was wondering if I could ask you a few questions about. . .

5. 考官回答问题时要认真听，并可就其回答问更多的问题。

6. 不要提大问题，要提具体的问题。如：

过于笼统：Can you tell me something about. . .

Can you give me some information on. . .

比较具体：When. . . ?

Who. . . ?

7. 不要用"How about / What about. . . "，如：

How about finding books?

如果使用，也应有更具体的问题跟随，如：

How about finding books? Is the catalogue on computer or what?

8. 不要用重复考官的回答来表示听懂(数字或日期除外)。不要用"You mean. . . "，然后重复考官说的话。如确有澄清的必要，可以 rephrase 考官的话。

9. 表达方法要自然。如：

不够自然：And another question. . . / The last question is. . .

比较自然：Another thing is. . . . / One last / more thing. . .

10. 不要问无关的问题。如果考官说"You can get more information from the general office"，你就不应接着问"Where is the general office"或"When is the general office open"这样的问题，因为考官前面的回答的意思是"I don't know about this"。

11. 不要过多地使用"Would you mind telling me. . . "或"Could you tell me. . . "结构(见前文)。

12. 用不着使用 Miss、Madam、Sir 这样的称呼，也不要在考官的每一个回答之后都说"Thank you"。

13. Role play 结束时，简单道谢。如：

Thank you very much for your help.

Thank you. You've been very helpful.

Thanks. It's been really useful talking to you.

（三）一些用过的提示卡(cur cards)、考生提问及考官回答举例

1.

You are going to be studying at a British college. You meet a student who studies in the same city as you hope to go to. Find out about the cheapest way to live there. Accommodation　　Food　　Entertainment Transportation　　Books　　Discounts for students Shopping

考生提问举例

To start:

Hi, I hear you've been here a while now. Can I ask you a few things about how to live cheaply?

a) **Accommodation**

What's the cheapest kind of accommodation I can get?

Is it cheaper to live in university or in private accommodation?

b) **Transportation**

What's the cheapest way of getting about town?

Would it be possible to buy a cheap bike somewhere?

Is taking taxis very expensive?

c) **Shopping**

Where's the best place to find cheap clothing/ household goods?

Do supermarkets tend to be cheaper than smaller shops?

d) **Food**

Would it be cheaper to eat in university

考官回答举例

a) **Accommodation**

Private sector — Renting a house or a large flat with 3 or 4 friends is often the cheapest way.

Individual flats are most expensive.

University accommodation — self-catering halls cheapest (shared kitchen).

Where to find it — university accommodation office, ads in local newspapers, notices on university notice boards.

b) **Transportation**

Bus — weekly/ monthly/ season bus passes.

Long distance — coach (National Express student coachcard).

Trains — expensive, especially at peak hours.

Bike — secondhand bikes advertised in local papers.

c) **Shopping**

Can buy cheap household goods, clothes, and fruit & vegetables at street markets and special discount stores.

Good secondhand clothing and furniture at charity shops (e.g. Oxfam 销售募集来的旧衣物、书籍等的慈善商店).

d) **Food**

Supermarkets tend to be cheapest and

dining halls or to cook for myself?

Where do students usually buy their food?

Are takeaways very expensive?

If I want to eat out, what are the cheaper kind of places?

e) **Books**

I've heard books are pretty expensive in Britain. Is there anywhere I can get them cheaper?

f) **Entertainment**

What's the cheapest night out here?

What do students usually do for a cheap night out?

g) **Discounts for students**

As a student, what kind of concessions can I get?

Can I get a discount for my travel?

most convenient. Also street markets.

Eating out — cafes, pubs. Can usually find cheap Indian / Chinese / Italian restaurant.

e) **Books**

Secondhand book stalls / shops.

University Book Exchange — can buy used textbooks and also sell your old ones.

f) **Entertainment**

University entertainments tend to be cheapest — films, discos, theatre, etc.

Bar prices usually the cheapest in town.

Cinemas / theatres give student concessions.

Often free sports facilities in parks.

g) **Discounts for students**

Travel — student railcard / coachcard (a third off normal price 普通价的三分之二).

Museum / cinema / theatre entrance fees.

2.

As part of your course at your college in the UK, you have to do a survey of British people. Your examiner is one of the people you are interviewing. Occupation   Family members Education   Hobbies / personal interests

考生提问举例

考官回答举例

To start:

Good afternoon (or: Good morning). I'm sorry to trouble you, but I'm doing a survey of British people as part of my college course. Would you mind if I asked you a few personal questions?

a) **Occupation**

What's your job?

b) **Education**

How many "A" levels (英国的高中课程) did you get?

Did you go on to higher education?

(Obviously you went on to higher education, did you go to university?)

c) **Family members**

Would you mind if I asked if you were married?

Do you have any brothers or sisters?

Are any of them married?

What do your parents do?

d) **Hobbies / personal interests**

Do you have any hobbies?

What do you do in your spare time?

How often do you do that?

a) **Occupation**

Primary school teacher (3 years).

b) **Education**

4 "A" levels, left school at 18, went on to teacher training college (4 years).

c) **Family members**

Unmarried. Two brothers, one married with two children. One sister, married, no children.

d) **Hobbies / personal interests**

Sports — windsurfing, horse-riding.

3.

> You have just arrived at your college in Britain and you hear about a party to welcome new students. You would like to go, so you go to the Overseas Students Office to get some more details. Your interviewer works there.
>
> | | | |
> |---|---|---|
> | Organiser | Cost | Activities |
> | Time | Partner | Transportation |
> | Place | | |

考生提问举例

To start:

Good afternoon (or: Good morning). I've just heard about the party for new students. Can I ask you a few things about it?

考官回答举例

a) **Organiser**

The Overseas Students Association. They do this every year.

b) **Time**

Friday evening, 8 pm.

a) Organiser

Who's the party been organised by?

b) Time

When's it going to be?

c) Place

Where's it going to be held?

d) Cost

Do I have to buy tickets for it?

e) Partner

Can I bring someone with me?

If I don't want to come on my own, can I bring a friend?

f) Activities

What kind of party is it going to be?

Is anyone going to give a speech?

g) Transportation

What time will the party finish?

Will there be any transport arranged back to the halls of residence?

h) Other

Will there be any food or drink?

How many people do you think will be there?

Will they be all overseas students?

c) Place

The Smithdown Bar in the basement of the Student Union building.

d) Cost

Free of charge. Don't have to get tickets.

e) Partner

Can bring a friend — doesn't have to be an overseas student.

f) Activities

Nothing special, just dancing, chatting, getting to know one another.

Members of the Overseas Students Committee will be there.

g) Transportation

As party will end at midnight, mini buses will be arranged for students who live in the halls of residence.

h) Other

Will be a bar with drinks at special reduced price. Snacks will be provided.

Around 200 students should be there, both from overseas and UK.

4.

You are going to write an article for the Student Union newspaper about your tutor. Ask him/her some questions. Your interviewer is your tutor.

Family	Childhood memories
School	Friends (still in touch?)

考生提问举例

To start:

I'd like to do an article on you for the Student Union's paper. I wonder if you'd mind if I asked you a few personal questions?

a) **Family**

Are you married, if you don't mind me asking?

Do you have any brothers or sisters?

What do your parents do?

b) **School**

What kind of school did you go to?

Were you a good pupil?

c) **Childhood memories**

What's your first childhood memory?

What event from your childhood left the deepest impression on you?

d) **Friends** (**still in touch**?)

Do you still keep in touch with any of your school friends?

What about your university / college friends?

考官回答举例

a) **Family**

Married.

One brother.

Parents both retired.

b) **School**

Went to state school.

Quite a good pupil.

c) **Childhood memories**

Being lost in a park aged 4.

Impression left by grandmother's sudden death.

d) **Friends** (**still in touch**?)

In touch with 3 school friends and several university friends.

5.

You have just arrived at your college in Britain. You hear that there will be a reception for new students to which you would like to go, so you go to the dean's secretary to find out more.

Held by (host)	Activities	Tickets
Time & place	Food & drink	Attendance compulsory?
Participants	Dress	Anything else

考生提问举例

To start:

Good afternoon (or: Good morning).

考官回答举例

a) **Held by** (**host**)

Dean of the department.

I've heard there's going to be a reception for new students. Can I ask you a few things about it?

a) **Held by (host)**

Who's it being held by? / Who's organising it?

b) **Time & place**

When's it going to be?

Where's it going to be held?

c) **Participants**

Who's going to be there?

d) **Activities**

(depending on who's going to be there)

Is the (vice chancellor) going to give a speech?

What's going to happen at this reception?

e) **Food & drink**

Is there going to be any food or drink?

f) **Dress**

Should I wear anything special?

g) **Tickets**

Where can I get tickets from?

h) **Attendance compulsory**?

Do I have to go to it?

b) **Time & Place**

Thursday 7 pm.

Abercromby Hall in the Student Union building.

c) **Participants**

Both old and new students in the department; staff members of the department, both teaching and administrative; the Vice Chancellor (英国的大学校长).

d) **Activities**

Vice Chancellor will give a welcome speech.

Staff members of the department will be introduced. Nothing special, chatting, socialising.

e) **Food & drink**

Drinks and snacks will be provided.

f) **Dress**

Smart but casual.

g) **Tickets**

Tickets are free, but must apply for them from the Dean's secretary.

h) **Attendance compulsory**?

Not compulsory, but good opportunity to meet students and staff.

6.

You were absent from your writing class yesterday in which the students were given an assignment. Your interviewer is one of your classmates. Ask him / her about the assignment. Topic / content　　Presentation　　Submission date Length　　Title page　　Place of submission

考生提问举例

To start:

I heard that you were given a writing assignment in yesterday's class

a) **Topic / content**

What does it have to be on? / What's it on?

b) **Length**

How long does it have to be?

c) **Presentation**

Does it have to be typed or can we hand-write it?

d) **Title page**

What does the title page have to look like?

e) **Submission date**

When's the deadline?

When does it have to be in for?

f) **Place of submission**

Where do we hand it in?

考官回答举例

a) **Topic / content**

Choose from the recommended reading list.

b) **Length**

2,000 to 3,000 words.

c) **Presentation**

Must be typed, double spaced.

d) **Title page**

Must include your name, tutor's name, title and course code.

e) **Submission date**

Before the last day of term (in four weeks).

f) **Place of submission**

Tutor's office. If not there, in a box outside office.

g) **Other**

Extensions must be granted by tutor, and only for exceptional circumstances. Will be returned in first week after vacation.

7.

> You have just arrived at your college in London and want to find out about the capital's entertainment. Your interviewer is a British student. Ask him / her about it.
>
> | | | |
> |---|---|---|
> | Cinema | Pubs | Sports |
> | Theatre | Restaurants | TV |

考生提问举例

To start:

Hi, I've been in London for just a few

考官回答举例

a) **Cinema**

Many cinemas — the Odeon, the Plaza,

days. Can I ask you something about entertainment here?

a) **Cinema**

Are there lots of good cinemas in town?

Do they show foreign films?

b) **Theatre**

I know London is famous for its theatres. Which are the best ones to go to?

Are they expensive?

Is there an opera house / ballet company in London?

c) **Pubs**

I've heard a lot about British pubs. Are there some good ones in town?

I really want to play darts / pool. Do most pubs have it?

Do they serve food?

d) **Restaurants**

Where are most of the restaurants?

Is there a Chinatown?

e) **Sports**

I really like football / tennis / rugby / cricket.

Do any good teams play in London?

Is there anywhere I can play...?

f) **TV**

I often relax by watching TV. How many channels are available?

ABC.
Showing both new releases and older films. To see alternative and foreign films, go to the Bluecoat Arts Centre.

b) **Theatre**

In the West End, all kinds — classics, drama, comedies, musicals.
The Barbican Centre — home of the Royal Shakespeare Company.
The National Theatre — 3 separate theatres in new building.
The Royal Opera House — home of National Opera Company and Royal Ballet.

c) **Pubs**

The most popular place for social activity in UK. Therefore many pubs in different styles — old, traditional / newer American style bars / with disco / attached restaurant.
Most have a darts board / pool table / dominoes, and serve bar meals.
Open from 11 am – 11 pm.

d) **Restaurants**

All kinds of national restaurants — mainly around Soho（伦敦商业中心的一个地段）. Large Chinatown.

e) **Sports**

Six top football teams in London. Tennis at Wimbledon in June. Rugby Union at Twickenham. Cricket at Lord's.
Many sports centres, swimming pools, and gyms in London.

f) **TV**

4 channels:
BBC 1 — general viewing programmes — films, documentaries, plays, comedies, soap operas.
BBC 2 — educational programmes.
ITV — commercial channel — light viewing.
Channel 4 — programmes for minority audiences.

8.

> You are a new student at a British College. You go to the Welfare Office to find out about health care provision in the UK. Your interviewer is a welfare officer there.
>
> | | |
> |---|---|
> | Health care facilities | Medical insurance |
> | Public / private health care | Emergencies |
> | Registration (doctor) | Prescriptions / medicine |

考生提问举例

To start:

Good afternoon (or: Good morning). I've only been here a few days and would like to know something about health care in Britain. Can I ask you about it?

a) **Healthcare facilities**

Does the college have its own health clinic?

b) **Public / private health care**

What's the difference between public and private health care?

Will I be entitled to treatment on the National Health Service?

c) **Registration**

Do I have to register with a doctor?

d) **Medical insurance**

What would medical insurance cover me against?

Is it expensive?

e) **Emergencies**

What should I do in an emergency situation?

考官回答举例

a) **Healthcare facilities**

University Health Clinic for all students. Doctors. Appointments in morning, morning surgery no appointments necessary.

b) **Public / private health care**

Public — free of charge (for students staying over 6 months).

Private — have to pay, expensive, but avoids waiting lists.

c) **Registration**

Register at University Clinic upon arrival, or with local GP (general practitioner 社区医院的全科大夫).

Unnecessary to register with dentist. Just go to one for treatment / check-up.

d) **Medical insurance**

Can take out cover for medical expenses (treatment, medicine). Will cover you against both illness and accident.

e) **Emergencies**

Dial 999 for ambulance / police / fire brigade. Book an emergency appointment with your doctor.

f) Prescriptions / medicine

Where do I get medicine from?

Do I have to pay for the medicine?

f) Prescriptions / medicine

Doctor will give you a prescription which you then take to a chemist's to get the medicine. Medicine free, but small prescription charge (about £5).

9.

You are a new student at a British college. You go to the college library to find out about its facilities. Your interviewer is a librarian who works there.

How to join	Finding books	Special facilities
Borrowing books	Layout	Opening hours
Fines		

考生提问举例

To start:

Good afternoon (or: Good morning).

Can I ask you a few things about the library?

a) How to join

How do I join the library? /How do I become a member?

b) Borrowing books

How many books can I borrow at one time?

For how long can I borrow them?

Can I renew them if I want them longer?

c) Fines

What are the fines for overdue books?

考官回答举例

a) How to join

By completing a form. Must produce your departmental student card.

b) Borrowing books

Post graduates may borrow up to 10 books at one time for up to 6 weeks. Can renew for another 6, unless books have been recalled.

c) Fines

10p per day per book.

d) Finding books

All catalogue is on computer. Can look up book under author or title, or do a search under subject index. Computers on all floors.

Catalogue also still on card index, but only under author.

Library staff will be giving tours of

What are the fines for books returned late?

d) Finding books

How do I go about finding books?

Is the catalogue on computer?

Where are the computers?

Will we be shown how to use them?

e) Layout

Is there a plan of the layout of the library anywhere?

Where are the books on (subject)?

f) Special facilities

Does the library have any special facilities, such as a room for viewing videos?

g) Opening hours

When is the library open?

Is it open during the vacation?

Do the opening hours change at exam time?

library and demonstrations on how to use the computers throughout Fresher's Week.

e) Layout

Plan on the wall, also lists of subjects on each floor.

Ground floor — short term loan collection, card catalogue, photocopiers.

1st floor — reference, periodicals, journals.

Candidate's subject on third floor.

f) Special facilities

Audio-visual area — video tapes can be viewed / audio tapes listened to.

Computer area — gives access to university computer network. Can also access other college networks, so can keep up to date with latest developments within your field.

Microfilm readers and printers.

Private study rooms for research students.

g) Opening hours

Mon. – Fri.: 9 am – 10 pm.

Saturday & Sunday: 9 am – 6 pm.

Vacation: 9 am – 5 pm.

10.

You have been notified of an urgent meeting of the Student Union, so you go to the Student Union Office to find out more details. Your interviewer is a secretary there.

Subject of meeting	Time & place	Attendance compulsory?
Participants	Length of meeting	Anything else
Chairperson		

考生提问举例	考官回答举例
To start: Good afternoon (or: Good morning). I've just heard about this urgent meeting...	
a) **Subject of meeting** ...Can I ask you what it's about?	a) **Subject of meeting** Proposed closure of the Stanton Library. Due to reduced government funding, the university authorities have had to make cuts, one of which will be the closing of this library. The library holds extensive specialist materials on science and technology.
b) **Participants** Who will be there?	b) **Participants** Vice chancellor, Student Union Executive Committee, students.
c) **Chairperson** Who will be chairing the meeting?	c) **Chairperson** The president of the Student Union.
d) **Time & place** When will it be? Where's it going to be held?	d) **Time & place** Wednesday 2pm in the Mountford Hall, Student Union building.
e) **Length of meeting** How long do you expect the meeting to go on for? / How long do you think it will last?	e) **Length of meeting** About an hour to an hour and a half.
f) **Attendance compulsory**? Does everyone have to go?	f) **Attendance compulsory**? No, but since it is very important, as many students as possible should go, particularly if science / technology student.
	g) **Anything else** Meeting will clarify situation and look at suggestions to make savings. Will also discuss possible actions against closure.

11.

You have been in Britain for a few days when you meet a second year student. Ask him / her about the local town.

Accommodation	Sports	Books
Transport	Food	Discounts for students
Entertainment	Shopping	

考生提问举例

To start:

Hi, I've just arrived here so I don't know anything about the local town. Can I ask you a few things about it?

a) **Accommodation**

Is it better to live in university accommodation or private?

If I wanted to find a flat or a room in a shared house, where's the best place to find one?

b) **Transport**

What's the best way of getting around town?

What time are the first and last buses?

Are taxis very expensive?

c) **Entertainment**

What do students usually do for a night out?

Are there any good theatres in town?

Is there a concert hall?

d) **Sports**

Are there any decent football teams in the town?

Is there a sports centre in town?

e) **Food**

Where are the best places to eat in town?

Is there a Chinatown?

Will I be able to find Chinese foodstuffs

考官回答举例

a) **Accommodation**

University accommodation — halls of residence, single or double room. Shared bathroom. No cooking facilities, eat in dining halls.

Self-catering halls — single rooms. Shared bathroom and kitchen.

Shared flats — with up to 10 other students, own room, share facilities.

Private —

(1) Sharing a house: cheap, own room, share facilities. Most students live in Smithdown area — cheapest area in city.

(2) Flat: 1/2 rooms. Own kitchen and bathroom.

Where to find it: University Accommodation Office / newspaper ads / college noticeboard.

b) **Transport**

Regular bus services — first bus 5 am, last bus 11 pm. Can buy weekly / monthly / season bus passes (pass: 通行证,此处指公共汽车周票或月票).

Black taxi cabs — minimum charge of 70p.

c) **Entertainment**

2 good theatres, opera house, concert hall, numerous cinemas, good pubs.

d) **Sports**

Premier League football team. Top tennis tournament in summer.

Sports centre with swimming pool, gyms, tennis, badminton, volleyball courts, five-a-side football, golf course.

e) **Food**

Most students shop at large supermarkets — quick and convenient.

Many good cheap restaurants near

to cook with?

Where's the best place to buy food?

f) Shopping

Is there a shopping centre in town?

Which are the cheapest supermarkets?

g) Books

Are there any good bookshops?

Are there any secondhand bookshops?

h) Discounts for students

As a student, what kind of concessions can I get?

college — Chinese, Italian, Indian, Mexican.

f) Shopping

Large shopping precinct in centre — department stores and specialist shops.

g) Books

Waterstones and Blackwells, 2 largest bookshops. Many secondhand bookshops.

h) Discounts for students

Cinemas, theatres, concerts all give concessions.

Student Railcard / Student Coachcard, both give a third off travel.

12.

You have just arrived in the UK and are staying in temporary accommodation, but you need to find something more permanent, so you go to the university accommodation office to find out what's available. Your interviewer works there.

Types of accommodation	Rent	Telephone
Location	Facilities	Notice period
Distance from college	Kitchen / bathroom	Possible to view?
Transportation	Possibility of sharing	

考生提问举例

To start:

Good afternoon (or Good morning). I'm looking for accommodation. I wonder if you can help me.

a) Types of accommodation

What kinds of accommodation are there?

b) Location

Whereabouts is it?

考官回答举例

a) Types of accommodation

2 types: (1) University halls (集体宿舍楼) or shared flats. (2) Private — bedsits (bedsitter: 卧室兼起居室) / flats / shared houses.

b) Location

Next to university precinct. Southfields. Student area.

c) **Distance from college**

How far is it from the college?

Is it far from the centre of town?

d) **Transportation**

Is there a bus stop nearby?

e) **Rent**

How much is the rent?

Is that inclusive of bills?

f) **Facilities**

Has it got central heating?

Is it gas or electricity?

Is there a garden?

g) **Kitchen / bathroom**

Do I have my own kitchen and bathroom or is it shared?

Is it an electric or gas cooker?

Is there a washing machine?

How is the water heated?

h) **Possibility of sharing**

Would it be possible to share the place with a friend?

i) **Telephone**

Does the place have a telephone?

j) **Notice period**

When I want to leave, how many weeks' notice should I give?

k) **Possible to view?**

Could I go and have a look at it?

l) **Other**

How much is the deposit?

Do I have to pay rent in advance?

c) **Distance from college**

2 minutes to Student Union Building, 15 minutes by bus to university, 10 minutes by bus to centre.

d) **Transportation**

Bus stop just outside halls. Bus stop 100yds down the road (buses every 15 minutes).

Taxi rank nearby.

e) **Rent**

University halls: £25.

Shared house / bedsit: £30 per week inclusive of bills.

Flat: £35 exclusive of bills.

f) **Facilities**

g) **Kitchen / bathroom**

Halls — launderette, TV room, games room, music room, sports ground.

Shared house / bedsit — 2 rooms, kitchen, bathroom, fully furnished, gassed central heating

Flats — TV, lounge, washing machine, small garden, fully furnished, gassed central heating.

h) **Possibility of sharing**

Halls — shared with 10 other students.

Shared house / bedsit — share both with 4 others (students).

Both types have washing machines.

i) **Telephone**

Halls — pay phones on all corridors.

Shared house — incoming calls only (只能打入、不能打出的电话).

Flats — pay phone.

j) **Notice period**

2 weeks, or 1 month.

13.

You have been informed of a conference that will take place next month. Go to the conference organiser's office to find out more details. Your interviewer works there.		
Topic	When & where	Social activities
Speakers	How to get there	Registration
Schedule	Accommodation	

考生提问举例

To start:

Good afternoon (or: Good morning). I wonder if I could ask you a few questions about the conference?

a) Topic

What's the conference going to be on?/ What's the conference about?

b) Speakers

Who will take part in the conference?

Who will the speakers be?/ Who will be giving papers?

c) Schedule

What is the schedule like?

d) When & where:

When's the conference going to take place?

Where's it going to be?/ Where's it going to be held?

e) How to get there

What's the best way to get there from here?

How do I get to the conference centre from the train/coach station?

考官回答举例

a) Topic

Candidate's field of study.

b) Speakers

Leading experts from that field.

c) Schedule

Friday: Registration.

Saturday: 9 am – 5 pm conference.

Sunday: 9 am – 12 smaller, optional. meetings on various topics of specialisation. 2 pm – 4 pm closing session.

d) When & where

Manchester Conference Centre.

In 2 weeks time (weekend of 21st).

e) How to get there

By train/coach.

Between 4 – 9 pm on Friday, special conference mini-buses will run from Piccadilly coach station & Victoria train station to conference centre. Otherwise buses No. 21/36.

f) **Accommodation**

Will accommodation be arranged for us?

g) **Social activities**

Are there any social events planned for the weekend?

h) **Registration**

If I want to go, do I have to register beforehand?

When do I have to register?

i) **Other**

Are participants expected to contribute a paper? Can I if I want to?

How many are you expecting?

f) **Accommodation**

Hotel attached to conference centre.

g) **Social activities**

Welcoming reception on Friday evening.

Cheese & wine party on Saturday evening.

h) **Registration**

Unnecessary to register now.

Register upon arrival in Manchester.

Registration fee: £20.

14.

You have been at your college in Britain for a few days when you go to the information office with a few questions about the college. Your interviewer works there.

Student Welfare Office	Health care	English language classes
Student counsellors / tutors	Insurance	Travel information

考生提问举例

To start:

Good afternoon (or: Good morning).

I've only been here a few days so I was wondering if I could ask you something about the college.

a) **Student Welfare Office**

What kind of services does the Student Welfare Office provide?

考官回答举例

a) **Student Welfare Office**

Information / advice centre — all aspects of college life and living in the UK, financial / accommodation / guidance for overseas students.

Leaflets / booklets on most common areas of enquiry.

b) **Student counsellors / tutors**

Counsellors — deal with academic / social / emotional / clinical problems.

Tutors — volunteer students assigned to new students to help them settle in.

b) Student counsellors / tutors

What's the difference between a counsellor and a tutor?

c) Health care

What health care facilities are there at the college?

Does the college have a health centre?

Do I have to register?

How do I get dental treatment?

d) Insurance

Where can I get information on taking out insurance?

e) English language classes

Have you any information on English language classes?

What kind of courses are available?

f) Travel in formation

Can I get travel information anywhere on campus?

c) Health care

University Health Centre — provides comprehensive medical service. Free if stay for more than 6 months. Register upon arrival. Appointments in afternoon only. Or register with local GP.

Dentist / Optician — registration unnecessary.

d) Insurance

Endsleigh Insurance — student insurance company. Branch in Student Union Building.

e) English language classes

English Language Unit — provides support and courses for overseas students.

(1) Intensive pre-sessional (正式课程开始前的预备课程): 1/2/3 months during July - Sept.

(2) English for academic purposes: 1 year, full time.

(3) In-session (正式课程开始后的) language support classes: held during lunch hour or late afternoon. Free. Maximum of 5 hrs per week. Contact the Language Unit for more details.

f) Travel information

Union Travel Shop in Student Union Building. Cheap travel. Open 9 am - 5 pm daily.

15.

On arrival at the university, your instructions are to proceed to the University Information Office. Your interviewer is the information officer on duty.

Location of your accommodation (booked in advance)	Joining the Student Union
Location of dining halls	English language test
Registration with the police	Location of your department

考生提问举例	考官回答举例
To start: Good afternoon (or: Good morning). I was told to come to this office when I arrived. . . .	
a) Location of your accommodation . . . Can I ask you where my accommodation is? I booked it in advance.	**a) Location of your accommodation** William Morris Tower (single study rooms), tall building just across square.
b) Location of dining halls Where are the dining halls? Are the dining halls near my place?	**b) Location of dining halls** Behind William Morris Tower — hexagonal-shaped building.
c) Registration with the police I've heard that I have to register with the police. When do I have to do that? Where's the nearest police station? What documents do I have to take with me? Do I have to pay?	**c) Registration with the police** All non-commonwealth & EC nationals must register with the police within 14 days of arrival in the UK. Two passport photos required. Cost: £35.
d) Joining the Student Union Where can I join the Student Union? Do I need to bring anything with me? Is it free?	**d) Joining the Student Union** Automatic, free membership. Recreational & social centre of college societies, clubs, bars, cafes, shops, music, games area, travel shop. Welfare advice. Collect Union membership card from sports hall during Fresher's Week. 1 passport photo required. Also serves as student ID to get concessions.
e) English language test I believe I have to take an English test. When will this be? How long will it take? What skills will it be testing? Will it affect my course at all?	**e) English language test** All non-native speakers must take English test upon arrival. Two aims: (1) to advise students on possibility of extra tuition; (2) to keep statistical check on overseas students' level of English. Takes 2 hours. Listening, reading, writing. Details sent later in week.
f) Location of your department Can you tell me where my department is? It's the . . . Department.	**f) Location of your department** Department is . . . ? On other side of campus. Monday 8:45 am, student tutor will take them to department and show around.

16.

> You have been at your university for a few days when you are introduced to a second-year student. Find out a bit about the university.
>
> Student Union　　Sports facilities　　Travel
>
> Union societies / clubs　　Campus entertainment

考生提问举例

To start:

Hi. I've only been here a few days and don't know much about the place. Can I ask you a couple of things?

a) **Student Union**

What are the benefits of joining the Student Union?

What does the Student Union do?

How often are the elections held?

b) **Union societies / clubs**

I've heard that there are many different societies and clubs at the college. Is there a... society?

How much is it, roughly, to join?

c) **Sports facilities**

I'd really like to do / play some... while I'm here. Will I be able to do that?

Is there a university team? Do they take part in competitions?

d) **Campus entertainment**

What's the night life like at the college?

Is there much going on in the evenings at the college?

Are there any films shown?

考官回答举例

a) **Student Union**

Recreational, social, cultural & political centre of college. Represents students' interests within the college and campaigns on their behalf.

Umbrella for union societies & clubs.

Films, theatre, concerts.

Welfare and support services.

b) **Union societies / clubs**

Religious, cultural, national, international, political, social, musical, sporting.

Elect own executive committees and manage own finances.

Usually nominal fee to join.

c) **Sports facilities**

All kinds: sports hall, outdoor / indoor pitches, courts, swimming pool, gymnasium, nearby sailing centre.

d) **Campus Eetertainment**

Theatre — student & professional performances.

Cinema — films twice a week.

Discos, parties, dances, concerts, rock groups.

Bars & cafes.

Do many students go to the union bars?

e) **Travel**

Where can I get travel information from?

e) **Travel**

Union Travel Shop — discounted travel.

17.

A Bank Holiday (许多西方国家的一种公假) is coming up and you would like to go somewhere for the weekend, so you go to the local tourist information office to find out what's available.		
What's available	How to get there	Entrance fees
Location	Opening times	Anything else

考生提问举例

To start:

Good afternoon (or: Good morning). I'm thinking of doing something this weekend. Could you give me some idea of things to do around here?

a) **What's available**

What kind of thing is available?

b) **Location**

Whereabouts is it / that?

c) **How to get there**

Can I get there by public transport?

d) **Opening times**

When's it open? / What are the opening times?

e) **Entrance fees**

How much is it to get in?

Are there any student concessions?

f) **Anything else**

How long does it take to get there (by train)?

Is there somewhere I can eat at the place?

考官回答举例

(1) **Museums**

(a) National Museum of the Moving Image

South Bank Complex.

History of film and TV, special exhibition on Eastenders (popular UK soap opera).

10 am – 6 pm daily.

Admission: £4. Concession: £2.50.
Tube station: Waterloo Lines, Bakerloo / Northern.

(b) The British Museum
Bloomsbury Avenue.
Exhibits from UK & abroad, past & present.
10 am – 5 pm daily except Sunday 10 am – 4 pm.
Admission: free.
Tube station: Bloomsbury Lines, Central.

(c) Science Museum
Exhibition Road.
Special display on Michael Faraday.
9 am – 5 pm daily.
Admission: £3. Concession: £2.
Tube station: South Kensington Lines: Circle / District.

(2) **Bodiam Castle**
East Sussex.
Most complete medieval fortress in Europe (built 1385). Museum & shop.
10 am – 6 pm daily.
Admission: £1.50.
Train: British Rail, Victoria to Bodiam (2 hrs). Other side of town (signposted).

(3) **Thorpe Park**
Staines Rd., Chertsey, Surrey.
Fun park, many different rides, log flume, roller coaster, Canadian Creek 1 Railway, Treasure Island. Restaurant & theatre.
Open 8 am – 8 pm daily.
Admission: £20. Concession: £15 includes all rides.
Train: British Rail, Euston to Chertsey (1 hr).
Regular shuttle buses operate between station and park.

(4) **Capital Radio Folk Festival**
Crystal Palace Bowl, Park Road.
Sponsored by London Radio Station.
Dance & music from around Britain. All day programme starting 10 am until 11 pm.
Admission: £10. Concession: £5.
Some events may incur extra charge.
British Rail: Waterloo to Putney (20 minutes), or Jubilee line to Crystal Palace.

(5) **Safari Park**
Windsor.
Just 3 miles from Windsor Castle, so could visit that too.
9 am – 5 pm daily.
Admission: £12.50. Concession: £8.50.
Train: British Rail, Kings Cross to Windsor (2 hrs).
Buses every half hour to park.

18.

> Your interviewer has won a competition. Ask him / her about the prize.
>
> Kind of competition　　Interviewer's feeling
>
> Prize　　Interviewer's intention

考生提问举例

To start:

So, I hear you've won some competition.

a) **Kind of competition**

What kind of competition was it? / What was the competition?

b) **Prize**

What did you win? / What was the prize?

c) **Interviewer's feeling**

That sounds really nice. You must be pleased!

d) **Interviewer's intention**

What are you going to do?

So you won't go, then?

考官回答举例

a) **Kind of competition**

Local supermarket. Had to complete an advertising slogan.

b) **Prize**

Dinner for two in local French restaurant.

c) **Interviewer's feeling**

Not pleased — doesn't want to go. Last time went, but was ill afterwards.

d) **Interviewer's intention**

Will probably give prize to friends.

19.

> Your colleague in the UK has won second prize in a competition. Ask him / her about it. The interviewer is your colleague.
>
> Second prize　　Kind of competition　　When / how long for
>
> First prize　　Organiser　　Travel arrangements

考生提问举例

To start:

So, I hear you've won some competition.

考官回答举例

a) **Second Prize**

2 weeks' vacation in the USA, plus

a) **Second prize**

What was the prize?

b) **First prize**

What was the first prize?

c) **Kind of competition**

What kind of competition was it?

d) **Organiser**

Who's going to be organising the trip?

e) **When / how long for**

When are you going?

How long for?

f) **Travel arrangements**

Are you flying from London? To where?

What kind of place will you be staying in?

Will you stay in one place, or visit different places?

Who are you going to take with you?

£500 spending money.

b) **First Prize**

3 weeks in the Caribbean.

c) **Kind of competition**

Geographical competition in magazine.

Had to answer general knowledge questions on various countries.

d) **Organiser**

The magazine.

e) **When / how long for**

Winners can choose when to go within a year.

2 weeks.

f) **Travel arrangements**

Fly from London Heathrow to Florida.

Spend a week in Miami, then on to Key West, visiting Disneyland. Stay in a 5-star hotel.

20.

> At your college in the UK, you have to work on a project with your tutor so you arrange a time to meet at his / her place.
>
> When he / she's available
> Where he / she lives
> Kind of accommodation
> Facilities
> Interviewer's feeling about accommodation

考生提问举例

To start:

Hi. I was wondering if we could arrange a time to meet to talk about this project.

a) **When he / she's available**

When's convenient for you? / When are

考官回答举例

a) **When he / she's available**

Next week, Thursday evening, 7 pm.

you free?

b) Where he / she lives

Perhaps we could meet at your place. Where do you live?

c) Kind of accommodation

That's a convenient area of town. Do you Live in a house or a flat?

d) Facilities

Has it got a garden?

e) Interviewer's feeling about accommodation

It sounds a really great place. Do you like living there?

b) Where he / she lives

In Toxteth area (near centre), 24 Lark Lane.

c) Kind of accommodation

Large, old terraced house.

d) Facilities

Large garden at back.

e) Interviewer's feeling about accommodation

Just moved into accommodation 2 weeks ago. Very pleased with it. Re-decorating at the moment, so a mess. Nice neighbours.

四、口试的一些注意事项

1. 报名表

考官在见到考生之前就已经拿到考生填过的报名表。因此,报名表要认真、准确地填写。要做到能够用英文回答所填写的内容。

2. 理解

如果听不懂,不要说“I don't understand”,而应说“I'm sorry?”或“Pardon?”“I'm sorry. I didn't quite catch that.”

不要沉默不语,好像在思考,然后突然说“What?”。如果听不懂,最好是马上表达。

3. 回答要贴切

听懂问题是正确回答问题的前提。有时会出现“大概听懂”,但没有全懂。这时很难贴切地回答问题。如“What do you see yourself doing in 10 years time?”不同于“What are you going to do when you return from the UK?”

4. 不要戛然而止

虽然有时可用 yes 或 no 来回答考官的问题,但应在简答之后有所扩展。如:

— Are you married?

— Yes, I've been married for five years now, and we have a four-year-old daughter.

— I see you teach at Beijing University.

— Yes, that's right. I'm mainly involved in teaching but I also do some research work.

再如:

—Do you like your job?

—Yes, very much. It's very stimulating...(etc.) though I do find the lack of research opportunities rather frustrating...

5. 难题或意外的问题

遇到这样的问题在所难免,在思考答案时不应沉默,可以使用所谓的"hesitation devices",如:"Well, you know, I'm really not sure...I'm no expert on this, but I think..."还可以从侧面回答某些问题,如:

— What do you think about the role of women in China today?

— Well, I'm sure that you're aware that the role of women has changed dramatically over the past few decades in China. My wife is a good example of a working woman who is also a mother. She ...

如确实是难题,可坦白地告诉考官。如:

I'm sorry, I really have no idea about that. I've not paid much attention to it. / I haven't been following it. / I'm not really very interested in politics / economics, etc.

6. 纠正错误

如你觉得自己的发言不妥,可以纠正自己的错误,但不宜太频繁,以致影响交流的流畅性。在口试中,有效的交流比"正确性"更为重要。

7. 采取主动

如果考官的话使你感兴趣或你希望考官澄清他的意思,你也可以问他问题。应把口试看成一个自然的交流机会,考生有时亦可采取主动。但不宜问太多问题或问需要很长的回答的问题。

8. 必要的 follow-up

在自然的交流中,会有很多的 follow-up。在口试中亦是如此。如:

— The library is open 9 – 5 Monday – Friday and 9 – 12 on Saturday.

— Oh, so it's not open on Sundays then?

9. 体态语言

口试时要尽量显得放松、自然。坐态要端正,背靠椅背。要与考官有频繁的目光接触。进门打招呼时和离场道别时要面带微笑。

10. 语法错误

不要过多地担心语法错误。自然而有效的交流才更为重要。但过多的错误会影响考官对你的看法。我们在口试中发现的非常典型的错误有 he / she 不分,第三人称单数动词未加"s",时态不一致等,望考生对这些问题特别注意。

第四章 阅读考试

一、阅读考试简介

雅思考试的阅读根据出国的目的分为两类。凡是计划出国留学，攻读学士、硕士或博士学位的考生应参加 Academic 类考试。申请移民，参加短期交流式培训的考生要考 General Training 类考试。这只是一般规律，会有一些例外。考生应根据自己的情况，尽快地了解该考哪一类，以及时做准备，因为这两类考试不仅在阅读文章的题材、难度等方面有很大的差别，在写作上也有差别。

（一）Academic 类（简称 A 类）

A 类阅读考试有三篇文章，至少有一篇文章为文科类型（与社会、经济等文科专业有关），另外两篇涉及理、工、农、医，一般与科技有关。每篇文章的长度为 800～1000 词，每篇文章有 12 至 15 道题，总共有 40 道题，个别试卷或多或少一两道题。所有的文章均出自英、美刊物或书籍，这些刊物和书籍的主要读者为母语是英语、受过高等教育的人。在十多年的雅思考试培训中，我们发现过一些雅思考试中使用的阅读文章的出处，它们是：*New Scientist*（英国，周刊）；*The Economist*（英国，周刊）；*Popular Science*（美国，月刊）；*Scientific American*（美国，月刊）。

虽然真题中使用的文章远不止这四本杂志，但可以通过阅读这些杂志中的文章来体会真题的难度。而且，阅读能力的进一步提高也是通过阅读原文文章（而不是经过改写或专为学习英语的人编写的文章）来完成的。

阅读考试的文章题材多样，题型不固定，考生之间的阅读速度、理解能力更是千差万别。因此，没有哪种方法是“最”有效的。考生应通过多做练习来达到熟悉题型、摸索适合自己的方法的目的。对多数考生来说，要以同样的细致程度完成三篇文章是有困难的，最好的安排是花 50 分钟左右将其中的两篇做得较细，以争取较高的正确率，将剩余的时间用在另一篇文章上。那么如何判断应先做哪两篇文章呢？拿到试卷后，最忌讳的就是翻到第一页开始逐字、逐行地读。首先，应看一下三篇文章的长度有多大差别，是否有图、表等 non-textual information，是否有 glossary（关键词），题型除较典型的 match the headings，yes / no / not given，summary 以外还有没有别的题型。通过一两分钟的浏览所得到的信息,判断每篇文章的题材,看看有没有太生疏的领域。做题时可先看一下文章的标题和文章的前两三行,如内容生疏则应马上换一篇,不要因为已经花了三分钟就一定要顶着头皮接着往下做。实际情况是,每篇文章的主题不同,很可能有一两篇的内容你较熟悉,如先做了你很不在行的那篇文章,多花了时间,正确率也得不到保障,最关键的是有可能因时间有限而把某篇对你来说可能是很容易的文章放弃了。因此,碰到不熟悉的主题一定要先放弃,待最后再说。

如果一篇文章有 summary,那应该在读文章之前先读 summary,虽然 summary 中有若干词,但由于它言简意赅,可以只花一两分钟就知道全文的大意,这样在读正文时就可以更加充分地调动脑子里与此文章有关的知识。如果不看 summary,在阅读时就有一个从完全无知到逐步进入角色的过程。缩短这个过程对于提高阅读速度和正确率均有帮助。

对于 match the headings 的题型,当然是先看段落,再从给出的一串 headings 中去找。用一个就划掉一个,这样可以使目光只在那些未使用过的 heading 上停留。一般来说,这类题都会把第一段作为例子给出答案,因此可以马上把与第一段对应的 heading (即 example)划掉。在指令中也许会有这样一句话:You may use a heading more than once,这会让人觉得某一 heading 同时适用于两个或更多的段落。这种情况也许会出现,但在多年的教学中,没有听说过哪个考生碰到过这样的题。

其他类型的题,如 yes/no/not given, who does what 等,都应该先看题,然后再看文章。当然,只能看一两道题,找到答案后再看后面的题。

总之,由于文章的难度、特殊的题型、有限的时间等因素,考生所习惯的阅读方法也许不能被有效地用于雅思的阅读考试。这不仅需要进一步提高阅读能力,也需要摸索自己的新方法。

(二) General Training 类(简称 G 类)

G 类的阅读分三个部分(sections),第一、二部分一般为功能性的短文,如广告、通知、产品说明、旅游日程安排等。第一部分的文章(其实不是文章,但因找不到更合适的词,暂且用“文章”一词)较短,有三至五篇,第二部分的文章稍长,一般为两篇。第三部分是一篇文章,其长度、难度、题型均与 A 类阅读的文章近似,只是题材更接近于生活,如教育、体育等。因此关于第三部分文章的所谓“应试技巧”,请参看本章的前半部分及 A 类的模拟试题。

考生在准备第一、二部分时所遇到的最大问题是没有足够的练习材料,因为目前市场上的大部分阅读教材都很传统,在体裁方面非常单一,全都是清一色的阅读文章,很少有诸如菜单、药品说明书等“另类”功能的材料,因此建议考生要多看原文报刊,如 *China Daily*、*Time* 等,特别注意其中的各种各样的广告。

另外，有一本叫做《读者的选择》(*Reader's Choice*)的教材在许多书店都有，其中部分章节有一定的相关性，建议考生选用。

这些所谓“功能性”文章的类别有限，前文已基本提到，多看一些报刊上的相关内容，多做几套模拟题，即可基本掌握各类别的特点，剩下的问题则基本与体裁生疏无关，而是对语言的基础知识，如词汇及习惯表达方法的掌握与熟练运用了。

二、A 类阅读模拟试题一、答案及题解

INTERNATIONAL ENGLISH LANGUAGE TESTING SYSTEM

PRACTICE TEST (Version One)

ACADEMIC READING

TIME ALLOWED: 1 HOUR

NUMBER OF QUESTIONS: 40

Instructions

ALL ANSWERS MUST BE WRITTEN ON THE ANSWER SHEET.

The test is divided as follows:

Reading Passage 1	Questions 1 – 15
Reading Passage 2	Questions 16 – 28
Reading Passage 3	Questions 29 – 40

Start at the beginning of the test and work through it. Your should answer all the questions. If you cannot do a particular question leave it and go on to the next. You can return to it later.

READING PASSAGE 1

*You should spend about 20 minutes on **Questions 1 – 15** which are based on Reading Passage 1.*

An "F" in World Competition

A President Bush calls his plan for fixing schools "Education 2000." In that year, he promises, American students will lead the world in math and science. But judging by the results of international achievement tests released last week, Bush may have to rename his program "Mission: Impossible." South Korean and Taiwanese students whipped Americans in the math and science exams for 9- and 13-year-olds. The United States ranked near the bottom. Americans did excel in one part of the test, a survey of leisure and study habits — although the distinction was nothing to be proud of. As U.S. Secretary of Education Lamar Alexander noted: "It was not among our six education goals to lead the world in the amount of TV our students watched."

Science Project

On the science test for 13-year-olds, Americans got an average of 67 percent correct; Koreans were first with 78 percent correct.

South Korea	78%
Taiwan	76%
Switzerland	74%
Hungary	73%
Russia	71%
Slovenia	70%
Italy	70%
Israel	70%
Canada	69%
France	69%
Scotland	68%
Spain	68%
United States	67%
Ireland	63%
Jordan	57%

B The tests, called the International Assessment of Educational Progress (IAEP), were administered by the Educational Testing Service, which also runs the Scholastic Aptitude Tests. The first IAEP, in 1988, included only six countries/regions; in this second test, 20 participated. (Notable nonparticipants: Germany, which didn't want to spend the money it cost each country to administer the test, and Japan, which dropped out when South Korea joined.) Other international tests have been criticized because of the difficulties of comparing students from different cultures. A major complaint has been that other countries test only their very best students while the United States tests a representative sampling. IAEP officials say the 175,000 students they tested last year were as comparable as possible.

C In math, the gap between the American and Asian youngsters was especially wide. Nine-year-old Americans got an average of 58 percent correct; the top scores, the Koreans, averaged 75. For 13-year-olds, the American average was 55, the Koreans' 73. Advanced curriculum helped. "Most of the countries that did well emphasized geometry and algebra, where our kids are still learning arithmetic," says Diane Ravitch, U.S. Under Secretary of education.

D Even the very best American students didn't measure up. The range of scores received by the top 10 percent of Americans was much greater than that of the top 10 percent of Asian students. For example , in the math test, the highest-scoring 10 percent of 13-year-old Koreans got 96 to 100 percent of the questions right; Taiwan's top 10 percent got 97 to 100 percent correct. But America's top 10 percent got only 83 - 97 percent of the questions right.

E There was one small bright spot, in science. Nine-year-old Americans came in third, after Korean and Taiwanese children. On average, Americans got 65 percent of the questions correct, compared with 68 percent for Koreans. This doesn't necessarily mean that U.S. schools do a good job of teaching science to young children. Test organizers say they believe U.S. kids may have done better because the 9-year-olds' science test concentrates on life sciences rather than physical sciences, and survey results indicate that U.S. teachers are more comfortable with biology than physics or chemistry. As they get older, U.S. kids fall way behind. Among 13-year-olds, they were again near the bottom in science.

F **Success recipe**: The tests' organizers say the results don't indicate any particular recipe for success. The U.S. school year is shorter than that of many other countries, but the school day is longer. American students actually spend more time in school than Koreans. Quality of time, not quantity, matters most, says Ravitch. "A lot of time in American classrooms is interrupted, with announcements about band practice or whatever." The countries with high scores used a wide range of teaching methods, from the highly structured to the progressive. Some (Israel, the Untied States) devoted a lot of money to education; others (China, Spain) spent less. Use of spare time was closely correlated with academic success, however. Students who read and did a lot of homework scored better than those who came home and plopped down in front of the TV for hours every day. Attitudes toward intellectual achievement are also important. In Asia, scholarship is admired. "In the U.S., we call our best students nerd or dweeb," says ETS President Gregory Anrig. "As a nation, I think we have conflicting feelings about people who are smart, and as parents, we send conflicting messages to our children about being smart."

G Despite the results, U.S. Education Secretary Alexander says he hasn't given up on American kids. Last week he announced that about $ 2 billion currently in the budgets of various federal agencies will go to math and science education, with the emphasis on retraining teachers. Ravitch says the program will be bigger and broader in scope than a similar initiative launched after Sputnik 1 in 1957. The national goal then was to be first on the moon. That, too, was once considered Mission: Impossible.

Questions 1 – 7

Do the following statements agree with the views of the writer in Reading Passage 1?

In boxes 1 – 7 on your answer sheet write

YES	*if the statement agrees with the writer;*
NO	*if the statement does not agree with the writer;*
NOT GIVEN	*if there is no information about this in the passage.*

Example:	Answer:
It is believed that American kids have better biology teachers than chemistry teachers.	***YES***

1. Neither Germany nor Japan took part in the latest IAEP.
2. South Korea sent their top students to participate in the IAEP.
3. American 13-year-olds did better than their Canadian counterparts.
4. American children spend more time watching TV than children from many other countries.
5. Scottish children have beaten the English kids in the latest IAEP.
6. The results of the 3rd IAEP indicate that Canada and France did equally well.
7. American 13-year-olds are not as intelligent as their 9-year-old brothers and sisters.

Questions 8 – 15

The following statements are related to some countries / regions, as mentioned in Reading Passage 1. Decide which country (countries) / region(s) each statement refers to and write your answer in the corresponding box in the answer sheet. If there is no information about this in the passage, write ***NOT GIVEN*** *in the corresponding box.*

Example:	Answer:
School days are longer.	***America***

8. 70% of the questions at the IAEP was answered correctly.
9. Teachers enjoy teaching physics better than chemistry.
10. A lot of money was spent on education after the Russians had sent off the first spacecraft.
11. The scores received by the top 10% students are more clustered together.
12. School time is not well spent.
13. Students do a lot of homework instead of watch TV for hours everyday.
14. Bright kids are ridiculed.
15. Refused to participate in the IAEP due to financial concerns.

READING PASSAGE 2

*You should spend about 20 minutes on **Questions 16 – 28** which are based on Reading Passage 2.*

Overtaking Concorde

1 The obvious response of airlines faced with overcrowded airports such as those in Tokyo, Osaka, Honk Kong and many others is to put more people into each aircraft, meaning that big is beautiful. For trunk routes, wide-bodied jets are the way to go for economic efficiency. Aircraft and engine manufacturers have done their bit by tweaking airframes to reduce drag and fuel-burn over the years, bringing basic operating costs down.

2 But this path of development is now approaching the end of worthwhile technological improvements, with only two new extensions left. First involves the Airbus A330 and the Boeing 777, both now being developed, which will both be seen in the colours of various Asian airlines in the mid to late 1990s. When these designs are pushed to their ultimate form over a few years of increasing engine power, both will be in effect twin-engined 747s so far as capacity is concerned — high-volume people movers ideal for Asia's regional trunk routes.

3 The second path is to scale up capacity using four engines, and Airbus and Boeing are both looking at designs for what will be effectively giant 747s, with 600 – 700 seats and either side-by-side double fuselages (Airbus) or a full-length double deck (Boeing). Neither type is expected to appear in less than 10 years, but when they do, among obvious applications will be trans-Pacific and Asia-Europe routes.

4 But the speeds of these new types will be in the same range as that of virtually all jet transports since their inception in the 1950s and 1960s: Mach 0.8 – 0.85 (80% – 85% of the speed of sound), a zone mandated by the limits of subsonic aerodynamics, the historic cost of materials and, latterly, environmental considerations such as noise and air-pollution from engines.

5 The only exception used in commercial service is the Anglo-French Concorde, still flying regular supersonic trips across the Atlantic 15 years after its introduction. But

Concorde has been the shoal on which other dreams of supersonic airliners have foundered: a spectacular technical success for its time, it was an equally spectacular commercial failure, with only 14 entering commercial service. It is too noisy, too small, drinks fuel and has only been viable — at premium fares — because its development costs were written off by the British and French governments.

6 The message for those with supersonic ambitions has been that if you cannot do better than Concorde, do not even try.

7 However, parts of the philosophy which led to Concorde still apply, and are leading to hopes that supersonic transport may be only a matter of 15 – 20 years away. First is that everyone would like to reach their destination faster, instead of spending boring hours confined in a metal tube. And second is that increasing an aircraft's speed also increases its potential productivity, meaning less units needed to do the same amount of work.

8 Various consortia in the US, Europe and Japan are now undertaking studies to define the market, the product and the technology necessary to bring this about, though the target date of 2005 is thought to be highly optimistic by most. Some of the efforts seem to focus on high technology for its own sake, with applications to be found later: Japan, for instance, has teamed up with four major Western engine manufacturers in an eight-year, US $ 224 million programme to develop a "variable cycle" turbo-ramjet capable of operating at Mach 5, or about 4,800 km per hour.

9 But a study by Boeing indicates that, for commercial success, a supersonic transport should fly at about half this speed, or only slightly faster than Concorde, for economic and environmental reasons. Boeing's thinking was the result of its involvement in a project with the US National Aeronautics and Space Administration to look at commercial supersonic flight in 1986. By 1988, impressed with the apparent potential shown by its studies, Boeing set up a team to do preliminary design work and look at technological development.

10 Boeing's market projections were based on worldwide passenger flows doubling by the year 2000 to 4.8 million passengers a day, or a rate of 5.9% a year — slightly higher than its own more recent estimate of 5.2%. Boeing then looked at the scheduled international market, which accounts for 23% of the total, and took out routes of less than 2,500 nautical miles as uneconomic for supersonic flight. It also eliminated routes which are mostly over land, because of concern about sonic booms. What remains in the year 2000, says Boeing, is a group of trans-Pacific, Asia-Europe and trans-Atlantic routes which will account for 315,000 passengers a day, a figure which will grow to 607,000 a day by 2015. This, according to Boeing, is a potential market for 1,000 – 1,500 supersonic transports with 5,000 nautical miles' range, a cruising speed of Mach 2.4 and a capacity of 250 – 300 passengers.

11 With this design basis, a non-stop Los Angeles-Tokyo trip would take only four hours and 18 minutes, compared with 10 hours 18 minutes today. And even with one stop on longer flights, the time saved is dramatic: Los Angeles to Sydney would be 7 hours 18 minutes, including an hour's stop in Honolulu, compared with today's non-stop subsonic flying time of 14 hours.

12 Major considerations for Boeing were that the supersonic aircraft should be able to use existing airports, comply with the latest noise regulations and not require exotic fuels such as liquid hydrogen. This means new technology for engines, and according to Boeing, various promising leads have been identified which should lead to meeting goals set for noise and exhaust emission standards. Boeing says that meeting the noise goals "will be a difficult but achievable task," and points to engine-manufacturers' research into ways of reducing emissions of oxides of nitrogen which harm the earth's ozone layer.

13 While use of supersonic aircraft from existing airports might help to cut the rate of growth of fleets, given that less units will produce more work, there is a downside to this argument. If a supersonic aircraft performs twice as many trips as its subsonic counterpart, it will be on the ground twice as often, and therefore taking up parking bays, immigration and customs facilities and other airport services for twice as long.

14 The need for additional airports and better facilities is therefore not going to disappear. Without them, the number of trips in which time spent in airports exceeds flying time will merely increase as aircraft speed rises.

Questions 16 – 19

In the box below are what are / were to be done in the aircraft making industry. Answer the following questions by choosing letters A – H in the box below. Please note that some questions need more than one letter. Write your answers in boxes 16 – 19 on your answer sheet.

A. Develop the latest models of four-engined jumbo jets.
B. Increase aircraft's productivity.
C. Send people to their destinations more quickly.
D. Renew study of and ultimately the production of supersonic jets.
E. Use liquid hydrogen as fuel to increase engine power.
F. Develop the latest models of two-engined jumbo jets.
G. Build more airports and improve airport facilities.
H. Improve technology for engines so as to reduce noise and oxide of nitrogen.

16. According to the passage, what three in the above list are actions taken to fly more people and fly them faster?
17. Which one in the above list is an action taken to produce better engines for supersonic jets?
18. Which one in the above list is an action to be taken to cope with an increase of passengers travelling by air?
19. Which two in the above list are reasons for future supersonic transport?

Questions 20 – 23

Complete the table below. Write your answers in boxes 20 – 23 on your answer sheet.

	departure	arrival	time	stopover(Y / N)
supersonic	Los Angeles	(20)	4 hr 18 min	N
subsonic	Los Angeles	Tokyo	(21)	N
supersonic	Los Angeles	Sydney	7 hr 18 min	(22)
subsonic	Los Angeles	Sydney	14 hr	(23)

Questions 24 – 27

Use **NO MORE THAN ONE or TWO WORDS** *to answer the following questions. Write your answers in boxes 24 – 27 on your answer sheet.*

Example:	Answer:
How many Concorde aircrafts are now in commercial service?	*14*

24. What is the likely speed that the new supersonic jets will fly at?

25. What is the capacity that Boeing is aiming at for the new supersonic jets?

26. What is the approximate number of passengers travelling by air today?

27. What is the number of passengers in the year of 2015 that Boeing is now thinking of when projecting the market potential for supersonic aircraft?

28. What is the main idea of Reading Passage 2?

Choose one letter from below and write it in box 28 on your answer sheet.

A. Concorde was a technical success but a commercial failure.

B. There is a renewed interest in commercial supersonic transport.

C. There are many problems to solve in order to improve supersonic aircraft.

D. Increasing concerns for environmental considerations mean good-bye to commercial supersonic transport.

READING PASSAGE 3

You should spend about 20 minutes on ***Questions 29 – 40*** *which are based on Reading Passage 3.*

Dante Tours the Inferno

1 It wasn't until refrigerator-size boulders began hurtling down from above that the scientists sitting in an Anchorage, Alaska, control room started to get seriously worried. Until then the robot known as Dante II had successfully negotiated a steep, muddy descent and ambled unconcernedly through hot steam and poisonous gases. But even a 3-m-tall, 770-kg automation has its limits, and multiton chunks of rock moving at high speed were beyond Dante's. "That big one," said Carnegie Mellon University robotics expert John Bares, pointing nervously at a video screen after a rockslide, "would've wiped us out."

2 In the end, it was a misstep, not a rock, that toppled Dante, and only after the robot had completed its main mission: a detailed study of the crater floor 90 m below the rim of Alaska's active Mount Spurr volcano that included a 3-D survey of the hellish terrain and an analysis of gases issuing from belching vents. Among the significant results: the first maps of the crater's surface, normally hidden by out-croppings and haze. Dante also discovered scant sulfur dioxide and hydrogen sulfide in the noxious air, implying that the volcano, which erupted in 1992, will probably stay quiet for a while.

3 But important as this news was to the volcano experts and the people of Anchorage, just 130 km from Mount Spurr, the volcano study was perhaps the least noteworthy part of the robot's mission. Despite the final slipup, which toppled Dante and left it stranded on the steep mountain slope, the 10-day trek went a long way toward proving the potential of a technology that could let humans explore a wide range of sites too hazardous to visit in person — other volcanoes, deep caves, the barren wastes of Antarctica, the ocean floor and even the surfaces of the moon and Mars. "The robot has performed like a champ," says David Lavery, manager of the Telerobotics Research Program at the U.S. National Aeronautics and Space Administration, which paid for most of Dante II's $ 1.7 million development cost.

4 Dante II is the brainchild of Bares and William Whittaker, the principal research scientist at Carnegie Mellon's robotics lab and a legend among robot designers. Whittaker helped design the machine that cleaned up the reactor in Three Mile Island, Pennsylvania, after its near meltdown in 1979, and he oversaw development of a system that will automatically inspect the heat-resistant tiles on NASA's space shuttles.

5 Dante is perhaps his most sophisticated product. Its vaguely spider-like aluminium body has eight legs, four of which are always on the ground; that provides maximum stability as the machine moves forward at a top speed of 90 cm per minute, stepping lightly over obstacles more than 1 m high. Eight on-board video cameras enable scientists to view the terrain. Even more useful is a laser-ranging system — a sort of light-based radar — that makes 30,000 distance measurements every second and generates a virtual-reality computer image of the landscape. Says Bares: "It gives us a very complete picture of what's around us."

6 What makes Dante II truly revolutionary, however, is its four computers and their controlling software. Although the robot was connected by cable to a power generator and transmitter at the crater rim, which let the scientists direct it via a satellite hookup to the control room, Dante II can operate independently at times and did for nearly half the mission, negotiating its own path through the boulders.

7 That skill will be crucial if a Dante-like robot is sent to another world. On Mars, for example, says Lavery, contact would probably be limited to once a day, and even then the enormous distances would result in a minimum 10-minute time lag in communications. Dante II is not quite smart enough for full autonomy, but considering that it took less than a year to design and build, it is remarkably close to self-sufficient. Says Lavery: "The consensus was, if we had another four or five months, we would have had that ability."

8 Another barrier to sending robots to the planets is weight: every kilogram sent into space is expensive. At nearly a ton, Dante II would break the bank. Whittaker is already thinking about lighter models, though. And while NASA's Lavery cautions that Dante II is still "far from any sort of flight opportunity," he acknowledges that much of the technology used aboard Dante II may find its way into future space missions. In fact, NASA wants to launch a robot explorer toward Mars as early as 1996. And a private company working with Carnegie Mellon scientists hopes to send a Dante-like robot to the moon in 1997. The purely commercial purpose: to gather images for a gamelike, virtual-reality tour across the lunar surface.

9 In the meantime, Dante II-type robots should be in hot demand from earthbound volcanologists, 11 of whom have died exploring active craters in the past few years. As for Dante III, or whatever Whittaker calls the next generation, its task will be to spare humans from facing even greater dangers on other worlds.

Questions 29 – 32

Complete the table of the details of Dante II below. Write your answers in boxes 29 – 32 on your answer sheet.

Item	Detail
Example: Height	*3 m*
Weight	(29)
(30)	90 cm per minute
Body material	(31)
Designed by	(32)

Questions 33 – 35

Choose the appropriate letter / letters and write it / them in boxes 33 – 35 on your answer sheet.

33. The on-board equipment of Dante II includes the following except ·

A. a laser-ranging system.

B. a power generator.

C. 8 video cameras.

D. 4 computers.

E. a transmitter.

34. Dante II has been used in which of the following areas?

A. To explore volcanos.

B. To explore ocean floor.

C. To clean nuclear contaminated areas.

D. To inspect the heat resistant tiles of NASA's space shuttles.

E. To explore the surface of the moon.

35. Dante II is not qualified for space expeditions because

A. it is not smart enough.

B. it does not go fast enough.

C. it is too bulky to be carried by a spacecraft.

D. it needs better heat-resistant materials.

E. it is not light enough.

Questions 36 – 40

Decide if the following statements are true or false according to the information provided in Reading Passage 3. If a statement is true, write **TRUE** *in the corresponding box in the answer sheet; if it is false, write* **FALSE**. *If there is no information about a statement, write* **NOT GIVEN** *in the corresponding box in the answer sheet.*

Example:	Answer:
A robot similar to Dante II has been made to inspect the heat-resistant tiles on NASA's space shuttles.	***NOT GIVEN***

36. Falling rocks damaged Dante II.
37. Dante II sent 3-D graphic images of a deep cave.
38. A modified version of Dante II will be sent to Mars in 1996.
39. Dante II had an accident after it had completed its main mission.
40. If the designers and builders had had more time, they would have made Dante II more intelligent and able to make all its decisions.

答案及题解

READING PASSAGE 1

文章标题中的 F 指美国学校的评分系统中的"不及格"。

Questions 1 – 7:

1. **Yes** 见 B 段括号中的话。

2. **Not Given** B 段的最后三句话似乎与此题有关,但前两句是在说其他的比赛,而不是 IAEP。最后一句话是惟一与此题有关的文字内容,但句中的 as comparable as possible 是一种非常松散的说法,几乎等于没说。因此答案是 Not Given。

3. **No** 表中列出了 13 岁孩子的成绩排列。加拿大的名次比美国靠前。

4. **Yes** 见 A 段的 Americans did excel in one part of the test ... 美国教育部长说:看电视领先不是我们的教育目标。

5. **Not Given** 文中说共有 20 个国家和地区参赛,但表中仅列出 15 个。英格兰是否参赛,参赛名次如何,均不得而知。如果有 15 个参赛,表中也列出了 15 个,但没有英国,这道题的答案就是 No,因为英格兰未参赛,自然也不会被别人领先。

6. **Not Given** B 段说到此赛事举行了两次,而题中说 the 3rd IAEP。因此答案为 Not Given。应以作者报导此事件的时间为出发点,在此之后举行的赛事本文章没有提到。

7. **Not Given** E 段说美国 9 岁的孩子的成绩优于 13 岁的孩子的成绩,并指出了这种结果的可能原因。但此题在文中未得到支持。

Questions 8 – 15:

此类题属于 who does / did what 类。但已知的是 what,要找出 who,因此有一定的难度。

8. **Slovenia, Italy, Israel**

9. **Not Given** E 段说美国的教师喜欢教生物,不喜欢教物理和化学。但本文中未就物理和化学之间做比较。

10. **The U.S.** 见 G 段。文中说 1957 年苏联的第一颗人造卫星(sputnik)升空后,美国开始大兴教育。

11. **Taiwan, Korea** clustered 意为集中的、成群的。见 D 段。题中用的比较级,因此仅 Taiwan 一词即可,亦可加上 Korea,但仅答 Korea 不能算对。

12. **The U.S.** 见 F 段中 Quality of time, not quantity, matters most 及此后的引语。band practice:乐队演练。

13. **Not Given** 文中说美国的孩子看电视多,但未说哪国的孩子做功课多,看电视少。

14. **The U.S.** 见 F 段中 Attitudes toward intellectual achievement are also important. In Asia, scholarship is admired. "In the U.S., we call our best students nerd or dweeb"。scholarship:这里指学问、学识,不是奖学金。nerd 和 dweeb 对许多学生来说是生词,但应能感觉到语

气、情感上的转折,并由此推断出这两个词不是夸奖、赞美的词,而是挖苦、讽刺的词。

15. **Germany**　　见 B 段。

READING PASSAGE 2

此文有约 1000 词,是真题长度的上限。真题的文章在 800 至 1000 词之间。

Questions 16 – 19:

16. **A,D,F**　　第 2 段提到 two new extensions,分别是发展双引擎和四引擎的客机,也就是说选项中的 F 和 A。第三条出路就是本文的主题,即发展超音速民用飞机,也就是选项 D。此种需要两个或更多字母作答案的题,如只部分答对则不记分。除顺序外,所有的字母必须与标准答案一致。

17. **H**　　见第 4 和第 11 段。

18. **G**　　注意此题的措词,大意为"乘飞机的人增加了该怎么办",不应将其理解为"想增加乘飞机的人,该怎么办"。

19. **B,C**　　见第 7 段的 First ... And second is ...。

Questions 20 – 23:

见第 11 段。

20. **Tokyo**

21. **10 hours 18 minutes**

22. **Y**

23. **N**

Questions 24 – 27:

24. **Mach 2.4**　　Mach:马赫数。Mach 2.4:音速的 2.4 倍。此题亦可答作 2.5 或 4800km/hour (见第 8 段最后一句和第 9 段的第 1 句)。

25. **250 – 300**　　capacity:载客量。见第 10 段最后几个词。

26. **2.4 million**　　见第 10 段第 1 句话(大意是"到 2000 年翻番,达到 4.8 百万",现在的人数为 2.4 百万)。

27. **607,000/day**　　为超音速客机做市场预测时,要抛掉许多群体:受旺、淡季影响的、路程短的、在陆地上空飞行的等等。详见第 10 段。the scheduled international market:定期航班的国际市场,即受旺、淡季影响的航班。

28. **B**

READING PASSAGE 3

Dante:但丁,意大利诗人,长诗《神曲》的作者。该诗分《地狱》、《炼狱》、《天堂》三个部分,以梦幻的形式描写作者游历"地狱"、"炼狱"、"天堂"的情景。在此文中为一机器人的名字。

inferno：地狱，在此文中指火山口。

Questions 29 – 40：

29．**770 kg / nearly a ton**　见第 1 段和第 8 段。

30．**Top moving speed**　见第 5 段。

31．**Aluminium**　见第 5 段。

32．**Bares and Whittaker**　见第 1、4 段。第 4 段的 Bares 是第 1 段提到的 John Bares。答题应对等，只用姓答，或用姓和名答。

33．**B，E**　见第 6 段第 2 句。

34．**A**　题中用的是完成时。文中虽提到此类机器人可用于其他用途，但文中所描述的是 Dante II 的"处女航"，此机器人尚未用于其他用途。

35．**A，E**　见第 7、8 段。

36．**False**　见第 2 段第 1 句。

37．**False**　Dante II 探索了火山口，不是山洞。

38．**Not Given**　题中的情态动词 will 表示即将、就要，表达势在必行、不可逆转的意思，而第 8 段用的是 wants to，与 will 意思不同。另外，题中明确了时间（1996），而文中用的是 as early as 1996，意思也不一样。

39．**True**　见第 2 段第 1 句。

40．**True**　见第 7 段后半段。

三、A 类阅读模拟试题二、答案及题解

INTERNATIONAL ENGLISH LANGUAGE TESTING SYSTEM

PRACTICE TEST (Version Two)

ACADEMIC READING

TIME ALLOWED: 1 HOUR
NUMBER OF QUESTIONS: 40

Instructions

ALL ANSWERS MUST BE WRITTEN ON THE ANSWER SHEET.

The test is divided as follows:

Reading Passage 1	Questions 1 – 13
Reading Passage 2	Questions 14 – 27
Reading Passage 3	Questions 28 – 40

Start at the beginning of the test and work through it. Your should answer all the questions. If you cannot do a particular question leave it and go on to the next. You can return to it later.

READING PASSAGE 1

*You should spend about 20 minutes on **Questions 1 – 13** which are based on Reading Passage 1.*

The Call of the Wild

A The monotonous shrill of cicadas fills the humid air as a dozen orange-colored apes swing from branches and vines. It is almost feeding time at the Sepilok Orangutan Rehabilitation Center, and the residents are impatiently waiting for their human caretakers to bring them their morning meal. Located 24 km from the city of Sandakan near the northern coast of Malaysian Borneo, this 4,000-hectare rain-forest reserve is a temporary home for orphaned young orangutans. Some were taken by Sepilok rangers from people who had been illegally keeping the apes as the pets; others were brought in from lumber camps where their mothers had been killed in logging accidents. The center's mission is to "rehabilitate" the orangutans by breaking their dependence on human beings and reintroducing them to the wild. The process can take years.

B Twenty-five staff members watch over the 80 animals at Sepilok and play host to the 150 or more visitors who stop by on most days. "The main thing is conservation," says Reynard Gondipon, 27, the center's veterinarian. "We try to get the local people to love the animals and become more conservation conscious."

C Newly-arrived orangutans are carefully examined and then placed in quarantine. In the beginning, they cry much of the time, seeking affection by stretching out their long arms toward anyone who walks by their cages. "It's difficult when the orangutans come in very young," says Gondipon. "I urge the rangers to hug them every now and then. But later on, we try to reduce contact, or else they will become too accustomed to us."

D After a few months of quarantine, the young orangutans are slowly introduced to the surrounding jungle. At first they spend about two hours a day playing in the open. Once they reach the age of two, they are allowed to roam freely, though they instinctively stay near the platform where they are fed. Imitating their elders, the youngsters learn to climb, swing in and jump from trees, build sleeping nests and search for food.

E At this stage, dependence on humans still runs deep. Twice a day, rangers lug red plastic buckets to the feeding platform to give the animals nourishing meal of bananas and milk; the fare is deliberately bland to force the young orangutans to look for other food for themselves. "During the fruiting season, we also decrease the amount," says Gondipon. "This encourages them to go into the forest to find their own." On this day, a dozen apes swing in from the jungle and pull themselves up to the platform. The rangers hand out bananas as the animals take turns sticking their heads in a bucket for gulps of milk.

F On most mornings visitors gather on a nearby knoll to watch the feeding , and after the meal are joined by some of the apes, interested in studying their human observers. Most, though not all, of the orangutans are so tame that they wrap their gangly arms around the guests. But there are exceptions. When a young ape, Boy ambles toward a woman and reaches for her purse, Sylvia Alsisto, 24, who heads the center's education division, shakes a stick at the ape and yells, "Boy!" "Excuse me," she tells the visitor. "Don't touch him. He'll bite." The woman pulls away, though not before the orangutan has grabbed and eaten her map of Sepilok.

G Because excessive contact with humans hinders rehabilitation, the staff discourages visitors from touching the animals. An exception is Jojo, 3, once a pet, who disdains the jungle life and is content with prancing and posing for a curious audience. "It is very hard trying to rehabilitate Jojo," says Gondipon. "he doesn't want to climb, and he once fell from a tree and broke his arm. So, rather than let the visitors touch all the other orangutans, we let Jojo do the job for them."

H By the age of nine, the apes are moved to a second feeding platform a kilometer away. Here they have little contact with people but are still brought food to supplement their diet. On a platform near the ground, two feeders bellow like orangutans as a way of telling the apes out in the forest that it is mealtime. A few people are waiting nearby, brushing off the occasional leech that tumbles onto them from the trees above. "Someone's up there," whispers Janet Liew, 31, who has come from Sandakan. "I see her." At first there is little response to the feeders' howls. Then the leaves rustle overhead. Down comes a female orangutan with an infant clinging to her. The mother accepts a few bananas and then some milk. As the excited visitors snap pictures, the orangutans retreat back up the tree.

I The rangers see the apes' flight from the cameras' flashes as a good sign: it shows that as the animals become less dependent on people for food, they are also less at ease with them. High above in the overhead canopy, the mother cradles her baby and carries it off into the forest.

Questions 1 – 3

Choose the appropriate letter / letters and write it / them in boxes 1 – 3 on your answer sheet.

1. The word "visitors" is used a number of times in the passage (paragraphs B, F, G and H). It is used to refer to

   A. people only.

   B. apes only.

   C. both people and apes.

2. The target population of the Orangutan Rehabilitation Center are (*please choose two*)

   A. orangutans formerly kept as pets by people.

   B. orangutans living in the wild.

   C. young orangutans whose mothers have been killed.

   D. wild animals in the area.

3. Which one of the following is not the rangers' effort to help the orangutans to be less dependent on people?

   A. Reduce rangers' physical contact with them.

   B. Reduce food during fruiting season.

   C. Limit the daily food.

   D. Move the feeding place.

   E. Brush off the occasional leech that tumbles onto them.

Questions 4 – 5

Reading Passage 1 has 9 paragraphs marked A – I. Answer questions 4 and 5 by writing the letter A – I of the appropriate paragraphs in boxes 4 and 5 on your answer sheet.

Example:	Answer:
Which paragraph mentions the geographic location of the Orangutan Rehabilitation Center?	*A*

4. Which paragraph says that some young orangutans can be dangerous?

5. Which paragraph mentions more explicitly that the rangers are achieving their purpose?

Questions 6 – 13

Complete the following summary of Reading Passage 1. Choose **NO MORE THAN THREE WORDS** *from the passage for each gap. Write your answers in boxes 6 – 13 on your answer sheet.*

A center to rehabilitate orphaned young orangutans is run by some conservation ...(6)... people in Sepilok, 24 km from the city of Sandakan, Borneo. A ...(7)... home for about 80 orangutans, it gives them a chance to learn to be less ...(8)... people for food and eventually be able to fend for themselves in ...(9).... On a platform near the ground, bananas and milk are offered to the orangutans ...(10).... After several years, the orangutans are moved to a second feeding platform ...(11)..., to further reduce their ...(12)... with people. They gradually become less ...(13)... with people, which is seen as an indicator of the rangers' success.

READING PASSAGE 2

*You should spend about 20 minutes on **Questions 14 – 27** which are based on Reading Passage 2.*

Terror on the Internet

A Thanksgiving weekend was quiet in the Long Island, New York, home of Michelle Slatalla and Josh Quittner. Too quiet. The phone didn't ring all weekend — which is unusual for a pair of working journalists. Nor did they hear the familiar beep of electronic mail arriving from the Internet, although Quittner tried several times to log on. It wasn't until their tenant complained about a strange message on their answering machine that the couple investigated and discovered all was not well in their electronic cocoon.

B "We'd been hacked," says Quittner, who writes about computers — and hackers — for his local newspaper *Newsday*, and will start writing for *Time* in January. Not only had someone jammed his Internet mailbox with thousands of unwanted pieces of electronic mail, finally shutting down his Internet access altogether, but the couple's telephone had been reprogrammed to forward incoming calls to an out-of-state number, where friends and relatives heard a greeting laced with obscenities. "What's really strange," says Quittner, "is that nobody who phoned — including my editor and my mother — thought anything of it. They just left their messages and hung up."

C It gets stranger. In order to send Quittner that mail bomb — the electronic equivalent of dumping a truckload of garbage on a neighbor's front lawn — someone, operating by remote control, had broken into computers at IBM, Sprint and a small Internet service provider called the Pipeline, seized command of the machines at the supervisory — or "root" — level, and installed a program that fired off E-mail messages every few seconds. Adding intrigue to insult, the message turned out to be a manifesto that railed against "capitalist pig" corporations and accused those companies of turning the Internet into an "overflowing cesspool of greed." It was signed by something called the Internet Liberation Front, and it ended like this: "Just a friendly warning corporate America: we have already stolen your proprietary source code. We have already pillaged your million dollar research data. And if you would like to avoid financial ruin, get the (expletive deleted) out of Dodge. Happy Thanksgiving Day turkeys."

D It read like an Internet nightmare come true, a poison arrow designed to strike fear in the heart of all the corporate information managers who had hooked their companies up to the information superhighway only to discover that they may have opened the gate to trespassers. Is the I.L.F. for real? Is there really a terrorist group intent on bringing the world's largest computer network to its knees?

E The Net is certainly vulnerable to attack. Last April a pair of publicity-hungry lawyers deluged more than 5,000 Usenet newsgroups with an unsolicited promotional mailing, triggering a flood of angry E-mail massive enough to knock them off the Net. A few years earlier a single "worm" program, designed by a Cornell University student to explore the network, multiplied out of control and brought hundreds of computer systems to a halt.

F Since then the Internet has become, if anything, an even more tempting target. According to the Pittsburgh, Pennsylvania-based Computer Emergency Response Team, which fields complaints from systems operators, hardly a day goes by without a computer assault of one sort or another—from filching passwords to trying to crack military files. In the first nine months of 1994, CERT logged 1,517 incidents — up more than 75% from 1993— some of them involving networks that link tens of thousands of machines. Two weeks ago, someone infiltrated General Electric's Internet link, forcing the company to pull itself off the network while it revamped its security system. "Every morning we find marks from people trying to pry open the firewall," says Michael Wolff, author of the *Net Guide* book series and founder of a small Internet service called Your Personal Network, a small Internet.

G Firewalls, for those not familiar with the jargon of electronic security, are computers that act like the guards in a corporation's front lobby. They are supposed to keep the tens of millions of people with Internet access from also having access to the company's internal computer system, where precious corporate assets may be stored. Firewalls typically use passwords, keys, alarms and other devices to lock out intruders. But though such obstacles are an essential feature of any well-designed security system, experts warn that the technology of firewalls is still in its infancy. "There is no such thing as absolute security," says Steven Bellovin, co-author of *Firewalls and Internet Security*. "There is only relative risk."

H And what about the folks on the receiving end of a mail bomb? "That's a tough one," says Vinton Cerf, an MCI executive who helped design the Internet in the late '60s. "If you know who was sending you the mail, you could install a filter to throw it away. But trying to discard thousands of messages when you don't know where they're coming from just isn't possible."

I The Internet was built to be an open and cooperative system. That's its strength—

and its weakness. "It's a fragile environment," says Pipeline founder James Gleick. "There's no cleverness in breaking a system like Pipeline. We're not MCI. We're exactly the kind of small-scale operation that gives the Internet its vitality and richness."

I That's what is so odd about the so-called Internet Liberation Front. While it claims to hate the "big boys" of the telecommunications industry and their dread firewalls, the group's targets include a pair of journalists and a small, regional Internet provider. "It doesn't make any sense to me," says Gene Spafford, a computer-security expert at Purdue University. "I'm more inclined to think it's a grudge against Josh Quittner."

K That is probably what it was. Quittner and Slatalla had just finished a book about the rivalry between a gang of computer hackers called the Masters of Deception and their archenemies, the Legion of Doom — an excerpt of which appears in the current issue of *Wired* magazine. And as it turns out, *Wired* was mail-bombed the same day Quittner was — with some 3,000 copies of the same nasty message from the I.L.F. Speculation on the Net at week's end was that the attacks may have been the work of the Masters of Deception — some of whom have actually served prison time for vandalizing the computers and telephone systems of people who offend them. But given the layers of intrigue and deception in the hacker wars, that could just as easily be disinformation broadcast to distract attention from a rival gang — or even a gang aspirant. It almost doesn't matter. Like many terrorist acts, this one seems to have backfired. The Internet today feels a little less "liberated," a lot less safe, and even more likely to be sectioned off with those firewalls the I.L.F. seemed so intent on destroying.

Questions 14 – 20

The following (14 – 20) are some people, companies or organisations mentioned in Reading Passage 2. In the box below are what these people / companies / organisations did. Match each name with what it did by choosing a letter from the box and write the letters in boxes 14 – 20 on your answer sheet.

Example:	Answer:
James Gleick	*D*

14. CERT

15. the Internet

16. a Cornell University student
17. two lawyers who wanted to attract attention
18. Quittner and Slatalla
19. I. L. F.
20. someone (in paragraph **F**)

A. sent off advertisements through E-mail that annoyed a lot of people
B. detected many attempts to gain access to internal networks
C. jammed somebody's Internet mailbox with electronic garbage
D. founded Pipeline
E. offers an open service to millions of users
F. tampered with the network and collapsed many computer systems
G. penetrated a big company's security system of computer network
H. had parts of a book published in a magazine

Questions 21 – 23

Use ***NO MORE THAN THREE WORDS*** *from Reading Passage 2 to answer the following questions. Write your answers in boxes 21 – 23 on your answer sheet.*

21. What do I.L.F. stand for?

22. What is the name of the world's largest computer network?

23. What are used to keep network from being attacked by infiltration attempts?

Questions 24 – 26

*Answer the following questions by writing the paragraph letters (**A** – **K**) in boxes 24 – 26 on your answer sheet.*

24. Which paragraph offers an explanation why Slatalla and Quittner suffered the disaster?

25. Which paragraph says there is an increase in the number of incidents to break into internal network?

26. Which paragraph explains how computer jamming could be done?

Question 27

Choose two letters and write them in box 27 on your answer sheet.

27. What happened to Slatalla and Quittner?

A. Their Internet access was shut down by the company.

B. Their E-mail mailbox was jammed.

C. They have been sacked by the *Newsday* and will start to work for *Time*.

D. Someone unloaded a truckload of garbage on their front lawn.

E. Their incoming telephone calls were diverted to another number out of New York State.

READING PASSAGE 3

You should spend about 20 minutes on ***Questions 28 – 40*** *which are based on Reading Passage 3.*

Perils of Electronic Radiation

1 Last October, a Nagoya businessman was surprised when the engine of his Mercedes Benz stopped as he was trying to make a call on his cellular telephone. Although investigations into the cause of the problem continue, the malfunction may have been due to microwaves from the telephone interfering with the car's electronic fuelinjection system.

2 In November, IBM announced that it planned to lower the electromagnetic radiation emitted on future models of video-display terminals (VDTs) used to communicate with its computers. The reason for the change, the company explained, was growing consumer concern about the safety of such terminals.

3 All electrical circuits emit unwanted radiation, or "noise", as it is sometimes called. As these two examples demonstrate, radiation can interfere with the operation of other circuits and may even pose health problems.

4 There is as yet no evidence for the latter. But, extraordinarily enough, given the number of people who spend much of their working lives sitting in front of VDT screens and several health warnings, there has been no systematic study carried out on electro magnetic emission. In 1987, the World Health Organisation recommended workers to position their terminals at least 1 m apart in order to avoid being exposed to radiation from more than one source. And a recent report sponsored by the US congressional Office of Technology Assessment said it was no longer possible to categorically assert that there were no risks to health from such radiation.

5 In Sweden, they are not waiting to find out one way or the other. In 1988, Swedish management and labour drew up strict standards on the amount of radiation VDTs were allowed to emit.

6 IBM's new terminals will be designed to meet or surpass the Swedish standards. Other makers are quietly following suit. In Japan, Sony says it is responding to calls from customers to lower the radiation emitted by its VDTs.

7 VDTs are exceptional products, in terms of the amounts of radiation they emit and their proximity to the user. But with the proliferation of electronically controlled devices in factories, offices, homes and cars, makers are beginning to adopt a more rigorous approach to the problem of electromagnetic interference, too.

8 One of the most common causes of interference, as anyone who has ever tried to listen to a radio or watch a television near a road knows, is the electromagnetic noise generated by a car engine's spark plugs. In addition, there are also domestic spark makers such as the igniters used to light gas stove and heaters. Other well-known culprits are the brushes of electric motors.

9 All digital equipment, such as personal computers, modems and compact-disc players, contains a noisemaker in the form of a "clock," which is actually an oscillator whose high-frequency pulses synchronise the operation of digital circuits.

10 How to prevent interference occurring among all this inaudible but ubiquitous cacophony? As in medicine, prevention is better than cure.

11 Circuits can be designed so that they cannot unintentionally act as antennas. Circuit boards can be laid out to minimise the potential for noise emitting parts to affect each other. In addition, devices can be located far enough away from other devices to make interference unlikely. (But this approach is not idiot-proof: the cellular telephone in the Nagoya businessman's car, for instance, was installed in an unforeseen position.)

12 Connectors and cables can be shielded from interference with special materials. Entire equipment cases can be shielded by coating them with special noise-absorbing paint.

13 It is an ill wind that blows nobody any good. Those benefiting from the new concern about reducing electromagnetic noise include Asahi Glass and construction company Taisei. Both of these Japanese companies market special shielding materials intended to protect corporate computer rooms and "intelligent" commercial office buildings.

14 Even more involved in the noise-reduction market are tape-maker TDK and materials-specialist Tokin. Both of these Japanese companies are strong in the technology of ferrite, an iron-derived material good at absorbing radiation. It is used, among other applications, to coat the edges of doors on microwave ovens.

15 Ferrite parts such as coils can be incorporated in circuits to filter unwanted frequencies. The substance is also used to coat the egg-box-shaped walls of special echo-free chambers. Makers use these chambers to measure how much electro-magnetic radiation their products emit. The ferrite absorbs radiation that would bounce back off ordinary wall and spoil the measurements.

16 An indication of how seriously Japanese makers take the problem of electromagnetic interference can be gauged from the fact that TDK sold about 40 of these chambers in 1989. The company says it expects to sell even more this year.

17 Demand for echo-free chambers in Japan is driven by standards issued by the Voluntary Control Council for Interference by Data Processing Equipment and Electronic Office Machines. Established in 1985 by four industry associations, the council has more than 300 members.

18 The standards are based on recommendations by the International Electrotechnical Commission. Japan appears to be the only country thus far to have implemented the recommendations, albeit only on a voluntary basis.

19 This initiative marks a departure for the Japanese, who hitherto have tended to lag behind other nations in adopting international standards. Akihide Sei of the Japan Electronic Industry Development Association, one of the council's sponsors, estimates that 60% – 70% of Japanese equipment covered by the council's recommendations conform to its standards.

20 "In the past, makers would have tried to ignore the issue until a problem occurred," Sei says. "Now they worry about the damage that would be done to their image if something went wrong with one of their products."

Questions 28 – 34

Do the following statements agree with the views of the writer of Reading Passage 3?

In boxes 28 – 34 on your answer sheet write

YES	*if the statement agrees with the writer;*
NO	*if the statement does not agree with the writer;*
NOT GIVEN	*if there is no information about this in the passage.*

Example: Answer:

The ferrite coating of echo-free chambers bounces back electromagnetic radiation. ***NO***

28. The US congressional Office of Technology Assessment feels that the general public are overreacting to electromagnetic radiation.

29. The WHO recommended that terminals should be placed a metre away from the operator.

30. Systematic research should be carried out to study electromagnetic radiation.

31. Both IBM and Sony have produced low radiation VDTs.

32. Even though there has been growing consumer concern about the safety of VDTs, it has not been proved that electromagnetic radiation emitted by them is a health hazard to terminal operators.

33. The example mentioned in the first paragraph shows that devices can be located far enough away from other devices to make interference unlikely.

34. Ferrite has recently been used to make low radiation VDTs.

Questions 35 – 38

Answer the following questions by choosing letters ***A – H*** *in the box below. Write the answers in boxes 35 – 38 on your answer sheet. Please note that some questions require more than one letter to answer.*

Example:	Answer:
Which of the following has drawn up strict standards on the amount of radiation VDTs are allowed to emit?	***E***

35. Which two of the following have had economic gains from concerns about electromagnetic radiation?

36. Which two of the following are improving the quality of VDTs so that they'll have lower electromagnetic radiation?

37. Which one of the following produces echo-free chambers?

38. Which three of the following are responsible for setting safety standards of electromagnetic radiation?

A. TDK
B. IBM
C. Sony
D. Asahi Glass
E. Swedish management and labour
F. International Electrotechnical Commission
G. Japan Electronic Industry Development Association
H. Voluntary Control Council for Interference by Data Processing Equipment and Electronic Office Machines

Questions 39 – 40

Answer the following questions by choosing letters **A – G** *in the box below. Write the answers in boxes 39 – 40 on your answer sheet. Please note that some questions require more than one letter to answer.*

39. Which two of the following do not produce electromagnetic radiation?
40. Which of the following is / are under greater scrutiny for its / their potential harmful radiation?

A. cellular phone	B. microwave oven
C. ferrite coils	D. VDT
E. car engine	F. echo-free chamber
G. compact-disc player	

答案及题解

READING PASSAGE 1

此文描述了工作人员如何帮助猩猩获得在野生环境中生存的能力。orangutan：猩猩，产于印尼。与此动物有关的另外两种动物是：chimpanzee（黑猩猩）和 gorilla（大猩猩），均产于非洲。

Questions 1 – 13:

1. **A**　B 段的 visitors 到底指人还是猩猩有些不清楚，但其他几处均明确指人，因此，此词在 B 段也是指人。
2. **A, C**　见 A 段。
3. **E**　工作人员的目的是帮助猩猩获得在自然中生活的能力，A、B、C、D 均为此目的。leech：水蛭。
4. **F**
5. **I**　explicitly：明确地，反意词是 implicitly（含蓄地）。
6. **conscious**　A 段最后一词。
7. **temporary**　A 段第 3 句。
8. **dependent on**　I 段
9. **the wild / the forest / the jungle**　见 A、E 段。
10. **twice a day**　E 段第 2 句。
11. **a kilometer away**　H 段第 1 句。
12. **contact**　见 C、G、H 段。
13. **at ease**　（随便的，放松的）　见 I 段。

READING PASSAGE 2

此文讲述的是网络安全、黑客等内容。

Questions 14 – 27:

14 – 20 题属于 who does / did what 类题，既然是与 who 有关，一般都涉及专有名词（人名、机构名）。利用大写字母更显著的特点，尽快在文中找到 who，根据上下文即可找到 what。

14. **B**　15. **E**　16. **F**　17. **A**　18. **H**　19. **C**　20. **G**

21. **Internet Liberation Front**　见 I 段。
22. **The Internet**　应有定冠词。
23. **Firewalls / passwords, keys, alarms**　见 G 段
24. **K**　25. **F**　26. **C**　27. **B, E**

READING PASSAGE 3

此文讲述了电脑显示器的辐射问题。

Questions 28 – 40:

28. **No** overreacting：小题大做、无中生有。见第4段最后一句。

29. **No** 题中说人机之间距离应为一米，文中（第1段中间）说两个显示器之间为一米。

30. **Yes** 见第4段第2句。

31. **No** 见第6段，... will be designed 和 responding to calls 均表示尚未生产出来。

32. **Yes** 见第3段和第4段第1句。

33. **No** 见第1段和第3段。

34. **Not Given**

35. **A, D** 答案D很明确，见第13段。答案C见第15、16段。egg-box-shaped walls：凹凸不平的墙，像超市装鸡蛋的盒子或托盘。

36. **B, C**

37. **A**

38. **E, F, H** 见第5、17、18段。

39. **C, F**

40. **D** under greater scrutiny：倍受审视。文章虽提到其他物体也产生电磁辐射，如手机、汽车发动机、VCD机和微波炉，但主要论述的是显示器的辐射问题。

四、A类阅读模拟试题三、答案及题解

INTERNATIONAL ENGLISH LANGUAGE TESTING SYSTEM

PRACTICE TEST（Version Three）

ACADEMIC READING

TIME ALLOWED: 1 HOUR
NUMBER OF QUESTIONS: 40

Instructions

ALL ANSWERS MUST BE WRITTEN ON THE ANSWER SHEET.

The test is divided as follows:

Reading Passage 1	Questions 1 – 13
Reading Passage 2	Questions 14 – 25
Reading Passage 3	Questions 26 – 39

Start at the beginning of the test and work through it. Your should answer all the questions. If you cannot do a particular question leave it and go on to the next. You can return to it later.

READING PASSAGE 1

You should spend about 20 minutes on ***Questions 1 – 13*** *which are based on Reading Passage 1.*

A Sizzling Scientific Debate

A Environmentalists staged Earth Day to dramatize a simple message: The planet is threatened by a host of man-made ills, from toxic landfills to ozone depletion. But at least one part of the message — the theory that the buildup of carbon dioxide and other greenhouse gases in the atmosphere will cause global warming — has come under considerable attack. A small but vocal group of scientists contends that the case for warming is sketchy and based on inadequate computer models.

B Forces in Washington, led by White House chief of staff John Sununu, have seized upon the debate and persuaded President Bush to take a cautious approach to the problem. While not dismissing the greenhouse threat, the President has emphasized the need for more scientific research to help determine the proper policy response. This go-slow approach has irritated government officials in several other countries, especially in Western Europe. As the Europeans point out, many scientists still fear that global warming could take place unless strong action is taken to prevent it.

C Last week representatives from 18 nations gathered in Washington for a global-warming conference set up by the White House. The Bush Administration had hoped to get a debate going on the uncertainties of the greenhouse effect. Instead, most of the delegates appeared to agree that the global-warming threat is real and potentially serious. In the face of this strong sentiment, President Bush denied that he was taking global warming too lightly. The President reconfirmed a U.S. pledge to cooperate in a United National agreement on dealing with climate change.

D The greenhouse dilemma illustrates the difficulty of setting policy based on uncertain projections of the future. Scientists generally agree that an unchecked accumulation of greenhouse gases will eventually lead to warming, but no one knows when it will start, how much will take place or how rapidly it will occur. The most widely accepted estimate is a rise in the earth's average temperature of 1.5℃ to 4.5℃ (3°F to 8°F) as early as 2050. An increase in the upper part of that range could produce disastrous climatic effects, including rising sea levels and severe droughts in some areas.

E But the computer models that make the projections may not accurately reflect such factors as the role of clouds and the heat-absorbing capacity of the oceans. As these phenomena are better understood, warming projections will undoubtedly be revised in one direction or another.

F Evidence that greenhouse warming has already started is at best tenuous. Even though some scientists believe the concentration of CO_2 in the air has shot up 25% since the early 1800s, the average global temperature has risen by no more than 0.5℃ (1.1°F), and even that measurement is suspect. Moreover, the rise has been uneven. From about 1940 to 1970, a cooling period inspired some forecasters to predict a return of the ice ages.

G Despite the uncertainties, there is a broad consensus that nations should slow down the rate at which they are changing the atmosphere. Said West German Environment Minister Klaus Topfer at the Washington conference: "Worldwide action against the climatic threat is urgently required, even if the complicated scientific interrelationships of climatic change have not been fully understood."

H To his credit, Bush has already taken several steps that will help combat global warming. Among other things, the White House has 1) earmarked $1 billion for global climate research next year; 2) committed the U.S. to phasing out production of chlorofluorocarbons, potent greenhouse gases, by the year 2000; and 3) vowed to plant a billion trees, which would absorb CO_2 from the air. But Administration officials admit that Bush advanced most of the measures for reasons other than reducing global warming. And environmentalists argue that the U.S. Government should do much more to discourage the burning of fossil fuels. Among the possibilities: raise the gasoline tax or use financial incentives to encourage people to buy smaller, more efficient cars.

The following are the last two paragraphs of Reading Passage 1. Fill in the blanks with ***NO MORE THAN ONE or TWO WORDS*** *taken from the previous paragraphs. Write the words in boxes 1 – 5 on your answer sheet.*

I The White House, however, worries about the economic consequences of forcing sudden, drastic curbs in uses of ...(1)... . From the Administration's point of view, draconian action seems highly debatable so long as the scientific evidence for the greenhouse effect is ...(2)... . "We are not at the point where we can bet the economy," says a Sununu aide.

J That may be so. The ...(3)... is wise to consider the possible economic damage before committing itself to a major reduction in ...(4)... emissions. But surely the U.S. Government can safely do much more than it has already done to spur energy conservation. It is possible to buy a great deal of insurance against ...(5)... without sabotaging the economy.

Questions 6 – 11

Do the following statements agree with the views of the "small but vocal group of scientists" (paragraph A)?

In boxes 6 – 11 *on your answer sheet write*

YES	*if the statement agrees with the group;*
NO	*if the statement does not agree with the group;*
NOT GIVEN	*if there is no information about this in the passage.*

Example: Answer:

Oceans have a great ability to retain heat and keep the atmosphere from warming substantially. *YES*

6. An increase of carbon dioxide levels in the atmosphere means a corresponding increase of temperature.

7. Talks of a return of ice age are groundless as evidence shows that temperature has been rising since the early 1800s.

8. Computer models truly reflect what is happening around the world.

9. Clouds, formed by water vapours because of warm temperatures, may have a cooling effect by blocking some sunlight.

10. More intensive study should be carried out to find alternatives to replace fossil fuels.

11. Scientific conclusions are political since they may affect economy.

Questions 12 – 13

12. Which paragraph gives an example of the idea that there is not sufficient evidence for global warming?

13. Which paragraph indicates that steps taken by the White House are more political than environmental?

READING PASSAGE 2

You should spend about 20 minutes on ***Questions 14 – 25*** *which are based on Reading Passage 2.*

Footing the Bill

1 Imagine a company whose shift rotas are determined a year in advance and whose workers, in return for accepting last-minute alterations, demand large bonus payments. It does not sound like a bulwark of Thatcherism — But yes, it's the police, whose inefficiencies have emerged from the 1980s largely untainted by the prime minister's dearest principles.

2 The cost of the police force has risen by 55% in real terms over the past ten years: three times the rate of growth in defence spending and six times that of the education budget. Though few politicians will publicly question the Tories' largesse towards the service, the laxity with which police expenditure is monitored offers critics an easier target.

3 The police have escaped both the government's barrels. As local forces, they have not felt the spending cuts in Whitehall; as partners in a special relationship with the Home Office, they have been cushioned against the pressure on local authorities' spending. Rigid police procedures, most conspicuously the hourly wage structure, have been protected by the Police Federation, the trade union for police officers. And attempts at external monitoring have, until recently, proved toothless.

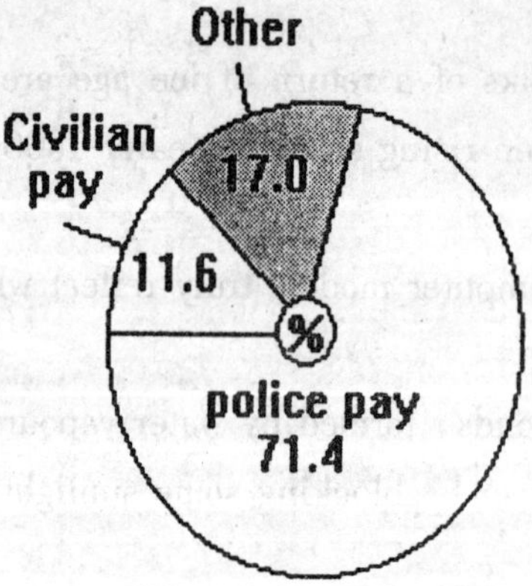

Estimated allocation of spending, 1989-1990

4 Take first the overall budget procedures. Each chief constable enjoys huge operational autonomy; yet in law he has less financial discretion over his force than the education bill is planning to give primary-school headteachers.

5 Control over current spending belongs to the local police authority. Half its revenue budget is reimbursed as a direct grant from the Home Office; in theory, this is reviewed by Her Majesty's Inspectorate — but no grant has ever been refused. Nor is the sum of these grants cash-limited like other items of public expenditure. It is like Whitehall is writing a blank cheque — value, in 1988 – 1989, £1.3 billion.

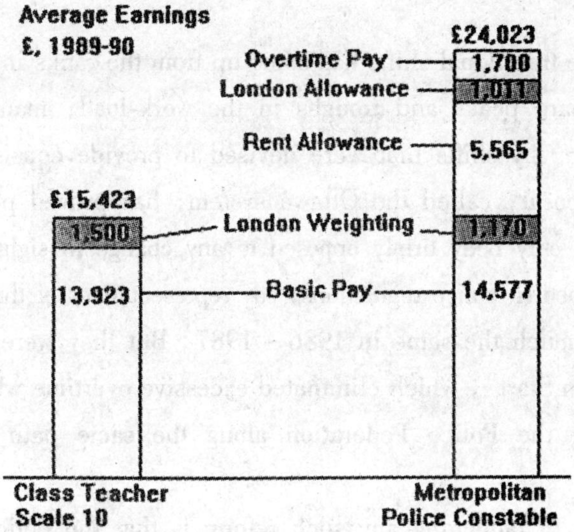

6 The other half of each local authority's spending on the police comes out of its block grant from the Department of the Environment. Here is another oddity. Whenever the home secretary — who controls manpower — allows a force to have more uniformed policemen, the block grant rises to pay for them and for some civilian support.

7 If the chief constable forgets about that support, he has won some spare cash. But what if he leaves his uniformed force unchanged in favour of recruiting cheaper (and more appropriately-skilled) civilians? The Home Office has urged this option, recognising that many police jobs do not require a policeman's authority. But these extra civilians will not bring more money. Their cost must come out of thc cxisting budget.

8 Where this disincentive means civilian recruitment is shelved — and the civilian staff of the police has stuck at just under 28% of total manpower since 1979 — the opportunity cost is high. Excluding pensions, the average cost of a Metropolitan police officer is estimated by the Home Office at £26,000 a year: twice the £13,000 cost of a member of the police civil staff.

9 Even without the increments paid in London, police officers are handsomely rewarded. In line with the formula fixed by Lord Edmund-Davies in 1978, their basic pay is linked to the Employment Department's all-earnings index — putting them in line with private-sector earnings in the 1980s and thus above the rest of the envious public sector. They also get housing allowances.

10 Recent home secretaries have cast a cold eye on both the formula and the allowances, without properly tackling either. But the real target for any pay reform would surely be the hourly wage, the sacred rota and the service's archaic shift structures that mean fat overtime payments.

11 Pressure to dump the traditional shifts has come up from the ranks in recent years. Modern policing dictates sharp peaks and troughs in the work-load: many officers are frustrated — and exhausted — by shifts that were devised to provide consistent manning around the clock. One proposal, called the Ottawa system, has proved popular after a trial run in Portsmouth. The only body firmly opposed to any change in sight is the Police Federation. Shifts are enshrined in police regulations, say representatives of the Federation.

12 Prison officers said much the same in 1986 – 1987. But they were persuaded to accept a new regime, "Fresh Start", which eliminated excessive overtime while promoting greater efficiency. Coaxing the Police Federation along the same path still looks a daunting job.

13 Part of the problem in launching any such reform is that the police are still so unaccustomed to external criticism. Local police authorities are conscientious but part-time, and unable to compare local practices with those of other forces. Her Majesty's Inspectorate, watchdog for a force of 175,000, has precisely 20 inspectors and administrators to do the job. It carries out continuous inspections but few of its reports have been published. Its impact is hard to discern, beyond the voluminous statistics it produces.

14 The Home Office's police department has inspired no reforms. Eight civil servants, set up as a special division last July, are mainly responsible for Met; but they continue to share financial control with other divisions — and their monitoring role with the National Audit Office — in a way that seems unlikely to make much of a dent on the force. Although there are mutterings about efficiency, guidelines to police forces along the lines that might be recognisable, say, to the middle manager on a commercial company, still seem remote.

15 The Police Requirements Support Unit (PRSU), part of the Home Office, is supposed to promote the standardisation of purchasing by police forces around the country. Thus, a few years back, it issued a strategy document on computerisation. Yet there is still astonishingly little co-ordination between police forces in their purchasing of computers. Indeed, there is little co-ordination over buying anything at all. No two forces today even share uniforms similar enough to allow pooled purchasing; and individual items of clothing vary hugely in cost from one force to another.

16 The PRSU believes that civilisation of the police has gone about as far as it can. The Audit Commission, which has a say in police matters as part of its brief to watch over local-government finances, takes a different view. It has produced its first four reports on the police over the past two years and is currently preparing a range of further studies. "There are many functions undertaken by police forces which police officers are not trained to perform," noted the commission in a review of the police force's vehicle-fleet management.

17 Initially wary, several chief constables have started to pay attention suggested of saving money. Perhaps other civil servants will start to take more of an interest in the subject too.

Questions 14 – 17

In the box below are names of offices / departments mentioned in Reading Passage 2. Answer Questions 14 – 17 by choosing the appropriate letters from the box and writing them in boxes 14 – 17 on your answer sheet.

A. Home Office	B. Whitehall
C. The Police Federation	D. Her Majesty's Inspectorate
E. Department of the Environment	F. The Employment Department
G. The National Audit Office	H. The Audit Commission
I. The Police Requirements Support Unit	

Example: Answer:
Who has the responsibility to monitor the police? ***D***

14. Which one of the above is said to be more resistant to reforming the police's payment scheme?

15. Which one of the above feels that some police officers need more training?

16. Which two of the above are partly responsible for monitoring the financial situation of the police?

17. Which two of the above are responsible for providing allocations to the police?

Questions 18 – 20

Answer Questions 18 – 20 by choosing an appropriate letter and writing your answers in boxes 18 – 20 on your answer sheet.

18. Which one of the following has had the biggest expenditure increase?
    A. National defence.
    B. National education.
    C. The police.

19. Which one of the following is thought to be paid reasonably and the pay brings efficiency?
    A. The chief constables.
    B. The uniformed police officers.
    C. Home secretaries.
    D. Prison officers.
    E. Members of the police civil staff.

20. What is the main idea of Reading Passage 2?
    A. Allocations to the British police should be increased.
    B. Modern equipment should be provided for the British police.
    C. The British police is spending too much money.
    D. Compared with education, the British police is functioning better.
    E. Home Office should be responsible for the poor quality of the police.

Questions 21 – 25

Use the information from Reading Passage 2 to answer the following questions with ***NO MORE THAN THREE WORDS****. Write the answers in boxes 21 – 25 on your answer sheet.*

21. Which part of the police spending is under greater scrutiny and needs to be reformed?

22. How much more do the uniformed police force cost as compared with the civilian staff of the police?

23. How much of the estimated allocation of spending of 1989 – 1990 was spent paying the police?

24. How big is the police force?

25. How much more is a police constable paid for serving in London as opposed to serving somewhere else?

READING PASSAGE 3

*You should spend about 20 minutes on **Questions 26 – 39** which are based on Reading Passage 3.*

The Reason Why

1 When underwater-salvage experts found the wreck of the ferry Estonia last week, they quickly confirmed what shipping experts feared most: the huge bow door of the 15,566-ton ship was gone, ripped away while the vessel plowed through a stormy Baltic Sea shortly after midnight on Sept. 28. The immediate consequence was the loss of the ship and more than 900 of the 1,051 passengers and crew on board. The longer-range result could be a financial disaster for shipowners since the accident has called into question the safety of thousands of similar ships worldwide. Several countries swiftly ordered bow doors welded permanently shut, and the U.N.'s International Maritime Organization launched an extensive study to determine what should be done about some 3,600 other roll-on roll-off ferries plying the seas from the Arctic coasts of Russia to the archipelagos of the Pacific. "Nothing will be excluded," said IMO spokesman Roger Kohn. "The public must be reassured that everything possible is being done."

2 The reassurance is needed, because the flaws that caused the Estonia to sink are shared by most other RO-RO ships. All are equipped with large doors forward and aft to permit quick loading and unloading of trucks, buses and cars, the feature that makes them among the most efficient and profitable vessels afloat. But as the Estonia showed — and as many naval architects have warned — huge doors so near the waterline are dangerous weak points. When such a door is in the bow, as on the Estonia, it is especially vulnerable to the pounding of stormy seas or the shock of collision. "The RO-RO ships are undoubtedly more dangerous than other ship types," says Danish shipbuilding consultant Jens Dalgaard. "The crew has to be highly conscientious; otherwise it can be fatal."

3 But even the most conscientious crew would have been hard pressed to save the Estonia that night. Murky underwater videos taken last week showed a broken locking pin hanging loosely where the huge, 60-ton bow door should have been attached. An inner door lay partly open, leaving a meter-wide gap that had let in enough water to destabilize the ship. Investigators surmised that the locking pin snapped unnoticed sometime during the scheduled overnight crossing from Tallinn to Stockholm. As the ship drove at 15 knots through 6-m seas, the broken pin allowed the visor-like door to gape open under the pressure of the waves and then slam shut several times before ripping away completely.

4 A surviving engine-room crewman, Margus Treu, recalled hearing "two or three strong blows" about half an hour before the capsize. "These blows shook the whole ship," he said. "This was not a natural sound . It was an alien sound." When he abandoned ship and watched it sink, he reported, the outer bow door was gone. The investigators said they had no inkling as to whether the captain and mate of the watch knew that the bow door had been lost, because the entire bridge crew perished. "But there's really nothing the crew could have done," said Tuomo Karppinen, a member of a three-nation investigative commission. "It would have been too late".

5 Once the water was cascading in, rapid doom was assured by the cavernous vehicle decks that are another essential feature of RO-RO design. With no bulkheads, or walls, to stop water from surging back and forth over the open decks, such ships are vulnerable to a sudden loss of stability. A relatively small amount of water — far less than would sink a regular ship — can turn a normal rolling motion into a complete capsize in only a matter of seconds.

6 Faced with the prospect of further accidents and loss of public confidence in RO-RO fleets, shipping authorities throughout Europe ordered emergency inspections, especially of bow doors. At least three ferries — in Denmark and Norway — were found to have fatigue cracks or faulty locking mechanisms in their bow doors and were barred from sailing until repairs are made. Sweden and Finland ordered that all bow doors on ships under their jurisdiction be welded permanently shut. That means loading and unloading will be through the rear doors alone, so operators must leave a large — and unprofitable — space to allow vehicles to turn around at the end of the trip. The alternative could be a loss of public confidence in the ships and official demands for extensive, costly modifications that would further reduce profits.

7 Welding the doors closed may be the maritime equivalent of closing the barn door, however, and the dangerous barn itself is still there in the form of the open vehicle decks. The failure of any waterline door — whether by accident or during a collision — could lead to the same fatal capsize that sank the Estonia. Many safety experts insist that RO-ROs can never be safe unless sturdy deck-to-ceiling bulkheads are installed to limit the movement of incoming water. But such bulkheads, costing a nearly prohibitive $ 900,000 per ship, would impede the movement of vehicles. Such vessels might be safe, but they would no longer be RO-ROs.

Questions 26 – 32

The following are what happened to Estonia, some of the people on board, and other similar ships. Indicate the chronological order of the events by writing 1, 2, ... 8 in boxes 26 – 32 on your answer sheet.

Example:	Answer:
The door was ripped away.	*4*

26. More than 900 people died.

27. The pressure of the waves forced the door open.

28. The ship capsized.

29. Bow doors were welded permanently shut.

30. A locking pin snapped unnoticed.

31. The ship sank.

32. Two or three strong blows were heard.

Questions 33 – 38

Decide if the following statements are true or false according to the information provided in Reading Passage 3. In boxes 33 – 38 on your answer sheet, write ***TRUE*** *if a statement is true, write* ***FALSE*** *if it is false. If there is no information about a statement, write* ***NOT GIVEN***.

Example:	Answer:
The disaster happened on a stormy night.	*T*

33. RO-RO ships are more efficient and profitable because they have a larger capacity for various kinds of cargo.

34. Fewer people would have died if more life-saving facilities had been available.

35. The owner of Estonia did not lose much because both the ship and the passengers' lives had been properly insured.

36. Welding the bow door permanently shut means financial loss because the ship will carry fewer vehicles.

37. Both the bow door and open vehicle decks pose safety hazards to RO-RO ships.

38. Open vehicle decks allow trucks, buses and cars to drive onto and off the ship, which is why it is called RO-RO ship.

Question 39

Which one of the following was the least likely cause for the disaster?

A. a door in the bow
B. doors near waterline
C. fatigue cracks
D. faulty locking mechanisms
E. open vehicle deck
F. sailing speed
G. stormy seas

答案及题解

READING PASSAGE 1

虽然全球气温升高是一个趋势，但一些科学家认为这种趋势被夸大，气温将继续升高的预测是根据计算机模型做出的，而这种计算方法不准确。

Questions 1 – 5:

大多数情况下此类题为一篇文章的概要，但有时也是文章的一部分，即其中的若干段落。

1. **fossil fuels**　见 H 段倒数第 2 句。
2. **sketchy / inadequate / uncertain / tenuous**　见 A、D、F 段。
3. **White House / Bush Administration / U.S. Government**　见 C、H 段。
4. **Carbon dioxide / CO_2 / chlorofluocarbons**　见 A、H 段。
5. **global warming**　见 A、C 等段。

Questions 6 – 11:

回答一般的 Yes / No / Not Given 题要从文章作者的角度来判断。但这 6 道题要从那批"人数虽少但呼声很高的科学家"的角度来判断。雅思考试的题型不固定，用哪类题主要取决于文章的内容。因此，看懂指令至关重要。

6. **No**　见 F 段。
7. **Not Given**　ice age 在 F 段提到，但此说法是否属于 groundless（无根据的）则未做说明。
8. **No**　见 E 段。
9. **Yes**　见 E 段。计算机模型未准确反映出云彩和海洋的作用，即这两者分别有阻热和吸热的功能。
10. **Not Given**
11. **Not Given**

虽然在这 6 道题中答案是 Not Given 的题占一半，但在大多数情况下，此类题的比重不足三分之一。因此，如果时间不够，可都答 Yes 或都答 No，但不宜都答 Not Given。

Questions 12 – 13:

12. **F**
13. **H**　见该段中的 ... for reasons other than ...。

READING PASSAGE 2

文章叙述了英国警察费用过高，主要表现在加班费上。

Questions 14 – 25:

14 – 17 题属于 who does / did what 类题。要先找到 what ,再找 who。

14. **C** 见第 3 段。

15. **H** 见第 16 段。

16. **A,G** 见第 14 段。Home Office: 内政部。

17. **A,E** 见第 5、6 段。

18. **C**

19. **D** 见第 12 段。

20. **C**

21. **Hourly wage / overtime payments** 见第 3、10 段。

22. **£13,000** 见第 8 段,文职警员为 £13,000,正式警察为 £26,000,多 £13,000。

23. **71.4%** 见饼图。

24. **175,000** 见第13段。

25. **£2,181** 见柱形图。因为伦敦是大都市,警察任务繁重,因此有 London weighting。另外,伦敦生活费用高,因此有 London allowances。两项相加为 2,181 英镑。

READING PASSAGE 3

滚装船"爱沙尼亚号"于 1994 年 9 月 28 日在从塔林驶往斯德哥尔摩的途中沉没,九百余人丧生。本文讲述了沉船经过、此类船的弊端及应采取的措施。

Questions 26 – 39:

26 ~ 32 题为排序题,此类题特别要注意例题。一般情况下,例题是若干步骤中较靠中间的一步,不仅作为范例,更主要的是一个界标。考生在排序时应根据例题推断其前、后的步骤,以防因为错一道题而导致后面的题都错。与这些题有关的段落是第 3、4、6 段。

26. **7** 27. **2** 28. **5** 29. **8** 30. **1** 31. **6** 32. **3**

33. **False** 不是用来装不同种类的货物,而是装汽车。

34. **Not Given**

35. **Not Given**

36. **True** 见第 6 段。

37. **True** bow door 的问题贯穿全文,open deck 见第 6 段。

38. **True** Ro Ro: roll on and roll off,即汽车开上开下。Ro-Ro ship: 滚装船。

39. **False**

五、A 类阅读模拟试题四、答案及题解

INTERNATIONAL ENGLISH LANGUAGE TESTING SYSTEM

PRACTICE TEST (Version Four)

ACADEMIC READING

TIME ALLOWED: 1 HOUR
NUMBER OF QUESTIONS: 40

Instructions

ALL ANSWERS MUST BE WRITTEN ON THE ANSWER SHEET.

The test is divided as follows:

Reading Passage 1	Questions 1 – 13
Reading Passage 2	Questions 14 – 27
Reading Passage 3	Questions 28 – 40

Start at the beginning of the test and work through it. Your should answer all the questions. If you cannot do a particular question leave it and go on to the next. You can return to it later.

READING PASSAGE 1

*You should spend about 20 minutes on **Questions 1 – 13** which are based on Reading Passage 1.*

Questions 1 – 6

*Reading Passage 1 has seven paragraphs **A** – **G**. Choose the most suitable headings for paragraphs **B** – **G** from the list of headings below. Write the appropriate numbers (i - xi) in boxes 1 – 6 on your answer sheet.*

***NB**: There are more headings than paragraphs so you will not use all of them. You may use any of the headings more than once.*

List of Headings

(i)	A conventional way to process drinking water
(ii)	Removals of bacteria and viruses
(iii)	New methods are called for
(iv)	An ambitious plan
(v)	The continuous microfiltration system
(vi)	The future of microfiltration plants
(vii)	New focus: environment-friendly technology
(viii)	Disadvantages of septic tanks
(ix)	The expansion of Memtec
(x)	Public's concerns for waste disposals
(xi)	A different approach to cleaning the filter

Example: Paragraph A Answer: ***iii***

1. Paragraph B
2. Paragraph C
3. Paragraph D
4. Paragraph E
5. Paragraph F
6. Paragraph G

Treatment of Waste from Water

A Conventional approaches to waste disposal are becoming untenable. Most systems bring sewage in from the surrounding areas to a central plant for treatment, then transport the processed waste to the nearest river or sea for disposal. This is inefficient, as it takes 1 million litres of water to transport 200 litres of waste. It also involves heavy investment in pipes. Indeed, transport accounts for about 80% of waste-disposal system costs, while treatment accounts for just 20%.

B This must change, especially as demands on treatment grow. Tap water is increasingly subject to pollution, from both the atmosphere and waste disposal. Regulations governing water quality are being tightened in response, but conventional treatment systems are not up to the job. These systems typically date back to the last century, and they are based on principles known to the Romans. For example, drinking water in Yokohama, Japan, comes from a plant that originated in 1887. At the plant, incoming water flows through a coarse filter to eliminate large particles, then through a sand filter to remove smaller particles and bacteria. But because viruses are small enough to slip through sand, the water still must be disinfected with chlorine and left to stand for several hours before it is drinkable.

C As population densities in cities increase, appropriate methods for treating waste water are needed urgently. In Japan, engineering companies are eyeing emerging markets for environmentally sound treatment systems. Authorities are also looking to upgrade backward infrastructure, as 44% of Japanese homes are connected to sewage systems and the remainder on septic tanks. But they would prefer not to spend a fortune on pipes. Japan's Health and Welfare Ministry began experiments to develop new technology for clean-water systems. The project's focus is to evaluate systems that use sophisticated filtration techniques based on membranes.

D Perhaps the most distinctive of the systems under trial is one developed by Memtec, an Australian company. Its continuous microfiltration system consists of a tube into which are packed thousands of thin polyethylene fibres. The walls of the hollow fibres are highly porous, allowing liquid to pass, but blocking particles larger than 0.2 micrometres. That is small enough to exclude bacteria and viruses.

E But the clever part involves how the filter is cleaned. Conventional microfiltration systems dislodge solids that have accumulated on the surface of their membranes by pumping filtered liquid back through them at high speed. This takes a lot of energy and means membranes must be replaced often. Memtec's system adopts a different approach. At regular intervals, say every half an hour, input to the filter is shut off, and all liquid except the amount trapped in the pores of the membrane is removed. Pressurised air is pumped into the filter on both sides of the membrane. Then a fast-activating valve is opened to reduce the pressure on the outside. The still-pressurised air inside the fibre bursts across the membrane, pushing the liquid out of the pores. The wall of water is powerful enough to lift the solids off the surface. In effect, the membrane cleans itself. And because it is not subject to stress, the filter lasts for several years.

F Memtec's system has been successful in low-volume, high value-added applications. It is used widely in the drinks business to filter fruit juice, wine, beer and sake. Now the company has scaled up its membranes for use in high-volume markets such as drinking water and waste-water treatment. It is trying to persuade other large engineering companies to design its filters into their integrated treatment systems. The company has already demonstrated that its membranes can be applied on a large scale. They form the core of what is believed to be the world's largest continuous microfiltration plant built at Blackheath in the Blue Mountains near Sydney. During 21 weeks of trials, the A $ 2.3 million (US $ 1.7 million) plant treated 3 million litres of sewage daily. Measurements showed that the filtered water contained no bacteria or viruses. In fact, it was cleaner than the river into which it was released.

G Plants such as this have the potential to revolutionise water-treatment infrastructure. Huge centralised plants connected by hundreds of kilometres of pipes can be replaced with compact units located next to the communities they serve, returning the water they treat to adjacent streams. Because the plants are energy-efficient, they will be cheap to operate. The benefits to the environment will be huge.

Questions 7 – 13

Do the following statements agree with the views of the writer of Reading Passage 1?

In boxes 7 – 13 on your answer sheet write

YES	*if the statement agrees with the writer;*
NO	*if the statement does not agree with the writer;*
NOT GIVEN	*if there is no information about this in the passage.*

Example: Answer:

Conventional treatment of waste water should be modernised. ***YES***

7. Septic tanks in Japan are part of the modern technology of waste-water treatment.

8. Compression and sudden decompression are the basic working principle for cleaning microfiltration filters developed by Memtec.

9. Conventional water treatment systems include microfiltration.

10. Japan is facing a more serious problem of waste-water disposal than Australia.

11. Onc of the conventional treatment systems is made up of coarse filter, sand, and chlorine.

12. Some viruses have evolved in such a way that they cannot be killed by chlorine.

13. Cleaning and replacing filters could be a technical and financial problem to many microfiltration plants.

READING PASSAGE 2

You should spend about 20 minutes on ***Questions 14 – 27*** *which are based on Reading Passage 2.*

Weight-Loss Nirvana?

A substance that makes fat mice thin just might work for humans too

1 In the U.S., where one in three adults is seriously overweight, the news carried by the journal *Science* last week — that Friedman and his colleagues at the Howard Hughes Medical Institute and New York City's Rockefeller University had discovered a magical potion that melts fat in a matter of weeks — resonated with unusual force. Momentarily, at least, it buoyed the spirits of millions of lifelong dieters and boosted the stock of Amgen, the biotechnical firm based in California that holds the license on the underlying technology. It is too early to predict, however, whether this rare elixir (called leptin, after the Greek *leptos*, meaning slender) will be a stunning pharmaceutical success or just another "miracle" cure that never pans out. Even if all goes well, it could be five to ten years before leptin is approved in the U.S. for human use. Researchers must first demonstrate that leptin benefits people as well as rodents and that it causes no serious side effects.

2 The search for leptin began in the 1960s, when Douglas Coleman, a researcher at the Jackson Laboratory in Bar Harbor, Maine, began studying a strain of obese laboratory mice. In a series of ingenious experiments, Coleman surgically joined the blood vessels of an obese mouse to those of a normal-size mouse, creating a sort of artificial Siamese twin. What happened then was astonishing: the fat animal immediately began to lose weight. This suggested that the blood of nonobese mice carried a potent biochemical messenger, one that played a vital role in regulating appetite and metabolism. But the mysterious agent was present in such minuscule quantities that no one was able to isolate it.

3 Friedman picked up the challenge, applying new tools developed by the field of molecular genetics. The secret factor, he reasoned, must be produced by a gene that was defective in the obese mice. So he began to hunt for such a gene, the *ob*, or obese, gene. Sure enough, late last year, after eight years of effort, Friedman and his colleagues pinpointed the *ob* gene in both average-weight and obese mice. They then inserted the normal gene into bacterial cells, providing at long last detectable quantities of the protein they called leptin.

4 By injecting leptin into obese mice, three separate teams of researchers, including Friedman's, have confirmed that this protein is indeed the blood factor that makes fat mice thin. But they are still trying to puzzle out just how it works. Friedman, for one, believes leptin is almost certainly a hormone that travels through the bloodstream to act on the brain. In fact, it appears leptin may act in a feedback loop like the temperature sensor in a thermostat — or in this case a "fatstat" — to tell the body whether to turn metabolism and appetite up or down. Thus when leptin is low, hunger pangs increase, body temperature drops, and metabolism slows. When leptin is high, everything reverses. In such fashion, the brain strives to keep body weight stable and fluctuations small.

5 Because leptin is produced in fat tissue, the fatter an animal is, the more leptin its cells should make. Normal mice then respond to weight gain by turning out more leptin. As a result, their appetites slacken and their energy consumption speeds up. But the obese mice cannot produce leptin, so their brains never receive this vital message. "These animals," marvels Friedman, "get fat because they think they're starving, and then when we give them the protein, they get thin because they think they're fat!"

6 What, if anything, does this have to do with people? Perhaps a good deal. For humans have an *ob* gene that is virtually identical to the mouse gene, and it is possible that at least some folks have trouble keeping off kilos because of a mutation in this gene. Most experts, however, concur that defects in the *ob* gene are not likely to be a major reason for obesity in people. But that does not mean leptin might not be therapeutically useful for many other overweight people. In last week's *Science*, for example, a team of researchers from the pharmaceutical company Hoffmann-LaRoche described how they plumped up lean mice by giving them unrestricted access to high-fat food. Then they administered leptin. The mice responded by cutting their food intake and shedding the extra grams, suggesting leptin may have value in reversing more typical cases of weight gain.

7 What about side effects? Injections of leptin do not, as one might fear, turn lean mice into starving wretches. After losing weight, researchers from Amgen reported, normal mice stabilize both their food intake and their metabolism. Obese mice likewise reach an optimal leanness, then stop losing weight. The pattern of weight loss is also encouraging. For unlike extreme calorie restriction, which can weaken muscle, leptin appears to dissolve fat while leaving lean tissue intact. On the basis of such data, Amgen (which paid Rockefeller University $ 20 million for patent rights to make products based on the *ob* gene) has announced that it hopes to begin conducting human trials as early as next year.

8 Many experts find these plans too optimistic. Just because researchers have not

noted worrisome side effects yet, critics say, does not mean that none will emerge. Leptin, they point out, is a serious drug, not the easy-to-swallow "thin pill" dieters have dreamed of for so long. To do its work, leptin would probably have to be either injected daily or implanted under the skin for life. In the laboratory experiments reported last week, the obese mice started regaining weight as soon as the injections stopped. Even with a boost from something like leptin, cautions Dr. Ahmed Kissebah, an obesity expert at the Medical College of Wisconsin, the formerly fat cannot afford to become less vigilant. "People will still have to lose weight the hard way," he predicts. "It'll be like diabetes: you still have to exercise and watch your food intake."

9 Regardless of what eventually happens in the marketplace, the discovery of leptin is occasion for celebration. It has provided scientists with a new avenue for exploring a still poorly understood metabolic pathway, one that probably consists of many other equally powerful compounds, each of which could lead to new drugs. To the millions of seriously overweight Americans, help with a frustrating condition — years of guilty eating and self-recrimination — may finally be on the way.

Questions 14 – 21

Complete the following summary of Reading Passage 2. Choose **NO MORE THAN THREE WORDS** *from the passage for each answer. Write your answers in boxes 14 – 21 on your answer sheet.*

In America alone, there are more than 50 million seriously ... (14) ... people, many of whom have been struggling to keep their weight in check. The news carried by *Science* is the best these people could hope for.

According to Dr. Friedman, he and his colleagues have discovered that mice have a gene that is responsible for controlling their weight. If ... (15) ..., this gene, the *ob* gene, keeps mice eating and gaining weight. Friedman and his colleagues have identified an obese-gene-related compound called leptin which adjusts ... (16) ... and appetite. Normal mice can produce leptin which keeps ... (17) ... and weight gain in balance. Obese mice, on the other hand, cannot produce leptin and therefore their ... (18) ... are led to believe that they need more food. After being given ... (19) ... of leptin, these mice start consuming less food and burning more fat. After reaching ... (20) ..., they stop losing weight.

Though leptin clearly has a weight-controlling effect, many experts believe that it is a serious drug and should be dealt with extra caution. It will not be a silver bullet in fighting ...(21)..., and, even after its successful trials on humans, overweight people will still have to watch their diet and exercise.

Questions 22 – 27

Do the following statements agree with the views of the writer of Reading Passage 2?

In boxes 22 – 27 on your answer sheet write

YES	*if the statement agrees with the writer;*
NO	*if the statement does not agree with the writer;*
NOT GIVEN	*if there is no information about this in the passage.*

Example: Answer:

Leptin is effective in reducing weight but it's many years away before human can use it. ***YES***

22. Leptin, after being approved by health authorities, will be available to people in need through doctors' prescriptions.

23. Both obese mice and normal mice have the *ob* gene.

24. Both obese mice and normal mice have leptin in their bodies.

25. Dr. Fricdman never found the gene that was believed to control weight. Instead, he found leptin.

26. If excess leptin is present, the brain signals the body to reduce food intake and to become more active, thus reducing the amount of fat.

27. The *ob* gene causes the fat cells to produce the hormone leptin. The more fat, the more hormone is produced.

READING PASSAGE 3

You should spend about 20 minutes on ***Questions 28 – 40*** *which are based on Reading Passage 3.*

Questions 28 – 33

Reading Passage 3 has seven paragraphs ***A – G****. Choose the most suitable headings for paragraphs* ***B – G*** *from the list of headings below. Write the appropriate numbers (i - xi) in boxes 28 – 33 on your answer sheet.*

NB: *There are more headings than paragraphs so you will not use all of them. You may use any of the headings more than once.*

List of Headings

(i) An educated mother often means educated children
(ii) Education and financial credit
(iii) Woman are still way behind
(iv) Puzzles of the sexes
(v) Areas in which women are better
(vi) Education is the most important
(vii) Great changes taken place in the last 20 years
(viii) Why women are in a disadvantageous position
(ix) Schooling and fertility rate
(x) Government action needed to help women
(xi) Mental differences between the two sexes

Example:	Paragraph A	Answer: ***iii***

28. Paragraph B
29. Paragraph C
30. Paragraph D
31. Paragraph E
32. Paragraph F
33. Paragraph G

Closing the Gap

A Striking progress towards sexual equality has been made in the past two decades, particularly concerning adult literacy, school enrolment, and maternal mortality rates. Nonetheless, among the 900m illiterate people in poor countries, women outnumber men by two to one; 60% of the 130m children with no access to primary school are girls; and women's wages are typically only 60% - 70% those of men. Few would deny that narrowing this gap yet further would make for a fairer society. But there is also a growing consensus among development economists that it would also do a great deal to promote faster economic growth, if women are provided with more opportunities for education, nutrition, access to credit and property rights.

B The empirical evidence is strongest in the case of education. Because it improves a country's stock of human capital, education is an important factor in raising output. As one would expect, economic theory suggests that a better-educated workforce, of both men and women, is likely to spur a country's growth. In the case of women's education, however, there seem to be additional, growth-promoting benefits. For a start, educating women seems to reduce fertility. For any given amount of investment, lower fertility implies more capital accumulation per worker — and this raises growth rates per head.

C Studies from individual countries point out that one year of female schooling can reduce the fertility rate by between 5% and 10%. A simulation study of 72 countries around the world shows that, if all other factors were held constant, doubling female secondary-school enrolments in 1975 would have reduced the average fertility rate in 1985 from 5.3 to 3.9 children and lowered the number of births by almost 30%. Better education reduces fertility in several ways. First, it increases the potential wages that women can command; in this way, it raises the value of women's time, and so adds to the effective cost of bearing children. Also, better-educated women tend to marry later, and know more about contraception.

D As well as having fewer children, educated women are more likely to have betterfed, and therefore healthier, children — who will themselves be better educated. Evidence from World Bank surveys in Nicaragua, Pakistan, Vietnam and Côte D'Ivoire suggests that the probability of a child being in school increases with the mother's own education. Education and nutrition are the clearest links connecting greater equality and economic growth, but the World Bank says that there may be other channels too. For example, women get disproportionately little access to credit from the formal banking system in most developing countries, largely because they are assumed to have no collateral to offer. In Latin America, for instance, women make up only 7% – 11% of borrowers. However, studies from Bangladesh, where a number of schemes steer credit to poor women, show that making it easier for them to borrow can do more to cut poverty and raise investment than lending to men.

E From a theoretical point of view, these findings raise an intriguing question. If improving the economic opportunities of women brings such benefits, why do sexual inequalities persist at all? Put another way, why do households themselves not allocate their existing resources accordingly, in the interests of increasing their income? To answer this question, it is necessary to understand how economic decisions within households are made.

F Economists have customarily thought of the household as a single, or "unitary", decision-making body. Households were thought to maximise their welfare by allocating income and other resources to the members that promised the highest rates of return, as reflected in wages and prices. So one rationale for the persistence of inequality, consistent with this view of household decision-making, is that markets fail to capture the full benefits to society of investing in women. These benefits, in turn, are not reflected in wages. Households therefore make choices that fail to maximise their well-being. Alternatively, and pretty obviously, this "unitary" model of household behaviour may be incomplete. Some economists have analysed the household as a "collective" entity—i.e., they assume that the welfare of the individual members does not necessarily move in parallel with the welfare of the household as a whole. Each family member has his own preferences. As a result, decisions reflect not just market rates of return, but also the bargaining power of different household members. Women, as a result of social and cultural norms, as well as because of outside factors, tend to be in a weaker bargaining position than men.

G Whether it is to address a market failure or to improve the relative bargaining position of women within the family, or both, there does seem to be a case for government action to help women. The World Bank concludes that governments should try, wherever possible, to change laws and regulations in ways that promote equal opportunities, and, if necessary, to intervene to correct sexual inequalities. This would be both fair and efficient — which is as close as economic policy gets to a free lunch.

Questions 34 – 40

Complete the following summary of Reading Passage 3. Choose ***NO MORE THAN THREE WORDS*** *from the passage for each answer. Write your answers in boxes 34 – 40 on your answer sheet.*

Woman's situation all over the world have improved. However, statistics show that they are sill in a much disadvantageous position when opportunities for education, access to credit and ...(34)... are taken into consideration. It has been found that education of women is the most important factor in improving women's economic status. Studies have indicated that the amount of education received by women correlates with ...(35)... — the more education they receive, the fewer children they have. Compared with illiterate women, educated mothers tend to have ...(36)... kids and these kids are more likely to ...(37)... . According to World Bank surveys, greater equality and ...(38)... can be achieved through other channels, too, such as access to credit.

Reasons for women to be in an unfair ...(39)... include, according to some economists, markets fail to capture the full benefits of society of investing in women, and women are in a weaker bargaining position because of social and ...(40)... .

答案及题解

READING PASSAGE 1

Questions 1 – 13:

1. **i** 2. **vii** 3. **v** 4. **xi** 5. **ix** 6. **vi**

7. **No** 见 C 段第 3 句。infrastructure：基础设施。sewage systems：下水道。septic：腐烂的。septic tanks：化粪池。下水道是先进的标志，septic tanks 是句中所说的要更改的落后设施。

8. **Yes** 见 E 段。

9. **No** conventional：传统的，这里指 B 段提到的水处理方法。microfiltration：微过滤，这里指 D 段和 E 段提到的水处理方法，是一种新技术。

10. **Not Given** 文中提到这两个国家，但未说明谁的问题更严重。

11. **Yes** 见 B 段。题中的 sand 应被认为是指 B 段中的 sand filter。

12. **Not Given** 文中未指是否有病毒演变、进化。

13. **Yes** E 段讲述了 Memtec 公司使用的独特清洗方法，此方法技术先进，也更加经济。其他 microfiltration 处理厂未用此技术，自然要有较高的成本。此外，题中的 could be 也是一种留有余地的说法，这种用法在多数情况下可被视为 Yes。

READING PASSAGE 2

此文讲述了科学家利用现代生物技术发现老鼠身上有一种分泌可调节食欲和代谢的物质的基因，即 *ob* 基因。肥胖老鼠身上的 *ob* 基因有缺陷，不能分泌此种叫 leptin 的物质，因此，这种老鼠不能控制食欲，总是认为自己处在饥饿状态。科学家给这类老鼠注射 leptin 后，它们就开始节食、减肥。

Questions 14 – 27:

14. **overweight** fat 有贬义，不好听。obese 为医学用词。

15. **defective / it is defective** 见第 3 段第 2 句。

16. **metabolism** 见第 2 段和第 4 段第 4 句。a feedback loop：反馈循环机制。thermostat：温控开关。fatstat：脂肪敏感开关。

17. **food intake** 题中的 keeps ... in balance 表示这是一对需要平衡的矛盾。矛盾的一方是题中的 weight gain，另一方应是食物的摄入量，而不是 appetite 或 energy consumption 等。见第 6 段最后一句。

18. **brains** 见第 5 段第 4 句。brain（单数）也出现过（在第 4 段），但题中要用复数名词。

19. **injections** 见第 7、8 段。

20. **an optimal leanness** 见第 7 段第 3 句。

21. **obesity** 这里要填的应是题中 fighting 的宾语，当然要用名词；根据文章内容应与肥胖症有关。fat 当名词用意为脂肪，fatness 又未在文中出现。见第 8 段提到的肥胖症专家 Dr. Ahmed Kissebah。

22. **Not Given**

23. **Yes** 文中说老鼠身体中有 *ob* 基因，只是肥胖老鼠体内的 *ob* 基因有缺陷，不能分泌 leptin。

24. **No** 见上一题的说明。

25. **No** 文中说 Friedman ... pinpointed the *ob* gene（见第 3 段）。

26. **Yes** 正常的老鼠体内总是要有一些 leptin，但如体重增减，体内的 leptin 水平过高，这些老鼠就会节食。

26. **Yes** leptin 是由脂肪细胞分泌的，老鼠越胖，分泌的 leptin 越多。文中用了 protein（第 4 段第 1 句）和 hormone（第 4 段第 3 句）来指 leptin。

27. **Yes**

READING PASSAGE 3

Questions 28 – 40:

28. **vi** 29. **ix** 30. **i** 31. **iv** 32. **viii** 33. **x**

34. **nutrition / property rights** 见 A 段最后一句。

35. **(their) fertility (rate)** 见 C 段。

36. **fewer / better-fed / healthier**

37. **be better educated / be in school** 注意 36、37 两题。D 段第 1 句表达了一种递进关系，即孩子的数量及质量，然后才是受更好的教育。因此，第 37 题一定要与受教育有关，才能反应文中的递进关系。

38. **economic growth** 见 D 段第 3 句。

39. **(bargaining) position** 见 F 段结尾和 G 段首句。

40. **culture norms** 见 F 段结尾。

六、G 类阅读模拟试题一、答案及题解

INTERNATIONAL ENGLISH LANGUAGE TESTING SYSTEM

PRACTICE TEST (Version One)

GENERAL TRAINING

TIME ALLOWED: 1 HOUR
NUMBER OF QUESTIONS: 40

Instructions

ALL ANSWERS MUST BE WRITTEN ON THE ANSWER SHEET.

The test is divided as follows:

Section 1	Questions 1 – 15
Section 2	Questions 16 – 27
Section 3	Questions 28 – 40

Start at the beginning of the test and work through it. Your should answer all the questions. If you cannot do a particular question leave it and go on to the next. You can return to it later.

Section 1 *Questions* 1 – 15

Questions 1 – 5
Read the notice below and answer the questions that follow.

> **Hilo Hattie Shopping Shuttle**
>
> Take one of these new trolleys to Hilo Hattie, "The Store of Hawaii," from 8:20 am to 3:20 pm daily, 365 days a year. The free rides are available from selected Waikiki pick-up points, call 537 – 2926 for details. From Hilo Hattie you can continue on the trolley to Dole Cannery, Aloha Tower Marketplace and Ala Moana Center or return to Waikiki.
>
> Hilo Hattie was recently awarded the Hawaii Visitors and Convention Bureau's "Best Hawaiian Retailer" Kahili Award for 1998. The award symbolizes Hilo Hattie's goal of providing their customers with a unique and fun shopping experience.
>
> As the world's largest manufacturer of Hawaiian wear, Hilo Hattie has sizes and styles for everyone! They also offer the largest selection of Hawaiian souvenirs, gifts, T-shirts and island jewelry, all at low manufacturer direct prices.
>
> Hilo Hattie is open from 7 am to 6 pm, daily at 700 Nimitz Hwy; and from 9:30 am to 9:00 pm, Mon. – Sat., and 10 am to 7 pm, Sunday, in Ala Moana Center.

Answer the following questions using ***NO MORE THAN THREE WORDS or NUMBERS*** *and write the answers in boxes 1 – 5 on your answer sheet. One has been done as an example.*

Example:	Answer:
When does the shuttle begin to run every day?	***8:20***

1. What is the phone number to call in order to find out the shuttle's pick-up points?
2. How many Hilo Hattie shops are listed in the advertisement?
3. What does Hilo Hattie specialise?
4. Where is the shuttle's starting point?
5. What award did Hilo Hattie receive?

Questions 6 – 10

Read the notice below and answer the questions that follow.

Volleyball Courses

Please note: There are no registration restrictions for volleyball classes. Due to high demand for volleyball courses, students are encouraged to list a second preference in the event that their first choice is closed. All volleyball courses require a $ 6.00 lab fee payable to the instructor at the first class session. Please do not include the lab fee with the registration fee.

Beginning Coed Volleyball

Study basic volleyball skills in a fun, no-pressure atmosphere. Practice strong fundamental skills: serving, passing, setting, spiking, blocking, and digging. Meet new volleyball friends. No previous playing experience required.

Course Info: Sept. 20 – Nov. 22 ● Mon. 7:00 – 8:30pm ● 10 Mtgs ● St. Johns High School Gym, 46 Princess Road ● $ 72 (Plus $ 6.00 lab fee.)
Instructor: Clyde L. Ching

Intermediate Coed Volleyball

Improve individual and team volleyball skills for fun or competition. Improve existing skills by practising drills integrated into sessions on honing new skills. Focus on volleyball awareness to further self improvement.

Course Info: Sept. 16 – Dec. 2 ● Thur. 5:45 – 7:15pm ● 10 Mtgs (no class Nov. 11 and 25) ● Salt Lake District Park, 115 Abraham Road ● $ 72 (Plus $ 6.00 lab fee.)
Instructor: Adam Lockwood

Indicate if each of the following statements is true or false according to the information from the notice of volleyball classes. In boxes 6 – 10 on your answer sheet, please write ***TRUE*** *if the statement is true; write* ***FALSE*** *if it is false. If the notice does not contain relevant information about the statement, please write* ***NOT GIVEN***. *An example has been done.*

Example:	Answer:
The instructors are retired professional players.	***NOT GIVEN***

6. Courses for both levels are held indoors.

7. To attend either course, one needs to pay $ 78.

8. It's Thursday on November 11 and 25.

9. The intermediate course is for people who have finished the beginning course.

10. Participants pay the lab fee first and then the tuition fee.

Questions 11 – 15

Read the advertisement below and answer the questions that follow.

ONLY S&M AID LENDERS
LET STUDENTS ACROSS AUSTRALIA SAVE AS MUCH AS 8%.

There has been a good deal of confusion about the relative cost of student loans. The fact is, while all Federal Stratford loans have basically the same terms, lenders nationwide who work with S&M Aid offer loans that actually cost less. With credits and interest rate reductions for borrowers who pay on time, S&M Aid makes it possible for students to cut the total amount they repay by as much as 8%.

S&M Aid customers also get the best, most flexible service in the business today. They can choose from a number of repayment options that are tailored to their needs — borrowers can even choose a payment plan based on monthly income. And, experienced customer service representatives are available 24 hours a day, seven days a week to help customers understand the benefits and costs of their repayment options.

In the past 20 years, S&M Aid has helped over 20 million students get the financing they needed to attend college. By purchasing student loans, we provide banks with funds to make more student loans.

To request more information please pick up the phone and give us a call (800 – 891 – 1410).

If you Borrow ...	...through Direct Lending you pay back	...from an Ordinary Bank you pay back	... from a S&M Aid Lender you pay back
$ 5,000	$ 7,359	$ 7,359	$ 6,967
$ 10,000	$ 14,718	$ 14,718	$ 13,852
$ 50,000	$ 73,952	$ 73,952	$ 67,645

These figure represent total repayment amount for Stratford loans disclosed at a 4.72% interest rate with a 10-year term and assume the borrower pays electronically with S&M Aid's Direct Replay Plan and participates in the Great Returns and Great Rewards Programs.

Decide if the following statements are true or false according to the information in A&M Aid's advertisement. In boxes 11 – 15 on your answer sheet, write ***TRUE*** *if the statement is true; if it is false, write* ***FALSE****. If relevant information is not given in the notice, write* ***NOT GIVEN****. One has been done as an example.*

Example:	Answer:
Federal Stratford specialises in educational loans.	***TRUE***

11. It is better to borrow educational loans from S&M Aid than from a bank.

12. S&M Aid's representatives work on Saturdays and Sundays.

13. S&M Aid offers a lower interest rate than Federal Stratford.

14. The annual interest rate offered by Federal Stratford is 8%.

15. Great Returns is a lending program offered by S&M Aid.

Section 2 *Questions 16 – 27*

Questions 16 – 21

Read the notice below and answer the questions that follow.

Cardiff College of University of Wales

Find credit and noncredit courses, certificate and degree programs scheduled to suit your needs — days, nights, weekends, and online. Move forward on your degree. Or move forward in life by keeping current and flexible. Discover a wide array of options to prepare you for the challenges of the new century.

Cardiff College Offers you —

CREDIT PROGRAMS

Credit courses and degree programs are offered throughout the year. The College also administers courses for special programs and specific student populations.

NONCREDIT PROGRAMS

Innovative and affordable noncredit courses assist you in updating professional skills or pursuing career or personal development.

COMMUNITY PROGRAMS

Often produced in collaboration with other organizations, programs provide statewide access to outstanding artists and scholars from Wales and other parts of the world.

INTERNATIONAL PROGRAMS

Foreign students gain fluency in the English language through popular day and evening classes. Seminars on special topics are available with translation services for international groups.

CONFERENCE CENTER

Experienced support in organizing and managing conferences, institutes, and symposia is offered to qualified groups.

ACADEMIC ADVISING

As the academic unit responsible for all unclassified students, Cardiff College provides general advising and student support services to University of Wales and students who are not currently in a degree program.

DISTANCE LEARNING

The College coordinates distance learning activity for the Cardiff campus and works in conjunction with UW departments and outside agencies to explore alternative ways of offering courses.

SUMMER SESSIONS

Each summer more than 1,100 courses are offered in all major disciplines. Students earn credits towards their degrees, enjoy noncredit workshops, and participate in lively public events.

SUMMER SCHOLAR PROGRAM

Qualified high school leavers get a head start on college and explore campus life at UW.

ELDERHOSTEL

For people over the age of 55, the UW Elderhostel Program offers unique educational and cultural experiences with a focus on Wales' past, present, and future.

Fill in the blanks in the following statements using ***NO MORE THAN THREE WORDS*** *from the above advertisement of Cardiff College of University of Wales and write the answers in boxes 16 – 21 on your answer sheet. One has been done as an example.*

Example:	Answer:
The college has both credit and ______________ programs.	***noncredit***

16. The college has a ______________ where meetings of all sorts can be held.
17. The ______________ center of the college is trying to bring tuition to people in need through channels like correspondence and the Internet.
18. The college offers ______________ English language classes to cater for the needs of non-native speaking students.
19. Young people who are newly accepted by the University of Wales can attend a ______________ before beginning university life.
20. Students can participate in the ______________ in order to finish their degree programs earlier.
21. The college has an ______________ section that can provide counselling to students in need.

Questions 22 – 27

Read the advertisement below and answer the questions that follow.

Make Your Cell Phone "Hands-Free" in Seconds!

It's a fact, more and more automobile accidents are being blamed on the use of cell phones while driving. The problem has become so bad that many countries have made it illegal to use a phone while driving unless it is equipped with a hands-free speakerphone. Until now, if you wanted to purchase an adapter for your car, you were forced to buy one from the phone manufacturers or cell phone carriers. Now, there's a great new product that lets you keep both hands on the wheel while using your cell phone: the Navigator Hands-Free Kit.

No more dangerous driving. Chances are, you've seen people driving down the road, cradling a cell phone on their shoulder, as they try to carry on a conversation while navigating traffic. With the increasing number of cell phone users on the road, the problem has gotten progressively worse. You've seen them, drifting across the center line while they're talking on the phone. For that very reason, some countries have enacted legislation banning the use of cell phones in cars, unless they are operated hands-free. Now, there's a great new way to carry on conversations that's safe, convenient and affordable. The Navigator Hands-Free Kit is a snap to install and incredibly easy to use. Now you can turn your cell phone into a car speakerphone. This enables you to keep both hands on the wheel while using your Motorola or Nokia cellular phone. No more cradling the phone between your ear and your shoulder ... and no more dangerous one-handed driving.

Installs in seconds. Simply plug the DC adapter into your car's cigarette lighter and set your phone in the cradle. A special connector in the base recharges your phone, saves your battery and converts your conversations to speakerphone mode. The speaker at the top of the cradle provides your in-car audio and the microphone at the bottom captures your voice. The unit also features a built-in volume control.

No installation required. You simply plug the holder into your car's cigarette lighter and place your cellular phone in the charger. You can enjoy a clear conversation and keep both hands on the wheel.

Navigator Hands-Free Holder / Charger....... £ 49.95/ £ 4.95 P&P

Please specify Motorola StarTAC or Nokia 6100 / 5100 series.

Wamstrad Technologies
56 Moss Lane West
Manchester EH6 8BH
England

Indicate if each of the following statements is true or false according to the information from the advertisement. In boxes 22 – 27 on your answer sheet, write ***TRUE*** *if the statement is true; write* ***FALSE*** if it is false. *If the advertisement does not contain relevant information about the statement, please write* ***NOT GIVEN***. *An example has been done.*

Example:	Answer:
It's illegal to use a phone while driving.	***TRUE***

22. It's more expensive to buy hands-free gadgets from cellular phone companies than from Wamstrad.

23. Accidents caused by drivers talking on the phone while driving are rare.

24. Qualified personnel should be contacted before installing the Navigator Hands-Free Kit.

25. Earphones are needed to use the Navigator Hands-Free Kit.

26. The Navigator Hands-Free Kit can recharge the phone battery.

27. Smokers don't like the Navigator Hands-Free Kit because it uses the cigarette lighter socket in their car.

Section 3 *Questions 28 – 40*

Read the passage below and answer the questions that follow.

Tour Industry Rediscovers the Diversity of Wild Areas

1 In the opinion of some, including Scott McNiven, an American aid worker who has visited every national park in Uganda during his spare weekends over the past two years, "Uganda is the best place to come for first-time visitors to Africa."

2 Both the government and the travel industry have been quick to redesign and relaunch their tourism marketing after the murder in March of eight foreigners by Rwandan Hutu Interahamwe guerrillas in Bwindi National Park.

3 Bwindi had been touted as Uganda's unique attraction, even though access was and is strictly limited — only 10 visitors per day are allowed to track the mountain gorillas in the park's impenetrable forest.

4 "The problem is that when we opened up tourism in this country, we used the gorillas as the bait in our strategy," says Ignatius Nakishero of the Uganda Tourist Board. "We have learned our lesson, and are busy promoting our other products: bird-watching, nature-walking, sport fishing and cultural tourism. Things have started gradually and are slowly picking up. People are making inquiries and, as long as nothing drastic happens, everything will be back to normal by mid-2000."

5 Tourism in Uganda is, in any case, about much more than gorilla tracking. The points in Uganda's favor, says Mr. McNiven, are the accessibility of game for viewing, the country's unusual diversity, the constant improvements in the country's travel facilities and the relative safety for travelers.

Alone with lions and leopards

6 "The parks are not so crowded as those in Kenya and Tanzania, where you can have 20 minibuses chasing one zebra," says Mr. McNiven. "Here, you can sit almost alone watching lions and leopards for more than an hour without interruption." He adds that there is an atmosphere of general safety and welcome throughout the country and a very low incidence of theft, especially compared with neighboring countries that attract hundreds of thousands of tourists every year.

7 Of the major game-viewing areas, Queen Elizabeth National Park has had no security problems in recent years. It contains a huge diversity of ecosystems, including lakes, forests and volcanic craters, with easy viewing of lions, elephants, chimpanzees and monkeys as well as hundreds of different bird species. The park is certain to become better known in the years ahead, especially since its 48-room travel lodge at Mweya has been completely refurbished at a cost of $ 9 million by the Madhvani Group, with the aim of rivaling the best lodges in Kenya.

8 "We hope that Mweya will be the focal point for tourism in Uganda," says the Madhvani project director, Farhan Nakhooda.

9 Murchison Falls National Park is also recovering popularity as its game population continues to recover rapidly from damage inflicted by dictator Idi Amin's soldiers in the 1970s. Recent visitors are especially enthusiastic about the availability of well-managed boat trips along the Nile near Murchison Falls. The craft allows viewing not only of the falls, where the Nile waters are forced through a gorge at places only 20 feet (six meters) wide, but also of the wide range of animals visible along the riverbanks. A high standard of accommodation is available at the new Sarova Paraa Lodge.

From the city to the wild

10 Around Kampala, too, more attention is being paid to weekend sports, game-viewing and cultural tourism within driving distance of the capital, which is itself only a few miles from the shores of Lake Victoria. Sailing, motorboating, fishing and island visits are all rapidly growing activities.

11 The hotel developer Sudhir Ruparelia is investing substantially in the Speke Marina, an out-of-town waterside resort. Beside the waters of the Nile, only two hours' drive away, is the Jinja Nile Resort, owned by Kenya-based Mada Hotels.

12 The Bwindi incident has made security in Uganda an even greater priority than before. The national park authorities have embarked on rigorous paramilitary training of

selected rangers, and the Ugandan army has increased its presence in the western corridor of parks, including Queen Elizabeth, Kibale, Ruwenzofi, Semliki and Murchison Falls.

13 "Security inside Uganda has improved in recent months," confirms a British diplomat, whose mission now updates its travel advice every two weeks, giving very specific local information.

14 The Foreign and Commonwealth Office's Web site for travel advice is http://www.fco.gov.uk/travel/countryadvice.asp.

Questions 28 – 32

The following is a list of names that are mentioned in the reading passage. Choose appropriate letters to answer questions and write the answers in boxes 28 – 32 on your answer sheet.

A. Elizabeth	I. Mweya
B. Idi Amin	J. Rangers
C. Kenya	K. Rwandan Hutu Interahamwe guerrillas
D. Kibale	L. Sarova Paraa Lodge
E. Lake Victoria	M. Speke Marina
F. Mada Hotels	N. Sudhir Ruparelia
G. Mountain Gorillas	O. The Madhvani Group
H. Murchison Falls	P. The Ugandan army

28. Which **two** in the above list brought damages to the travel industry in Uganda?
29. Which **two** in the above list have contributed to the safety of tourists?
30. Which **three** in the above list provide tourist facilities in Uganda?
31. Which **three** in the above list are names of Ugandan national parks?
32. Which **two** in the above list are names of tourist resorts?

Questions 33 – 40

Do the following statements agree with the view of the writer of the passage? In boxes 33 – 40 on your answer sheet, write

YES	*if the statement agrees with the view of the writer;*
NO	*if the statement does not agree with the view of the writer;*
NOT GIVEN	*if there is no information about this in the passage.*

Example: Answer:

Tour industry in Uganda is prospering. ***YES***

33. Scott McNiven likes Uganda.
34. The killing of eight foreigners was a political move of some guerrillas.
35. Uganda is safer than countries around it.
36. Ignatius Nakishero believes more activities should be offered to tourists.
37. The major activity for tourists was, for some time, tracing gorrilas.
38. Murchison Falls has had no major security problems.
39. There is no sign of recovery of tourism from the damage caused by the Bwindi incident.
40. Britain is doing more to help the Ugandan travel industry than America does.

答案及题解

SECTION 1

Questions 1 – 5:

从广告中可看出，Hilo Hattie 是一家服装厂，专营夏威夷服装，拥有几家零售店（700 Nimitz Hwy 和 Ala Moana Center），并在城里有免费购物班车（free shopping shuttle）。

1. **537 – 2926**
2. **Two**
3. **Hawaiian wear**
4. **Waikiki**　　见第 1 段最后一句。
5. **Best Hawaiian Retailer**

Questions 6 – 10:

coed：男女混合编班，来自 co-educaion（男女同校）。

一些排球术语：serve：发球；pass：传球；set：二传；spike：扣球；block：拦网；dig：救球。

6. **False**　　中级班的地点是 Salt Lake District Park，显然不在室内。
7. **True**　　72 元的学费，6 元的 lab fee。
8. **True**　　见中级班的时间安排。共十次课（mtgs: meetings），每周四上课，9 月 16 日到 12 月 2 日，共 78 天，跨 12 周，11 月 11 日和 25 日不上课，因此这两天一定是星期四。
9. **False**　　初级班明确说不要 previous experience，中级班未明确这一点。但从 students are encouraged to ...（第 1 段第 2 句话）可看出此题为 false。
10. **False**　　文章虽未明确说明，但 lab fee 是要在上第一节课时交给教练。第 1 段第 2 句的 in the event that their first choice is closed 指出有名额限制，因此肯定是先报名，后上课。

Questions 11 – 15:

S&M Aid 是一个提供教育贷款的机构，利息比其他有同样功能的机构低。

11. **True**
12. **True**　　见第 2 段的 seven days a week。
13. **True**　　见第 1 段的第 2、3 句话中的数字。
14. **Not Given**　　第 1 段末尾处提到 8%，这是 S&M Aid 所能达到的最大减幅，不是利率。
15. **True**　　见表下的说明。

SECTION 2

Questions 16 – 21:

文章介绍了一所学院的组成部分及其功能。先确定每道题与哪类功能有关，在文中找到此类功能，填空所需的相关词也就找到了。

16. **conference center**　　题中的 meetings of all sorts 与 conference 紧密相关。
17. **distance learning**　　题中的 correspondence（刊授、函授）和 the Internet 均与远距离教育有关。

18. **day and evening**　题中的 non-native speaking students（不讲当地语言的学生）一般需要提高英语水平，这就是 International Programs 的部分功能。从题中可看出此空应填的内容应是 English language classes 的定语，文中有四个词：popular day and evening，因只能用三个词作答，用后三个词更好。

19. **summer scholar program**　题中的 young people 指的就是文中的 qualified high school leavers（合格的高中毕业生）。

20. **summer session**　如想提前毕业，就要多拿学分。文中说可在暑期拿学分。

21. **academic advising**　counselling：咨询，与 advising 意思相同。

Questions 22 – 27：

文章介绍一种驾车时可安全使用手机的装置。此装置插在点烟器的插座中，装置上有喇叭和麦克风，还有音量调节。

22. **Not Given**　文中虽提到 phone manufacturers（第 1 段），但未提到价格，

23. **False**　从第 1 段的 the problem has become so bad that ...和第 2 段两次提到的 you have seen...可看出，此类事故并不罕见。

24. **False**　安装此装置易如反掌（... is a snap to install），甚至是即插即用，根本不用安装（no installation required）。

25. **False**　The speaker（喇叭）at the top of the cradle provides your in-car audio，由此可见，用不着耳机。

26. **True**　（A special connector in the base recharges your phone.）

27. **Not Given**　此装置要占用点烟器插座，但文中未提到吸烟者是否会因此不喜欢用这个装置。

SECTION 3

Questions 28 – 40：

这是一篇关于乌干达的旅游业正在逐步发展的文章。

28 ~ 32 题属于 who does / did what 类型。因已知 what，要从文中找出 who，所以比较难。做题时先从文中找到 what，然后根据上下文找出 who。

28. **B，K**　见第 2 段和第 9 段第 1 句话。

29. **J，P**　见第 12 段。

30. **F，N，O**　见第 11 段和第 7 段最后一句话。

31. **A，D，H**　见第 7 段第 1 行，第 12 段最后 1 行，第 9 段第 1 行。

32. **I，L**　tourist resorts：（有吃、住、玩的）旅游胜地。lodge：旅游胜地的旅馆。见第 7 段最后一句和第 9 段最后一句。

33. **Yes**　见第 1 段。

34. **Not Given**　第 2 段说有数名游客被杀，但未说明原因。

35. **Yes**　见第 6 段。

36. **Yes**　见第 4 段。

37. **Yes**　见第 4 段。

38. **No**　见第 9 段第 1 句。

39. **No**　见第 2、4 段。

40. **Not Given**

七、G 类阅读模拟试题二、答案及题解

INTERNATIONAL ENGLISH LANGUAGE TESTING SYSTEM

PRACTICE TEST (Version Two)

GENERAL TRAINING

TIME ALLOWED: 1 HOUR
NUMBER OF QUESTIONS: 40

Instructions

ALL ANSWERS MUST BE WRITTEN ON THE ANSWER SHEET.

The test is divided as follows:

Section 1	Questions 1 – 15
Section 2	Questions 16 – 28
Section 3	Questions 29 – 40

Start at the beginning of the test and work through it. Your should answer all the questions. If you cannot do a particular question leave it and go on to the next. You can return to it later.

Section 1 *Questions 1 – 15*

Questions 1 – 5

Read the rate list of a hotel below and answer the questions that follow.

Rate List of Hotel Neptune

Single rooms with shower	£ 20
Twin rooms with shower	£ 30
Double rooms with bath	£ 40
Studio rooms (1 pers.)	£ 15
(2 pers.)	£ 25
Suite with sitting room, bedroom, private bath and balcony	£ 70
Extra beds	£ 10 per day
Children under 12 years	50% reduction

Rates include breakfast.

All rates subject to variation.

Groups: one night's deposit required 4 weeks prior to the date of arrival. With a minimum group of 20 paying passengers, one person will be granted free accommodation.

Choose the option from the four alternatives A, B, C and D that best answers each of the following questions and write the corresponding letters in boxes 1 – 5 on your answer sheet. One has been done as an example.

Example:

How many beds are there in a twin room?

A. 1. B. 2.

C. 3. D. 4. Answer: *B*

1. How much does it cost for a couple to stay for two nights in a double room?

A. £40. B. £50.

C. £70. D. £80.

2. Two brothers traveling together would most probably stay in a ________.

A. single room B. twin room

C. double room D. suite

3. How much do a mother and her 8-year-old daughter need to pay for staying one night?

A. £21.5. B. £22.5.

C. £23.5. D. £24.5.

4. To receive a concession for groups, there should be at least ________ guests.

A. 20 B. 21

C. 22 D. 23

5. How long in advance should the hotel be contacted if a group of 20 want to stay for three nights?

A. One day. B. One week.

C. 20 days. D. One month.

Questions 6 – 10
Read the notice below and answer the questions that follow.

How do I withdraw from a noncredit course and/or get a refund?

Withdrawal/refund requests must be made in person or by writing to Outreach College; correspondence must be received or postmarked (if mailed) by the refund deadline date. Faxed withdrawal requests must include student's signature. No refunds are permitted after the refund deadline. Failure to attend class or notify your instructor of your intent to withdraw does not constitute an official withdrawal from the class.

For courses 6 weeks or longer, full refunds are permitted if requests are made on or before the 5th working day (including the first class session) after the class begins. For short courses 1 to 5 weeks in length, full refunds are permitted up to the last working day before the course begins unless otherwise specified. Students registering with a purchase order are billed regardless of attendance unless notification of withdrawal is made by the specified refund deadlines.

Non-attendance due to cancellation or changes in flight schedules by airline or travel agencies does not constitute a withdrawal, and Outreach College will not issue a refund. Refunds for check and cash payments are processed within 4 to 6 weeks. For charge payments, refunds are credited to the account originally charged and reflected on your monthly statement. If you have a question regarding your refund, call the Outreach College Business Office at 956 – 7773.

Indicate if each of the following statements is true or false according to the information from the above notice about refunding. In boxes 6 – 10 on your answer sheet, write ***TRUE*** *if a statement is true; write* ***FALSE*** *if it is false. If the notice does not contain relevant information about the statement, please write* ***NOT GIVEN***. *An example has been done.*

Example:	Answer:
The refund deadline is negotiable.	***FALSE***

6. Partial refunds are possible as long as a request is received before the course begins.
7. Failure to arrive at the college because of flight cancellation is an acceptable reason for a refund request.
8. It takes more days to process refunds by checks than refunds in cash.
9. If a course of three weeks begins on a Monday, refund can be granted if requests are received on Friday the previous week.
10. If a course of six weeks begins on a Monday, refund can be granted if requests are received on Friday the same week.

Questions 11 – 15

Read the notice below and answer the questions that follow.

Free Public Seminar

Due to the rapid growth of MICROSOFT NT™ network here in Brisbane, demand for qualified systems professionals and developers is skyrocketing. Employers seek qualified people, and recognize Microsoft-certified individuals as a source of quality support. Richmond College is pleased to present technical training courses in cooperation with Computer Training Company, Inc. (CTC), an authorized Microsoft Technical Education Center.

Microsoft offers one of the most comprehensive training programs for its products and technologies. Certified courses develop technical expertise and help participants to prepare for certifying examinations. Courses at CTC utilize state-of-the-art facilities and feature Microsoft-certified trainers.

***Technical Training Can*:**

Enhance your job performance;

Provide you with the knowledge to attain Microsoft certification;

Improve your career and earning opportunities.

Students are invited to attend a FREE seminar to learn more about Microsoft certification and the training courses. For more information on the free seminar and a complete list of the courses, visit www.richmondcollege.edu.au/mstraining.htm

Decide if the following statements are true or false according to the information in the seminar notice. In boxes 11 – 15 on your answer sheet, write ***TRUE*** *if a statement is true. If it is false, write* ***FALSE****. If relevant information is not given in the notice, write* ***NOT GIVEN****. One has been done as an example.*

Example: Answer:

There has been a growing need for networking professionals. ***TRUE***

11. The content of the seminar concentrates on the latest development in computer technology.
12. The seminar will take place in Richmond College.
13. The training courses offered by CTC teach people how to pass exams.
14. CTC has trainers certified by Microsoft.
15. People interested should use the Internet to find out more about the seminar.

Section 2 *Questions 16 – 28*

Questions 16 – 21
Read the advertisement below and answer the questions that follow.

Wireless Phone Jack Transmitter and Receiver

You can add telephone extensions with a remarkable new device — the Wireless Phone Jack. It converts phone signals into FM signals and broadcasts them over your existing electrical wiring. Just plug the transmitter into a phone jack and an electrical outlet. Then insert a receiver into any household outlet.

Clear reception at any distance. The Wireless Phone Jack uses your home's existing electrical wiring to transmit signals. So the sound quality far exceeds that of cordless phones. If you have an outlet, you can turn it into a phone jack—no matter how far away it is. The advanced noise reduction features guarantee crystal-clear reception throughout the largest homes. You can use the Wireless Phone Jack in any electrical outlet in or around your home even if it is on a different circuit than the transmitter.

Unlimited extensions. Most phone lines with regular jacks can only handle up to five extensions. But not the Wireless Phone Jack. All you need is just one transmitter, and you can add as many receivers as you want. Plus, you'll never get a monthly charge for the extra receivers.

Works with any phone device. This breakthrough technology can meet all of your single-line phone needs. It has a special digital interface for use with a fax machine or modem. You can even use it with your answering machine just by plugging it into the Wireless Phone Jack receiver.

Direct offer. We're offering a special introductory factory direct package. For a limited time, the transmitter is just $ 49. One transmitter works an unlimited number of receivers priced at $ 49 for the first one, $ 39 for each additional. Plus, with any Wireless Phone Jack we'll throw in a phone card with 30 minutes of long distance (a $ 30 value) for only $ 9.95!

Risk-free. Wireless Phone Jack is backed by our exclusive 90-day risk-free home trial. If you're not satisfied, return it for a full "No Questions Asked" refund. It's also backed by a one-year manufacturer's limited warranty. Most orders are processed within 72 hours and shipped via UPS.

Wireless Phone Jack transmitter	$ 49, $ 4 S&H
Wireless Phone Jack receiver	$ 49, $ 4 S&H
Save $ 10 on each additional receiver	*$ 39*
30-minute long distance phone card	$ 30
$ 9.95 with Wireless Phone Jack purchase	

For fastest service call toll-free 24 hours a day: 800 – 992 – 2966

COMTECH INDUSTRIES
2820 Waterford Lake Drive, Suite 106
Toronto, Canada

Indicate if each of the following statements is true or false according to the information from the advertisement. In boxes 16 – 21 on your answer sheet, write ***TRUE*** *if a statement is true; write* ***FALSE*** *if it is false. If the advertisement does not contain relevant information about the statement, please write* ***NOT GIVEN****. An example has been done.*

Example:	Answer:
The shipping and handling charge for a transmitter is four dollars.	***TRUE***

16. The Wireless Phone Jack allows up to five receivers.

17. Power lines in the wall help transmit FM signals.

18. Fax, modem can not be connected to the phone jack receivers.

19. The current price is valid for ninety days.

20. If someone buys two receivers, he needs to pay $ 88 exclusive of S&H.

21. Purchasers of the Wireless Phone Jack receivers don't get phone cards.

Questions 22 – 28
Read the directions for a medicine and answer the questions that follow.

***Zyrtec®* (*Cetirizine hydrochloride*)**
film-coated tablets

Composition
Each film-coated tablet contains cetirizine hydrochloride 10 mg.

Dosage Form, Route of Administration and Packaging
Box containing 5, 10, 20 or 100 film-coated tablets for oral use.

Indications
Symptomatic treatment of seasonal rhinitis and conjunctivitis, perennial allergic rhinitis as well as pruritus and urticoria of allergic origin.

Dosage and Directions for Use
Adults and children of 12 years and older. In most cases, the recommended dose is one 10 mg tablet daily. It is advisable to take the drug with a little liquid during the evening meal since the symptoms for which the product is given usually appear during the night.

Side Effects
When ZYRTEC is administered at recommended doses any side effects that may occur, such as agitation, dry mouth, drowsiness, or headache, do not differ significantly from placebo.

Special Precautions
At therapeutic doses, ZYRTEC does not potentiate the effect of alcohol (at a blood level of 0.8 g/l). Care should, however, be taken.

Pregnancy and Lactation
Teratology studies in animals have not demonstrated any special adverse effects. As a precaution, however, ZYRTEC should not be administered to pregnant women during the first three months of pregnancy, nor should women who are breast-feeding take the drug.

Drug Interactions
To date, there are no known interactions with other drugs. Nevertheless, ZYRTEC should be used with caution if sedatives are also being taken.

Overdosage
Drowsiness can be a symptom of overdosage, occurring from administration of 50 mg of ZYRTEC as a single dose. To date, there is no specific antidote. In the case of massive overdosage, gastric lavage should be performed as soon as possible.

Storage
Store below 25°C in a dry place.

Stability
The expiry date on the package, found after the mention "Exp." should not have been exceeded.

UCB S.A. PHARMA SECTOR
BRAINE-L'ALLEUD, BELGIUM

Fill in the blanks in the following statements using ***NO MORE THAN THREE WORDS*** *from the directions for Zyrtec. Write your answers in boxes 22 – 28 on your answer sheet. One has been done as an example.*

Example:	Answer:
The drug is made in ______________.	*Belgium*

22. The drug is mainly for treating ______________ reactions.

23. It's better to take the drug ______________ evening meals.

24. Possible side effects include headache and ______________.

25. The recommended dose is ______________ tablet(s) each day.

26. Women who are ______________ should not take the drug.

27. The drug is generally safe but care should be taken if the patient is taking ______________.

28. If someone has taken too much of the drug, he should be given ______________.

Section 3 *Questions 29 – 40*

Read the following passage and then answer the questions that follow.

Expanding Work-Search Web Sites Fuel the Job-Hopping Trend

1 A mere two years into his career on J.P. Morgan & Co.'s high-technology trading floor on Wall Street, John Parker got the itch. "I needed to make a move," he said. "I needed new challenges." Almost on a whim last April, he posted his résumé at Monster.com, the gigantic job-searching site on the Web. By the next morning, his phone started ringing wildly, and he began averaging 10 responses a day.

2 "I was overwhelmed," he said. By the time the frenzy subsided two months later, Mr. Parker, 36, had agreed to take a cut in salary to become the new director of Web production at Freeride.com, a start-up that offers loyalty points to frequent Web shoppers and stock options to frequent job hoppers.

3 Thousands of similar stories are being played out every day on more than 500 career sites. These include Web-only ventures like Monster.com and Hotjobs, as well as sites like Careerpath.com and Classified Ventures, in which newspaper companies are seeking to expand their lucrative classified advertising business into cyberspace.

4 Initially viewed simply as a new tool for both job seekers and corporate recruiters alike, these new services are starting to accomplish something more significant: They seem to be changing the very dynamics of the employment marketplace.

5 Never before have so many new career opportunities freely presented themselves — and never before have so many workers been able to attract such serious attention to their résumés. "I didn't realize this," Mr. Parker added, "but it gives you so many channels that you wouldn't otherwise have."

6 As a result, the sites are encouraging a habit that employers dread: job hopping. "It's really a mixed blessing," said Tina Evangelista, a group manager in Intel Corp.'s human resources department.

7 On the one hand, because Intel must recruit about 7,500 experienced managers, sales engineers and technical staff members annually, the new job-posting sites save tons of money. For about $ 10,000 a year, Ms. Evangelista said, Intel can post an unlimited number of want ads on sites with names Career Mosaic, Hotjobs and Headhunter.com. Compared with paying independent recruiters as much as 25 percent of a new employee's

salary, or compared with $ 25,000 for a full-page ad in the Sunday edition of *The San Jose Mercury News*, she said, that is quite a bargain.

8 On the other hand, Ms. Evangelista is convinced that this new environment is actually encouraging the practice of frequently switching jobs. "Company loyalty is becoming an oxymoron," Ms. Evangelista said, adding that she saw a potential for the on-line job market to become so hot that it could melt down. "At some point, managers aren't going to look at these résumés anymore," she said. "Why invest in someone who only stays at their job from four to six months? We just have to keep retraining."

9 And yet, many of those who operate these career sites believe that some corporations are getting their just desserts. "It's corporate America's fault," said Jeffrey Taylor, chief executive of Monster.com, which typically has more than 70,000 job listings at any given time. "The 1980s set the stage when corporations were treating products as more important than people," Mr. Taylor said. "And I think the current backlash among workers will continue."

10 Whether the Web sites are stoking worker restlessness or responding to it, the on-line job bazaar does seem to be intensifying what employers see as an already worrisome trend. The U.S. Bureau of Labor Statistics has been reporting a steady decline in median tenure among the nation's workers for years. Among men ages 35 to 44 — a key category because it provides an apples-to-apples look at mid-career employees over the years — the typical time on the current job had shrunk from 7.3 years in 1983 to 5.5 years in 1998. And among some types of information technology professionals, who are very much in demand these days, the generally accepted turnover rate hovers around 50 percent. That means the average worker switches jobs every six months, essentially on a project-to-project basis.

11 Certainly, the temptations to move are ever present. At Freeride.com, for instance, Mr. Parker has moved into an office that was recently vacated by Seth Price. Mr. Price had worked there, in a business development position, and left after only six months on the job. "Nowadays," Mr. Price said, "if things aren't going so well at work, you just type a few keys. The knowledge that there is always a choice is right in your face."

12 With his brief Web start-up stint now under his belt, Mr. Price, who is 30 years old and had previously worked as a corporate lawyer and then helped found a company called ezCD.com before hopping to Freeride, now hopes to head back to the mainstream corporate world and said he was weighing several job offers.

13 It is not simply stock options dangled by Internet start-ups that are causing all the job movement. Intel, for one, has been offering stock options to all employees for more than three years now, Ms. Evangelista said. Even so, she added, the problem of attracting and retaining new recruits becomes tougher and tougher every year. That is why, to combat high turnover, Intel is starting to weed out recruits who fit the profile of today's on-line job-hopper. The telltale signs, according to Ms. Evangelista, include a recent career history chock full of short stints and a résumé that appears on several — if not dozens — of major job sites at once.

14 Her advice to potential employees is pick your spots. "I think there's a difference between poking around once in a while at the online listings and throwing your hat into every pool out there," she said. "We've changed how we do it. Instead of recruiting the active job seekers, we are trying to find the casual lookers."

15 Certainly, Mr. Price was cautious when looking to land a serious management position. Yes, he scanned the Web's job boards to see what was out there and to get a good sense of the market. But instead of posting his résumé on-line, he first sent out quieter feelers to friends and close business contacts. That yielded some interesting leads and word soon spread to the right recruiters for the right companies. "I felt this was a better option for this stage of my career," he said.

16 For that matter, Mr. Parker also agrees that human recruiters will still play a key role in the age of Internet job listings. In fact, it was a real live headhunter who spotted his on-line résumé and worked to place Mr. Parker in his current job. "Actually," he said, "Freeride itself has no idea how they first found me."

Question 29

Which one of the following names does not fall into the same category as others do?

Write the appropriate letter in box 29 on your answer sheet.

A. Monster.com

B. Hotjobs

C. Careerpath.com

D. Career Mosaic

E. Headhunter.com

F. Freeride.com

Questions 30 – 33

John Parker, Tina Evangelista, Jeffery Taylor and Seth Price are names mentioned in the passage. The following sentences are summaries of their opinions that are expressed explicitly or implicitly. Match the person with the sentence that is his / her opinion. Please note that there are sentences that are not of anyone's opinion. Write the answers in boxes 30 – 33 on your answer sheet.

A. Employees don't have the same commitment and dedication to their company as before.
B. It is amazing how many people visit job-posting sites.
C. You cannot blame the job-hopping trend on the workers; they are making it even.
D. If you do not like your job, find another one.
E. Many people are attracted to jobs that are related to computer technology.
F. The Internet gives workers new opportunities to have their résumés read with attention.

30. John Parker: ____________________
31. Tina Evangelista: ____________________
32. Jeffery Taylor: ____________________
33. Seth Price: ____________________

Questions 34 – 40

Answer the following questions by writing the name of the person concerned. Write the answers in boxes 34 – 40 on your answer sheet.

34. Who is thinking of finding a new job?
35. Who worked on a job for only a few months and then got a new job?
36. Who is doing a personnel administration job?
37. Who is the boss of a job-posting site?
38. Who got his job through a recruiter?
39. Who has shown a dislike for frequent job hoppers?
40. Who got a new job with a lower salary than the previous one?

答案及题解

SECTION 1

Questions 1 – 5:

这是一家旅馆的房价。

single room:	单人房间,有一张单人床。
twin room:	双人房间,有两张单人床。
double room:	双人房间,有一张双人床。
suite:	有套间的房子。

1. **D** Rate List 中的价格为每天的价格,因此 £80 为正确答案,即 double room 的费用(£40)乘以 2。
2. **B** 兄弟二人旅游,住一间 twin room 可能性大。
3. **B** 母女二人一般会住 twin room。女儿不满 12 岁,可享受 50%的优惠。
4. **B** Rate List 中的最后一句话大意是,如有 20 位付费的客人,第 21 人可获免费。问题中有"at least",因此答案为 B。
5. **D** Rate List 中的倒数第 2 句话的大意是,团体客人应于到达之日四周前预付一天的费用。因此 D 为答案。

Questions 6 – 10:

此文是一所学校关于退费的规定。

6. **False** 第 2 段的前两句明确了与退全费(full refund)有关的最后期限(deadline),使人感到如符合其他规定,可以部分退费(partial refund)。但第 1 段的 no refund are permitted after the refund deadline 说明第 2 段中的 deadline 仅适用于退全费,不再有其他的 deadline。因此答案是 False。
7. **False** 见第 3 段的第 1 句话。
8. **Not Given** 第 3 段第 2 句说明了处理退费所需的时间,从这句话中无法判断支票与现金支付形式在时间上的差别,因此答案为 Not Given。
9. **True** 见第 2 段第 2 句。如果课程周一开始,"the last working day before the course begins"指前一个周五,因此答案为 True。
10. **True** 见第 2 段第 1 句话。如果课程周一开始,"on... the 5th working day after the course begins"指该周五。因此答案为 True。

Questions 11 – 15:

11. **False** 从第 1 段和第 2 段可得知,Richmond College 和 CTC 将联合举办颁发微软证书的技术培训。但此次免费讲座只是对上述内容做介绍(见最后一段),而不涉及计算机技术的最新发展。因此答案为 False。

12. **Not Given** 文中未提及讲座的地点。

13. **True** 见第 2 段第 2、3 句。

14. **True** Courses at CTC ... feature Microsoft-certified trainers：CTC 的课程有获微软证书的教员主讲。state-of-the-art facilities：反映本行业现状的设备，即最先进的设备。feature：由 ...... 主讲／主演。

15. **True** 见最后一句话。

SECTION 2

Questions 16 – 21:

这是一则广告，介绍一种以无线方式使住宅或办公室可以接很多个并列的电话机的装置（即同一个电话号码的分机），它的信号的发射和接收是通过电源线进行的。换言之，房内的电源线起着天线的作用。

16. **False** 第 3 段说，大多数电话线最多只允许有五个并列电话机，但这种装置则可有 unlimited 并列电话机。

17. **True** 见前文。

18. **False** 第 4 段说此种装置可连接传真机、调制解调器和留言机。

19. **Not Given** 第 5 段说此装置的售价为厂家的直销价，期限有限，但未说明将持续多长时间。第 6 段中提到的 90 天是无条件退全款的期限，不是价格的有效期。

20. **True** S&H(shipping and handling)：运费及服务费用，美国用法。英国用 P&P (packing and postage)。接收器的价格：第一个为$ 49，其余的为$ 39。如买两个接收器，应付$ 88 (49 + 39)。exclusive of ...：不含 ......。

21. **False** 第 5 段的最后一句话的大意是无论是买发射器还是买接收器，均可以$ 9.95 的价格购买价值为$ 30 的电话卡。

Questions 22 – 28:

这 7 道题要求用不多于二个词填空，所用的词一定得是原文中使用的词，且拼写与原文中完全一样，包括名词的单、复数，动词的各种时态等。

这是一则药品说明书。一些常用词如下：

composition:	组成，构成
contradictions:	禁忌症
directions for use:	服法，用法
dosage:	剂量
expiry date / validity:	有效期
indications:	适应症
properties:	特性
side effects:	副作用

special precautions:　　　　警示

storage:　　　　储存

22. **seasonal / allergic**　从 Indications 看,此药主要用于过敏引起的一些病症。许多过敏反应与季节有关,因此 seasonal 也是正确答案。

23. **during**　见 Dosage and Directions for Use。

24. **agitation / dry mouth / drowsiness**　见 Side Effects。

25. **one**　见 Dosage and Directions for Use。

26. **breast-feeding**(母乳哺乳)　用奶瓶喂奶是 bottle feed。Pregnancy and Lactation 说,怀孕后头三个月的妇女及哺乳的妇女不应服用此药。言外之意是怀孕三个月以后的妇女可以服用此药。因此不能用 pregnant。

27. **sedatives**　见 Drug Interactions。

28. **gastric lavage**(洗胃)　见 Overdosage。

SECTION 3

Questions 29 – 40:

由于有了很多网上招聘的网站,人们有了更多的找工作的机会,跳槽的人也越来越多。文章讲述了不同的人对此的不同态度。

29. **F**　除 F 以外,其他的选项均与网上招聘有关。

30. **F**　见第 5 段。

31. **A**　见第 8 段。

32. **C**　见第 9 段。making it even: 报复,摆平。

33. **D**　见第 11 段。

34. (**Seth**) **Price**　见第 12 段。

35. (**Seth**) **Price**　见第 11 段。

36. (**Tina**) **Evangelista**　见第 6 段。

37. (**Jeffery**) **Taylor**　见第 9 段。

38. (**John**) **Parker**　见第 16 段。

39. (**Tina**) **Evangelista**　见第 8 段。

40. (**John**) **Parker**　见第 1、2 段。

这 12 道题均与人名、网站名有关,这一点用几秒钟的浏览就可看出。在阅读文章时用笔将所有的人名、网站名划出,能很容易地找出大部分题的答案,关键是能否很快地意识到文章中专有名词的重要性。

八、G 类阅读模拟试题三、答案及题解

INTERNATIONAL ENGLISH LANGUAGE TESTING SYSTEM

PRACTICE TEST (Version Three)
GENERAL TRAINING

TIME ALLOWED: 1 HOUR
NUMBER OF QUESTIONS: 40

Instructions

ALL ANSWERS MUST BE WRITTEN ON THE ANSWER SHEET.

The test is divided as follows:

Section 1	Questions 1 – 15
Section 2	Questions 16 – 27
Section 3	Questions 28 – 40

Start at the beginning of the test and work through it. Your should answer all the questions. If you cannot do a particular question leave it and go on to the next. You can return to it later.

Section 1 *Questions 1 – 15*

Read the notice about a course below and answer the questions that follow.

MIBE Courses: Business Ethics

Contrary to popular belief, "business ethics" is not a contradiction in terms! Examine this vital topic with classmates via MIBE (Manchester Interactive Business Education).

How often have you experienced conflict between your personal value system and the values of the market, whether it's as a consumer compromising environmental concerns within the limits of your pocketbook, or as an employee compromising personal values to satisfy the boss? Explore how ethical values play out in the marketplace and the different ways the phenomenon of morality can be analyzed.

Instructor: Dr. Sharon Rowe has taught at MBS (Manchester Business School). Her specialties include the application of moral theory to problems of contemporary social and political concern, and the philosophy of law and feminism.

Dates: October 27 – December 2.

Time: Tuesdays and Thursdays, 19:00 – 21:00

Location: Kensinton Hall 201, MIBE.

Cost: £ 80 for registered MBS students, £ 200 for others.

Registration Deadlines: 20% off before August 31. Full tuition September 1 – October 23. Registration closes October 24 and onwards.

Further information can be obtained at the General Office of MIBE, 520 Oxford Road, or please phone 071 – 565 – 7266.

Questions 1 – 5

Decide if the following statements are true or false according to the information in the notice of MIBE courses. In boxes 1 – 5 on your answer sheet, write ***TRUE*** *if the statement is true. If it is false, write* ***FALSE****. If relevant information is not given in the notice, write* ***NOT GIVEN****. One has been done as an example.*

Example: Answer:
The General Office of MIBE is not open on Saturdays. ***NOT GIVEN***

1. The course is part of an MBA course.
2. The course content concentrates on the issue of environmental protection.
3. The instructor is a staff member of MIBE.
4. The classes are in the evenings only.
5. An MBS student needs to pay £ 64 if he signs up before the end of August.

Questions 6 – 10

Read the notice about a school below and answer the questions that follow.

MANOR HALL SCHOOL

Pound Hill Norwich

Independent Boarding School of Boys 10 – 17 *Years*

WE OFFER—

- Small classes and much individual attention from qualified staff.
- Good residential accommodation.
- Challenging courses for the bright and much help and encouragement for the not-so-bright.
- Good facilities, including a well equipped computer centre and three science laboratories and an art / craft and design complex.
- Courses leading to "O" level and CSE examinations.
- A special unit for boys with dyslexia and similar learning difficulties.
- A wide range of activities, enabling senior boys to take Duke of Edinburgh Awards.
- A full games programme including rugby, soccer, hockey, swimming, athletics and other minority sports.
- A balanced education for pupils of discipline in a caring environment. Most boys are full boarders but a few day boys are accepted.

Please write or telephone for a copy of the school prospectus.

Indicate if each of the following statements is true or false according to the information from the notice. In boxes 6 – 10 *on your answer sheet, write* ***TRUE*** *if the statement is true; if it is false, write* ***FALSE***. *If the notice does not contain relevant information about the statement, please write* ***NOT GIVEN***. *An example has been done.*

Example:	Answer:
The school accepts boys only.	***TRUE***

6. Each class has no more than 20 students.
7. The school caters for the needs of students with learning difficulties.
8. The school has various kinds of sports facilities.
9. The school doesn't accept day students.
10. The school is a private school.

Questions 11 – 15
Read the notice about a school below and answer the questions that follow.

Tips for Home Savings

Going green is good for your house and your pocketbook.

By using energy efficiently, you conserve natural resources, delay the need for new power plants, reduce emissions of gases that cause air pollution and acid rain, and reduce carbon-dioxide emissions that may contribute to global warming. Here are some helpful hints for making your home more energy efficient.

Washers and Dryers

Use cooler water when running your clothes-washing machine.

Remember that faster spin speed in the washer can reduce energy required for drying.

Clean your dryer's lint filter after each load. Check the exhaust pipe for leaks or blockage, and make sure they're vented outside. Some hardware stores sell a simple kit to vent dryer heat indoors in winter.

Don't overdry. It harms clothes and wastes energy. If your dryer has a moisture sensor, use it to turn off the unit automatically when clothes are dry.

Refrigerator / Freezer

Automatic defrost uses more energy than manual defrost models.

Ice-cube makers and through-the-door water dispensers are convenient but they increase energy use.

Side-by-side models use more energy than those with freezer on top.

Dishwashers

When selecting a dishwasher, compare water-consumption levels — some use as little as 8 gallons of hot water per cycle, others use as much as 12.

Look for a dishwasher with a heat booster that will raise the water temperature to 140 degrees, thus enabling you to turn down the thermostat on your water heater.

Decide if the following use ***LESS*** *energy or not. If it uses less energy, write* ***YES****. If it uses more energy, write* ***NO****. If the text doesn't contain information about the statement, write* ***NOT GIVEN****. Write your answers in boxes 11 – 15 on your answer sheet. One has been done as an example.*

Example: Answer:
Use cold water when doing the laundry. ***YES***

11. Let the dryer spin faster.
12. Let the fridge defrost automatically.
13. Use the through-the-door water dispenser.
14. Use a dishwasher with a 12 gallon water consumption.
15. Use a dishwasher that has a heat booster.

Section 2 *Questions 16 – 27*

Questions 16 – 27

Read the following passage about Tylenol and answer the questions that follow.

News about Pain Reliever Safety from the Makers of Tylenol

Serious Medicine: Use Only as Directed

Recently, there's been some discussion about the safety of over-the-counter pain relievers. To help you make an informed decision about the right pain reliever for you, it's important to have as much information as possible. Over-the-counter medicine is serious medicine, and it's important for you to read and follow the information on the label and stay within the recommended doses.

Tylenol Is Different

You may be surprised to know just how different pain relievers can be. There are two types: the ingredient in Tylenol, and NSAIDs (non-steroidal anti-inflammatories) such as aspirin, ibuprofen and naproxen sodium. All these pain relievers provide effective pain relief, however, one key difference between Tylenol and NSAIDs has to do with side effects. NSAIDs all work in the same way and tend to cause, to varying degrees, the same side effects. With so many pain relievers to choose from, it's especially important to read their labels and understand their possible side effects. For example, if you or someone in your family is among the tens of millions of people who suffer from asthma or ulcers, if you're aspirin sensitive or taking certain medications, choosing the right pain reliever is even more important. Doctors will tell you Tylenol is your wisest choice.

Of course, your best source of information regarding your choice of pain reliever is your own doctor or pharmacist.

A Word about Alcholol

You may have seen some reports in the media about the consumption of alcohol and pain relievers. If you regularly consume significant amounts of alcohol, you should talk to your doctor or pharmacist about any medication you're taking and, most definitely, follow the instructions on the label.

That's why the makers of Tylenol agree with a Food and Drug Administration (FDA) Advisory Committee that all pain relievers should carry a warning about the use of these medications and alcohol. In fact, we began adding the following warning on Tylenol packages last year and we urge all manufacturers of pain relievers to do the same: If you generally consume 3 or more alcohol-containing drinks per day, you should consult your physician for advice on when and how you should take Tylenol and other pain relievers.

You can be assured, if you're an occasional moderate drinker, you can use Tylenol with confidence. When you weigh the relative risks of using other pain relievers compared to Tylenol, you can understand why doctors recommend Tylenol more than any other pain reliever, even for those who drink alcohol. Tylenol is their first choice.

Making the Right Choice

When used as directed, you can be confident knowing Tylenol is the safest type of pain reliever you can buy.

Indicate if each of the following statements is true or false according to the information from the news above. In boxes 16 – 21 on your answer sheet, write ***TRUE*** *if the statement is true; if it is false, write* ***FALSE****. If the news does not contain relevant information about the statement, please write* ***NOT GIVEN****. An example has been done.*

Example:	Answer:
Tylenol is an over-the-counter medicine.	***True***

16. Aspirin and naproxen sodium are of the same type of pain relievers.
17. Naproxen sodium is an over-the-counter medicine.
18. Aspirin is better than ibuprofen for people suffering from asthma.
19. Some people are sensitive to aspirin and therefore should take Tylenol when in need.
20. The FDA Advisory Committee recommends Tylenol to moderate drinkers.
21. Heavy drinkers need pain relievers more than moderate drinkers.

Questions 22 – 27

Below is a list of words or phrases taken from the passage that follows. Read the passage and fill in the blanks with appropriate letters and write your answers in boxes 22 – 27 on your answer sheet. The first one has been done as an example.

A. locked	G. described below
B. adjust	H. in loose clothing
C. up and about	I. international travels
D. irritation	J. time zone
E. regulates body temperature	K. need medication
F. meal and sleep	L. long distance

Jet Lag

If you are feeling worn out after arrival and cannot seem to remember whether you ...(*example*)... the hotel room door or not, or where you placed your documents or why you are feeling lethargic when everyone else is ...(22)..., take heart. Join the thousands of travellers who face this inconvenience in their travels around the world. The symptoms described above refer to the after effects of air travel, commonly known as "jet lag".

Jet lag refers to the readjustments made by our body to changes in light, temperature and climate. Our body has two biological clocks: one controls the wake/sleep cycle and the other ...(23)... . When these mechanisms are disrupted through the crossing of multiple time zones, our bodies react with fatigue, disorientation, broken sleep patterns and we become irrational or unreasonable.

Prevention

Here are some suggestions to overcome some of the effects of jet lag. Before departure, adjust your ...(24)... times to the new time zone. Get plenty of exercise days before departure. Get a good rest the night before. If you are on a long haul and can go either direction, go westward as it causes less jet lag.

During the flight drink plenty of water to combat dehydration. Dress comfortably ...(25)... and slippers. Get up and walk often. Do small twisting/stretching exercises in your seat to reduce swelling of legs and feet. At stopovers, get out to walk or take a shower to get the muscles and circulation going again.

On arrival, expose yourself to the morning or afternoon light to help your body systems ...(26)... . Limit your first day's activities. Relax. Adapt your meal times and activities to those of your destination as soon as possible.

Treatment

Ask your doctor for a short-acting benzodiazepine if you ...(27)... . Over-the-counter antihistamines tend to work very well. Acupressure is said to work if done while travelling. Homeopathic treatments are also available. There is a lack of definitive clinical studies on melatonin so one should use it selectively and not over long periods.

Bon voyage!

Example: A　　22.____　23.____　24.____　25.____　26.____　27.____

Section 3 ***Questions 28 – 40***

Read the advertisement below and answer the questions that follow.

"My TV reception is so clear, you'd think I had a 50-foot antenna on my roof!"

Emerson's ingenious new antennas are hard to spot, easy to install and provide clear, powerful reception of broadcast signals... without rabbit ears.

1 I'm amazed at the way technology has improved television. Developments in electronic circuits have resulted in TV sets that have sharper pictures, brilliant colors and clearer sound. From the smallest portables to wide-screen home theater systems, televisions continue to work better and better as optical innovations are introduced. Unfortunately, a television's picture is only as good as the broadcast it's receiving, and even the world's best televisions cannot make up for a weak or distorted signal. Antenna technology has not kept pace with television design, and the rabbit ears from the 1950's are not far removed from what's available today. Well, there's finally been a quantum leap in the design of antennas, and it's the result of two patented components developed by scientists. These improvements are the secret behind Emerson's revolutionary new antennas.

2 Cable subscription solves the problem of getting the signal to your television, but storms and other factors can result in cable outages. If you prefer not to pay the rising monthly fees for cable or live in an area where it's not available, your picture is likely to be weak, undefined and distorted.

3 One way to improve your reception would be to mount a large antenna on your roof. Unfortunately, most roof antennas are not particularly pleasing to the eye and may even be prohibited in the area where you live. Rabbit ear antennas don't improve your picture to any great degree and make your room look like something from an earlier decade. Most antennas need to be aimed at the source of the broadcast and require turning mechanisms to pick up the signal clearly.

4 Whether you live miles out in the country or in a concrete building next door to a broadcast tower, bad reception can rob you of the definition and color you were intended to see. The Optima antenna gives you the signal-grabbing power of a large antenna in an inconspicuous, low-profile size.

5 In the past, creating an antenna with optimal reception meant making it big, with a large amount of surface area. This resulted in products that were large and unsightly or small and ineffective. Either way, the aesthetic look of your room or house suffered. Research and development tended to focus on the television, not on signal reception ... until now.

6 Recently, a brilliant scientist in Colorado developed an antenna that would maximize reception without being overly conspicuous. Emerson, a leader in electronic technology, has now made this innovation available to the public.

7 At a lab in Colorado, they developed two patented design improvements that made the Optima antenna possible. First, they created a flexible circuit board with a serpentine antenna, resulting in a large surface area confined to a small space. Second, they developed a technique that converts the copper shielding on the attached cable to an additional signal receiver. This greatly enhances the antenna's reception power and allows you to tune the antenna by simply moving the cable! The antenna works best at a range of up to 30 miles from the signal source. We recommend an amplifier for reception up to 45 miles away. Ask your representative for details.

8 The handmade assembly is encased in aircraft-grade plastic and high-density foam. The weather-resistant cover is a neutral white and can be painted to match the color of the house or room. Plus, the omnidirectional design allows you to mount the unit anywhere you please. The Optima's universal design makes it adaptable to any component, and installation is a snap. So sit back, relax and enjoy the clearest picture you can get from your television.

9 Call now to order the small antennas that get big reception. They both come with a 90-day manufacturer's limited warranty and Comtrad's exclusive risk-free home trial. Try them, and if you're not completely satisfied, return them within 90 days for a full "No Questions Asked" refund.

Indoor / Outdoor Antenna	$ 69.95	$ 8 S&H
Dishmate UHF / VHF Antenna	$ 69.95	$ 8 S&H

The Dishmate Antenna will work with 18″ dishes from RCA, Toshiba, ProScan, GE, Eurorat, Uniden, Sony and Hughes DSS Satellite systems. Please specify model when ordering.

Please mention promotional code 3693 – 13947.

For fastest service, call toll-free 24 hours a day: 800 – 992 – 2966

To order by mail, send check or money order for the total amount including S&H. To charge it to your credit card, enclose your account number and expiration date.

Attention mini-dish owner: If you own a mini-dish satellite system, you are aware of the off-air issue and are probably wondering how you can pick up local broadcasts. After all, what good are hundreds of channels if you can't find who won the local city council election. The Dishmate harnesses the same technological innovations as the Optima TV antenna to give you a powerful omnidirectional antenna that is virtually invisible. It is compatible with a variety of systems and is easy to install.

Virginia residents only *— please include 4.5% sales tax.*

Comtrad Industries, 220 Waterford Lake Dr., Midlothian, Virginia 23113, USA

Questions 28 – 40

Do the following statements agree with the content of the advertisement? In boxes 28 – 40 on your answer sheet, please write

YES	*if the statement agrees with the content of the advertisement;*
NO	*if the statement does not agree with the content of the advertisement;*
NOT GIVEN	*if there is no information about this in the advertisement.*

Example :
Emerson produces TV antennas.

Answer:
YES

28. Rabbit ear antennas are old fashioned but are still in use.

29. Cable TVs have good pictures but users need to pay to watch the programs.

30. For aesthetic reasons, people want their antennas to be conspicuous.

31. A TV can have poor reception even if it is near the signal sources.

32. The headquarters of Emerson is located in Colorado.

33. Like a roof antenna, the Optima antenna brings the best reception when it is on the roof.

34. With an Optima antenna, users can receive programs from satellites.

35. Emerson produces satellite dishes.

36. For a full refund, the Optima antenna must be returned within 90 days after purchase.

37. To install Optima antennas, buyers should contact qualified personnel.

38. The $ 69.95 price doesn't include S&H and sales tax.

39. 800 – 992 – 2966 is the phone number of Emerson.

40. Local broadcast can be received through satellite dishes.

答案及题解

SECTION 1

Questions 1 – 5:

这是一个系列讲座的通知,讲座的主题是商务伦理(business ethics)。

1. **False** 听这个系列讲座须单独付费,由此可推断,此讲座不是某个单位课程的一部分。

2. **False** 讲座主要内容是商业道德。第2段中所举的例子之一是消费者遇有环保的考虑与个人利益冲突时该怎么办。

3. **Not Given** 文中只说明 MIBE 举办此讲座,讲课教师在 MBS 工作过,但未说明讲课教师目前的工作单位。

4. **True** 每周二、四的19点至21点。

5. **True** MBS 学生的听讲费为 £80,但如在8月31日之前报名可享受八折优惠。20% off:在标价上削去二成。

Questions 6 – 10:

这是一所男生寄宿学校(boarding school)的广告。

"O" level:初中课程,高中课程是"A" level。

CSE (Certificate of Secondary Education):(英)中学教育证书。

Full boarders:食宿均在学校的学生,与"full"相对是只在学校吃饭、不住在学校的学生(day students)。

6. **Not Given** 文中说是 small classes,但未明确每班人数。

7. **True** dyslexia:诵读困难。

8. **True** rugby:英式橄榄球。soccer:足球。hocky:曲棍球。美式橄榄球:American football。

   football 一词在美国英语里指美式橄榄球,在英国英语里指足球,为了不造成混淆,这两种英语均常用 soccer 指足球。

9. **False** 见文中 a few day boys are accepted。

10. **True** 文中用了 independent,未用 private,这只是为了好听的缘故。实际上 independent 是指独立于公立教育体系的学校,即私立学校。

Questions 11 – 15:

这篇文章讲的是一些如何在家里省水、省电的秘诀。

green:绿色的,环保的

pocketbook:钱夹

through-the-door water dispenser：安在冰箱门外部用来方便取冷水的水龙头

11. **Yes** 见文中 faster spin speed ... can reduce energy required ...。

12. **No** 见文中 automatic defrost uses more energy。

13. **No** 见文中 ... through-the-door water dispenser ... increase energy use。

14. **No** 洗碗机使用大量热水，12 加仑当然比 8 加仑耗能多。

15. **Yes** 见文中 look for a dishwasher with a heat booster ...。

SECTION 2

Questions 16 – 21:

这是一种非处方药的介绍，药名为 Tylenol，译名为泰诺。

over-the -counter medicine：柜台上可买到的药，即非处方药，简称 OTC 药。处方药是 prescribed medicine。

FDA：（美国）食品与药品管理局

16. **True** 第 2 段说止痛类药分两类，一类是泰诺所含的成分，另一类是 NSAID，题中的两种止痛药均属第二类。

17. **True** 此文主要谈泰诺的特点以及其他各种 OTC 类止痛药。

18. **Not Given** 第 2 段最后两句话的主要内容是：对于许多患哮喘的病人，对于阿斯匹林过敏的人，对于在服用其他某些药物的人，选择正确的止痛片至关重要。对于这几类病人，大夫一般会推荐泰诺。

19. **True** 见上一题的解释。

20. **Not Given** 从文中可看出，FDA 的一个顾问委员会认为所有的止痛药均应带有警示说明，但文中没有说明该委员会是否推荐某类止痛药。

21. **Not Given** 文中虽有一部分专门谈饮酒者应如何使用止痛药，但并未说哪类人更需服用止痛药。

Questions 22 – 27:

这是一篇关于由时差所导致的身体不适及如何克服不适的文章，由于已将填空用的选择列出，做题时应主要考虑两个因素：1）语法； 2）内容。

22. **C** up and about：（病人）已起并走动。take heart：鼓起勇气，振作起来。
此空应与前面的 is 构成系表结构，能起此作用的惟一选择就是 C。

23. **E** 此空所需的词应与句中的 controls 相呼应，因此，应找一个结尾加 s 的动词，E 是惟一的选择。

24. **F** 此空所需的词应起修饰 times 的作用，即定语。定语一般由形容词、名词、代词、数词组成。从前面的动词看，应与作息、起居时间有关，因此选 F。

25. **H** 从动词 dress 和后面的名词 slippers 来看，所选的词组应有介词 in。另外，comfortably 亦与 loose clothing 呼应。因此选 H。

26. **B** 从前面的 help your body systems 来看，此处需要一个原形动词，因此选 B。

27. **K**　此空应为条件从句 if you 的谓语。另外,前面的 benzodiazepine 应为某种药,亦与 K 中的 medication 呼应。

SECTION 3

Questions 28 – 40:

这是一篇广告,介绍一种电视天线。这种天线既不是室内的 V 形天线(文中用的是 rabbit ears),也不是较常见的耸立在房顶上的那种天线(large antenna on your roof)。从下文的 Attention mini-dish owner 来看,它亦不是碟形卫星天线。因此,它是某种新产品,大部分读者未见过其外貌,做题时相应有一定难度。

28. **Yes**　见第 1 段中的 The rabbit ears from the 1950s are not far removed from what's available today。

29. **Yes**　第 2 段的 subscription 和 pay the rising monthly fee 均表示须付费,... solves the problems of getting the signal to your television 表示图像清晰。

30. **No**　见第 5 段。unsightly: 不雅观的。aesthetic: 美学的。

31. **Yes**　见第 4 段的第 1 句。另外,仅从 can 一词上也可基本判断答案为 Yes,因为此词表示"可以",所表达的意思留有余地,不绝对。其他类似留有余地的词有 may、probably、sometimes、could 等。相反,如果是意思绝对的词,如 never、always、completely 等,则该句话很可能为 No。

32. **Not Given**　headquarters: 总部。文中提到两个州名,Colorado 和 Virginia,但未指出 headquarters 的所在地。

33. **No**　见第 8 段第 3 句话。

34. **No**　此天线与普通天线(室内的 V 形天线和室外的高架天线)具有同样的功能,都是用来接受地方电视台通过发射塔发送的电视讯号的(见第 7 段最后三句话)。对于只有碟形卫星天线的住户来说,可以购买一个 dishmate 来接收当地电视的讯号。

35. **Not Given**　广告所介绍的天线是 Emmerson 的产品,文中未说明是否还有其他产品。

36. **Yes**　见第 9 段第 2 句。

37. **No**　见第 8 段 installation is a snap(安装非常容易)。如果需由专业人员安装,文章不可能用 snap 一词。

38. **Yes**　天线均为 69.95 元,但要付 8 元的运费和服务费,如是本州人(即 Virginia 州)购买,还需付 4.5%的税。

39. **No**　此电话为销售商 Comtrad Industries 的电话。

40. **No**　碟形卫星天线只能用来接收卫星电视讯号,不能接收当地电视讯号。

九、G类阅读模拟试题四、答案及题解

INTERNATIONAL ENGLISH LANGUAGE TESTING SYSTEM

PRACTICE TEST（Version Four）

GENERAL TRAINING

TIME ALLOWED: 1 HOUR
NUMBER OF QUESTIONS: 40

Instructions

ALL ANSWERS MUST BE WRITTEN ON THE ANSWER SHEET.

The test is divided as follows:

Section 1	Questions 1 – 14
Section 2	Questions 15 – 25
Section 3	Questions 26 – 40

Start at the beginning of the test and work through it. Your should answer all the questions. If you cannot do a particular question leave it and go on to the next. You can return to it later.

Section 1 *Questions 1 – 14*

Questions 1 – 5
Read the following hotel notice and answer the questions that follow.

Queen's Hotel, Southsea, Tel: (Portsmouth) 0705 – 62314960

ACCOMMODATION	ROOM CHARGE ONLY		
	1st & 2nd Floors	3rd Floor	4th Floor
Sea View Bedrooms			
Single with Bath or Shower	£ 25	£ 23	£ 21
Single with Bath or Shower and Toilet	£ 27	£ 25	–
Twin or Double with Bath or Shower	£ 36	–	–
Twin or Double with Bath or Shower and Toilet	£ 39	£ 36	–
Rear View Bedrooms			
Single with Bath or Shower	£ 18	–	–
Single with Bath or Shower and Toilet	£ 20	–	–
Twin or Double with Bath or Shower	–	£ 28	–
Twin or Double with Bath or Shower and Toilet	£ 33	£ 30	–
Private Suites			
One Single with Private Bath and Toilet, Sitting Room and Balcony	£ 80	–	–
One Twin or One Double with Private Bath and Toilet, Sitting Room and Balcony	£ 100	–	–

Double or Twin-bedded Rooms let as Singles — Single Rate plus £ 5.
Twin or Double Suite let for Single Occupancy — £ 90.

Please vacate room by 12 noon on day of departure.

Indicate if each of the following statements is true or false according to the information from the listed rates of the hotel. In boxes 1 – 5 on your answer sheet, please write ***TRUE*** *if the statement is true; write* ***FALSE*** *if it is false. If the notice does not contain relevant information about the statement, please write* ***NOT GIVEN****. An example has been done.*

Example:	Answer:
Rooms on the 4th floor are the least expensive.	***TRUE***

1. A room with twin beds costs the same as one with a double bed.
2. The cost doubles if the guest wants to have a room with a better view.
3. Rooms on the top floor have a better view than rooms on the lower floors.
4. All suites are for two persons.
5. There's a reduction if one person has a suite or a room for two to himself.

Questions 6 – 9

Read the notice below and answer the questions that follow.

Photography: Digital Imaging with Photoshop

Designed around the needs of photographers and artists who work with visual images, this hands-on workshop introduces participants to the fundamental image editing and manipulation tools available in Adobe Photoshop. Areas covered include scanning, rile size and resolution, color balancing and grey scale adjustments of contrast and density, manipulation of images for creative effect or to remove unwanted elements, and combining words and images. The electronic imaging chain, from input (scanning) to output (printing), is discussed. Participants leave with a working knowledge of many of the tools and capabilities of Adobe Photoshop.
Prerequisite: Basic familiarity with the Macintosh environment. No prior experience with Photoshop necessary.

Section A: Oct. 15 – 16, Fri. / Sat., 9:00am – 4:00pm—2 Mtgs.
Room 101, Computer Centre, Salford Community College, $ 200.
Instructor: David Ulrich

Section B: Nov. 15 – 16, Mon. / Tues., 9:00am – 4:00pm—2 Mtgs.
Room 101, Computer Centre, Salford Community College, $ 200.
Instructor: Dan Doemer

Decide if the following statements are true or false according to the information in the notice for the workshop. In boxes 6 – 9 on your answer sheet, write ***TRUE*** *if the statement is true. If it is false, write* ***FALSE***. *If relevant information is not given in the notice, write* ***NOT GIVEN***. *One has been done as an example.*

Example: Answer:
Knowledge of Macintosh environment is needed for attending the workshop. ***TRUE***

6. The classes concentrate on the use of computers to retouch photographs.
7. Participants in each class meet four times.
8. More people are likely to be attracted to Section A because it meets on Friday and Saturday.
9. The classes are for people who have used Photoshop before.

Questions 10 – 14
Read the advertisement below and answer the questions that follow.

BTB BUS COMPANY

The BTB Bus Company serves all parts of the city, and also provides an extensive service to nearby towns and villages.

BTB CITY BUSES are usually **orange**, and operate from 06:30 to 23:30. There are four kinds of tickets you can use:

Tourist Ranger is the ideal ticket for tourists and visitors to the city. The tickets are valid for 2, 3, or 5 days, and can be used on all city buses. They cost £4, £5.50 and £7.50.

Monthly Season — Going to work by bus? This is the one for you! For only £26.50 you have the freedom of the city for a whole calendar month.

Bus Card — lasts for one day. For £2.50 you can travel anywhere on the bus system for one day — but you must clip your card in the machine every time you board a bus.

Single Journey — 50p, valid for just one journey. Clip the ticket when you get on the bus. Books of ten tickets also available.

These tickets are only valid on BTB City Buses. They are available from post offices, tobacconists and BTB offices. TICKETS CANNOT BE PURCHASED ON THE BUSES.

BTB COUNTRY BUSES (which are usually **blue**) serve the towns of Conby, Rashville and Grill as well as numerous villages in the area. Services run from 07:00 to 21:30.

Tickets are bought on the bus. The minimum fare is 75p, increasing with distance. Buses depart from the main railway station and Goshley Square.

A MAP of the routes for both City and Country buses can be obtained (price 20p) from the BTB offices at the main railway station or 27 Part Square. Timetables for both services can be found at the bust stops.

Answer the following questions using ***NO MORE THAN THREE WORDS*** *from the advertisement of BTB Bus Company and write your answers in boxes 10 – 14 on your answer sheet. One has been done as an example.*

Example:	**Answer:**
How much is a single journey ticket for riding a city bus?	***50p***

10. If you are staying in the city for 2 days and want to see the city as much as possible, which ticket is the best for you?
11. What is the best ticket to buy if you want to show your visiting friend around on a Saturday?
12. Where should one go in order to buy tickets for the orange BTB buses?
13. Where are the tickets for the blue BTB buses sold?
14. Where should one probably go if he wants to catch a bus to Rashville?

Section 2 *Questions 15 – 25*

Questions 15 – 19

Read the directions for a medicine below and answer the questions that follow.

Elomide™

(Lodoxamide 0.1 %)

Sterile Ophthalmic Solution

INDICATIONS AND USAGE:

Elomide Ophthalmic Solution (EOS) is indicated in the treatment of the ocular signs and symptoms associated with certain allergic ocular disorders.

WARNINGS: FOR TOPICAL USE ONLY — NOT FOR INJECTION.

Do not touch dropper tip to any surface as this may contaminate the solution.

PRECAUTIONS:

As with all preparations containing benzalkonium chloride, users of soft (hydrophilic) contact lenses should refrain from wearing lenses while under treatment with EOS. The recommended frequency of administration should not be exceeded. EOS is unlikely to affect a patient's ability to drive or to use machinery.

ADVERSE REACTIONS:

EOS has been generally well tolerated. In controlled clinical studies, the most common side effect reported was mild and transient discomfort upon instillation (8.7% of patients) expressed as burning, stinging, itching or tearing.

OVERDOSAGE:

There have been no reports of EOS overdose following topical ocular application. In the event of a topical overdose, flush from the eye with running water.

DOSAGE AND ADMINISTRATION:

The dose for adults and children two years of age or older is one or two drops in each eye, four times a day at regular intervals.

Patients should be advised that the effect of therapy with EOS is dependent upon its administration at regular intervals, as directed.

The safety and effectiveness of EOS in children younger than 2 years of age have not been established.

STORAGE:

Store upright at room temperature (15℃ – 27℃). Keep out of the reach of children. Do not use after the expiration date. The content and bottle should be discarded one month after opening the container for the first time.

Elcon Pharmaceuticals, Switzerland

Fill in the blanks in the following statements using ***NO MORE THAN THREE WORDS*** *from the above directions for Elomide and write your answers in boxes 15 – 19 on your answer sheet. One has been done as an example.*

Example:	Answer:
The drug is made in ________________.	***Switzerland***

15. EOS is for ________________ only.

16. EOS should not be used more than ________________ a day.

17. EOS does not produce more serious ________________ than itching or tearing.

18. In case of overdose, eyes should be washed with ________________.

19. It is important that EOS is used at ________________.

Questions 20 – 25

Read the notice below and answer the questions that follow.

English Courses for International Students

Foreign students, short-term visitors from abroad, and Sydney's international residents can benefit from diverse study options for language, cultural, and professional enrichment through the International Programs of Outreach College.

The **N**ew **I**ntensive **C**ourses in **E**nglish (**N. I. C. E.**) program accommodates a wide variety of interests and time schedules. Courses emphasize spoken communication in English. Options for full-time or part-time study are available.

INTENSIVE SPOKEN ENGLISH (**I. S. E.**) prepares students for successful communication in Australian University courses and in the local or international business world. Classes include grammar, listening, oral production, and Canadian culture, with a choice of an academic or business focus in the advanced level.

10-week courses. 20 hours per week, morning classes.

ENGLISH FOR CONVERSATIONAL PURPOSES (**E. C. P.**) prepares students for successfully using practical English in everyday life and social and recreational settings. Classes focus on improving both conversational accuracy and fluency.

10-week courses. 20 hours per week, afternoon classes.

1999 – 2000 I.S.E. & E.C.P. Term Dates:

Term 113: October 8 – December 17, 1999

Term 114: January 7 – March 17, 2000

Term 115: April 7 – June 16, 2000

Winter and **S**ummer **N.I.C.E.** are four-week courses in English conversation and Australian culture. They offer an alternative to students who have only a short time to study English.

4-week courses. 20 hours per week.

2000 Winter Term: January 31-February 25

2000 Summer Term: July 24-August 18

N.I.C.E. AT NIGHT offers residents and visiting non-native speakers opportunities to perfect their English skills in the evening. Classes focus on language needs of individuals who wish to improve their language skills in order to communicate more effectively at work, in school, or in the community. To register for these courses, complete the attached Registration Form.

Special **E**nglish **P**rograms (**S. E. P.**) are designed for groups (foreign students from educational institutions or business personnel) who want to learn English while experiencing Canadiah culture. Programs can be designed to meet the unique needs of each group and may be combined with International Seminars to include content area study in addition to English.

International Seminars Program provides groups of foreign students and professionals exposure to current Australian perspectives and practices in their area of study or profession. Highly qualified professors and community professionals speak on topics requested by the sponsoring organization, with translation or in the participants' native language.

For more information on these classes, contact:

International Programs of Outreach College
University of Eastern Canada
2500 Dole Street, Krauss Hall 004
Toronto, Canada
Tel: (296) 956-7753 Fax: (296) 956-3421
E-mail: nice _ info@outreach.uea.edu.ca
Website: www.nice.uea.edu.ca

Indicate if each of the following statements is true or false according to the notice. In boxes 20 – 25 on your answer sheet, write ***TRUE*** if the statement is true; write ***FALSE*** *if it is false. If the notice does not contain relevant information about the statement, please write* ***NOT GIVEN***. *An example has been done.*

Example: Answer:
Outreach College is part of University of Southern Australia ***TRUE***

20. None of the courses include a writing component.
21. A student who needs to improve academic reading should study E.C.P.
22. A higher level of English is needed to study E.C.P. than to study S.E.P.
23. To study for a degree, one should complete S.E.P.
24. I.S.E. courses are more expensive than E.C.P. courses.
25. An I.S.E. course has more hours than an E.C.P. course.

Section 3 *Questions 26 – 40*

Questions 26 – 35

The passage "*Why Go to Canada*" *has eleven paragraphs* ***A – K***. Choose the most suitable headings for paragraphs ***B – K*** *from the list of headings below. Write the appropriate numbers (i – xiii) in boxes 26 – 35 on your answer sheet.*

NB: *There are more headings than paragraphs so you will not use all of them.*
You may use any of the headings more than once.

List of Headings

(i) Boosting chances of success
(ii) Anticipating problems
(iii) Two types of immigrants
(iv) Immigrants' contribution to Canada
(v) Lessons to be learned from extreme cases
(vi) Hire professionals to apply on your behalf
(vii) Improving chances if not qualified
(viii) Apply for immigration directly to the government
(ix) A land of attraction
(x) Avoiding costly mistakes
(xi) Either way, you make a choice
(xii) Highlighting qualifications
(xiii) Assessing chances of success

Example: Paragraph A Answer: ***ix***

26. Paragraph B ________
27. Paragraph C ________
28. Paragraph D ________
29. Paragraph E ________
30. Paragraph F ________
31. Paragraph G ________
32. Paragraph H ________
33. Paragraph I ________
34. Paragraph J ________
35. Paragraph K ________

Why Go to Canada?

A Huge, scenic and sparsely populated, Canada was rated by the United Nations Human Development Index as the best country to live in. The land of new hopes and opportunities attracts people worldwide — visitors, migrants and overseas students — and offers its permanent residents the sweetest benefit package who in turn contribute significantly to its economic growth, and bring customs and traditions, rituals and culture to the forefront of current government.

B Very few people really understand or know anything about the process of immigration application. First of all a potential immigrant needs to know something about the rules and regulations. The Canadian Government has designed a point system to assess potential independent immigrants. Emphasis is placed on education, practical training, experience and the likelihood of successful settlement in Canada. This means that people with a bachelor degree of some kind and advanced technical or other skills that are in demand in Canada are more likely to be accepted. The Government also adds weight to an application if the individual is fluent in Canada's official languages, English and French. Therefore someone with a good command of either English or French will have a better chance. Another way to immigrate to Canada is via the immigrant investor program. This provides an opportunity for experienced business persons to immigrate to Canada after making a substantial investment in a provincial government-administered venture capital fund.

C If you think you fulfill all the criteria you can easily apply for immigration by yourself. The Canadian Government clearly states: "Any one can apply without the help of a third party". As often happens in these situations, unscrupulous agents can take advantage of people who think that the only way they can immigrate is by paying huge amounts of money. People who want to become immigrants should carefully investigate the reputation and qualifications of third parties who offer their services for a fee. So why bother to use an immigration agent if application is easy?

D Actually there are many good reasons why so many intending migrants use such services. What the least competent and reliable professionals do is simply fill out the forms and send them to the Canadian Embassy with the required fees and documents! Some individuals (who can be referred to as "unscrupulous agents") may fail to send in the correct documents, delay the clients' application delivery, talk an unqualified candidate into buying their services despite the high possibility that the visa application will be refused or even suggest their clients supply fraudulent documents that are often discovered by the Canadian Embassy. Conversely, a highly qualified and reliable professional service justifies its costs for the comprehensive services it provides. A professional and reliable immigration firm should provide these five services for its clients:

E 1. An intending immigrant must first be well aware of his chances of success. A substantial amount of necessary payment and the potential impact on an applicant's life (i.e. thinking they will be accepted) can be avoided. A highly experienced immigration professional is capable of assessing a client's chances of success with an extremely high degree of certainty. In the case of a most unfavorable application, he discourages the client's application.

F 2. Depending on an effective interpretation of the selection rules as well as accumulated experiences, an experienced immigration professional highlights the applicant's qualities and helps persuade visa officials that the applicant is worthy of selection and meets all the selection criteria. If a person doesn't seem qualified, the adviser tries to find out other alternatives that may exist to make him a successful applicant. Such instances where qualified persons were discouraged from making applications are numerous. For example, a computer programmer whose professional skills are highly sought after in the Canadian labor market may be considered unqualified by the variance of their job description to the specifications in the National Occupational Descriptions published by the Canadian Government. An experienced immigration professional avoids areas of potential misunderstanding and best ensures that all the documents submitted and answers given at an interview will support a successful application.

G 3. The presentation or package of the application often makes a decisive impression on the visa officer. An experienced immigration professional identifies what type of information can be supplied that is most likely to favorably impress the visa officer considering the application.

H 4. In the case of a person who simply does not qualify, an immigration professional indicates the reasons that may lead to their visa application refusal and tries to find out ways to improve their circumstances so they become qualified.

I 5. Sometimes even highly qualified candidates finally end up in dismay for want of knowledge on migration affairs or misinterpretation of Canadian migration rules. In may cases, due to unnecessary concealing of certain facts that often lead to discovery, a supposedly successful application will be rejected and the applicant's personal credibility in future applications is ruined. A migration professional explains and convinces the visa officers that a person is highly qualified despite some minor factors that may be unfavorable to his application.

J 6. A seasoned immigration professional helps identify potential problems and provides advice in advance. An immigration professional is expected to be familiar with immigration law, s/he advises the applicant whether or not to submit certain complimentary documents, what evidence needs to be acquired to help support the candidate, and what should be avoided that may cause a negative impact on the application.

K Additionally, in the case of a refused application, a reliable immigration consulting firm should effectively defend its applicants from uneven interpretation, misapplication or even breaches of regulations. So, if you are interested in immigrating, you could try to apply on your own, or if you want to save yourself all the stress and confusion of applying, you could go for one of the reliable, professional immigration firms.

Questions 36 – 40

Complete the following summary of the reading passage. Choose ***NO MORE THAN THREE WORDS*** *from the passage for each answer.*

Many people from various countries are now thinking of emigrating to Canada. They can apply to the immigration authorities of the Canadian Government which has adopted ...(36)... to evaluate immigration applicants. The criteria for evaluation include education, training, skill and language, which means that people with a higher education background and having a skill that is needed in Canada plus good ...(37)... have good chances to emigrate.

There are two ways to apply for immigration. The first is to apply without the help of ...(38)..., which means the applicants contact the Canadian Embassy directly. Alternatively, applicants can hire professionals to apply on their behalf. This usually means to pay a substantial amount of money to immigration firms which in turn contact the Canadian Government and work through the application process. Though the former way costs much less, applicants may have difficulties or ...(39)... because the whole process can be complicated. Professional immigration firms, on the other hand, have the experience in dealing with legal matters that are part of the application process. The most important thing is to find the right firm, since there are ...(40)... firms that are not competent to represent applicants and will lead to applicants' loss of money and opportunity.

答案及题解

SECTION 1

Questions 1 – 5:

这是一家旅馆不同类型客房的价格表。

single 指 single room。同样,twin 和 double 分别指 twin room 和 double room。见模拟试题二 1 ~ 5题的说明。

1. **True** 表中的 twin 和 double 标价相同。
2. **False** 从常理上讲,海边的旅馆朝海一面的房间的景色好于另一面,这就是题中 a room with a better view 的所指。但从价格上看,这类房间(sea view bedrooms)的价格并未在不朝海的房间(rear view bedrooms)的价格上翻番。
3. **Not Given** 文中表明面向海和背向海客房价格不同。但从楼层上看,楼层越高,价格越便宜。因此无法判断顶层的房间是否有更好的景致。
4. **False** 价格为 £80 的套房就是单人套房。
5. **True** 见表下的两行说明。

Questions 6 – 9:

这是一篇电脑培训班的文章,教大家如何用 Photoshop 软件来加工照片。

6. **True** retouch:对文章、图片等进行修描、润色。
7. **False** Mtgs: Meetings。每个班只上两次课。
8. **Not Given** 此题虽有一定道理,但在文中没有文字上的支持。
9. **False** 参加者应对苹果系列电脑(Macintosh)有所了解,但并不需要有使用 Photoshop 的经历。

Questions 10 – 14:

这是某城市的一个公共汽车公司的运营说明。

10. **Tourist Ranger** 逗留二至五天的顾客买此票最划算。
11. **Bus Card** 此票一天有效,哪趟车都能坐,乘坐次数不限。
12. **Post office(s) / tobacconists**(街上的烟店)**/ BTB office(s)**
    公共汽车有两种颜色,市内车为橙色,市郊车为蓝色。市内车的各种车票可在上述三处购买,但不能在车上买。
13. **On the bus** 市郊车的票在车上买。
14. **(main) railway station / Goshley Square** Rashville 是市郊的一个镇。
    市郊车的起点站有两处:火车站和 Goshley 广场。

SECTION 2

Questions 15 - 19:

这是一种滴眼药的说明。

15. **topical**(局部的) **use**

16. **4 times**

17. **side effect / adverse reactions**

18. **running water**

19. **regular intervals**

Questions 20 - 25:

这是某学校为留学生开设的语言课程的介绍。

20. **Not Given** N.I.C.E.课程注意口语(emphasize spoken communication),但未必排斥其他,如阅读。S.E.P.课程可根据学生需要专门安排,但全文中均未说包括有写作内容。

21. **False** E.C.P.是口语课程。

22. **Not Given** 文章对这两类课程的难度或起点未做说明。

23. **False** 文中所有课程均不与学位课程挂钩。

24. **Not Given** 文中未提及任何一门课程的费用。

25. **False** 这两类课程的学时相同,均为 200 学时(10 周 × 20 学时)。

SECTION 3

Questions 26 - 40:

这是一篇某移民中介公司的宣传文章。

第 26 至 34 题为 match the headings。见前文关于这类题的说明。

26. **iii** 27. **viii** 28. **vi** 29. **xiii** 30. **xii** 31. **i** 32. **vii** 33. **x** 34. **ii**

35. **xi** 36. **a point system** 37. **English or French** 38. **a third party**

39. **confusion** 40. **unscrupulous**

第五章 写作考试

A类考生和G类考生都要在60分钟内完成两篇作文(见表2),但这两类考生的作文在体裁和题材方面均有所不同。A类考生的两篇作文是:1. 描述一个图或表中若干变量的趋势;2. 就某一种观点阐述自己的意见。G类考生的两篇作文是:1. 写一封信;2. 就某一种观点阐述自己的意见。两篇作文分别被称为Task 1和Task 2。Task 1的分量较轻,建议考生在20分钟内完成;Task 2的分量较重,建议考生在40分钟内完成。在评分上,Task 1占三分之一的比重,Task 2占三分之二的比重。A类与G类考生的Task 1完全不同,而Task 2虽然作文题目不同,所要完成的都是一篇论说文。下面将分别从A类和G类的Task 1以及两类的Task 2三个方面谈一些值得注意的问题。

	Task 1 主题	建议用时	评分比重	Task 2 主题	建议用时	评分比重
A类	描述图表	20 min.	1/3	论说文	40 min.	2/3
G类	写信	20 min.	1/3	论说文	40 min.	2/3

表2 两类考生的写作任务

一、A类的 Task 1

考生须描述一张图(柱形图、曲线图、饼图等)或由许多数字组成的表。首先,考生应先发现一些有意义、值得去描述的趋势及变量之间的关系,然后尽量详细的描述这些趋势及关系。描述时要避免重复使用单词或表达方法,要用多样的方法去描述增、减趋势。除了人人都熟悉的increase, decrease, rise, fall等几个最常用的词以外,考生还应掌握其他的表达方法,如slow down, level off, pick up speed, maintain, drop, the trend reverses, decline, gain / lose momentum等,见下面的几个例句。

The trend / momentum / increase slowed down in August.

八月份起,趋势(势头、涨幅)开始减缓。

The trend of reducing working hours began to gain momentum in the late 1960s.

60年代末,减少工时的势头开始走强。

The momentum of the drive for a cleaner environment accelerated from 1992.

1992 年起，清洁环境的运动的势头开始加强。

The rise lasted for three months and then began to level off in May.

增势持续了三个月之后于五月份开始走平。

Replacement of leaded gas with unleaded one picked up speed at the beginning of 1991.

1991 年初，无铅汽油取代含铅汽油的步子开始加快。

Though prices went up by 3%, the number of smokers maintained.

虽然价格上浮百分之三十，但烟民的数量未减。

不仅要用不同的方法来表述增、减，这些增、减的幅度也应尽量用不同的形容词或副词来形容。例如：

There was a minor drop in price in July.

七月份价格略有下降。

The trend reversed from mid 1980s: a steady increase was replaced by a decline.

80 年代中期情况开始反转，稳步的增长变成下降。

The cost went down and the sales went up accordingly.

成本下降，销量也相应增加。

The increase was slow but steady.

涨幅缓慢但稳健。

There was a dramatic drop of the number of accidents caused by drunk driving.

酒后开车引起的事故突然下降。

The fall lasted for six months but the reduction was negligible.

虽然连续六个月下降，但降幅微不足道。

There was a substantial increase of the consumption of decaffed coffee since the end of 1983.

1983 年末起，不含咖啡因的咖啡的消费量出现实质性增长。

Though there was a slight increase of rice production, the number of people affected by shortages of food continued to grow.

稻米产量虽略有增加，但受食品短缺影响的人数继续增加。

在写作时，特别要注意不要因字数不够而去分析势趋变化的原因。这部分考的就是描述能力，而不是分析能力。如一定要分析，切注意口吻，要留有余地，不能强加于人。例如：

The decline of sales figures was probably caused by the worsening of economic situation in nearby countries.

销售数字的下降可能是由周边国家的经济情况的恶化引起。

Fatigue may have been the reason for the sudden increase of the number of traffic accidents after 11 pm.

晚 11 时后交通事故数量突然增加的原因也许是疲劳。

The growth of the number of postgraduate students could be accounted for by decreased working opportunities.

就业机会减少,这也许是研究生数量增加的原因。

The shrinking of real estate markets could be attributed to the rise of interest rate.

不动产市场的萎缩也许是利息增长所致。

以上四个例句中的 probably, may have been the reason, could be accounted for, could be attributed to 均表现了留有余地、不强加于人的口吻。

另外,所分析出的原因(如周边国家的经济情况)也许未在图中得到显示,因此,还是应以描述为主。

例 1:

WRITING TASK 1

You should spend about 20 minutes on this task.

The table below is the income statement of a company. Write a report for the company's board of directors describing the information shown in the table.

You should write at least 150 words.

The Income Statement of OrpusTech Company for the Years 1996 – 2000 ($ 000)

	1996	1997	1998	1999	2000
Revenue Net sales	63,386	77,711	86,346	94,886	100,943
Costs and expenses					
Cost of sales	49,238	59,837	63,996	71,818	75,808
Selling expense	7,470	9,234	10,935	11,437	13,104
Administrative expense	2,684	3,867	5,490	5,795	7,038
Engineering expense	1,342	1,689	1,832	1,949	2,109
Gross income	2,652	3,084	4,093	3,887	2,884
Income taxes	1,081	1,281	1,630	1,505	1,254
Net income	1,571	1,803	2,463	2,387	1,630

The table is the income statement of the OrpusTech Company for the years 1996 - 2000. It shows figures of net sales, costs and expenses, gross income, income taxes and net income. Costs and expenses are further divided into cost of sales, selling expense, administrative expense and engineering expense.

It is shown that net sales grew steadily in the five year period, from $ 63,368,000 to $ 100,943,000. The profit, however, fluctuated. It went up three years in a row till 1998, which was the most profitable year, with a dramatic rise from $ 1,803,000 in 1997 to $ 2,463,000 in 1998. This is an increase of 37 percent. Then the profit declined in the following years. The biggest drop of net income occurred in 2000, which saw a decrease of 31 percent, from $ 2,387,000 to $ 1,630,000.

Attention should be drawn to the rise of selling and administrative expenses for the year 2000. Though net sales went up $ 6,057, increases of expenses on sales and administration were disproportionately large. (164 words)

简评：

表的数字很多，增减幅度、有意义的趋势不一目了然，这就需要更仔细地观察，有时还需做一点幅度或比例的简单计算。但最重要的还是指出最明显、最有意义的变化。利润自然是每个公司的最重要的指标，因此 Net income 的变化应是本报告的重点。另外，最后一年的利润大幅下降，指出销售及管理开销过高也是必要的。

例 2：

WRITING TASK 1

You should spend about 20 minutes on this task.

The diagram below shows changes of educational backgrounds of the employees of a company. Write a report for the company's general manager describing the information shown in the diagram.

You should write at least 150 words.

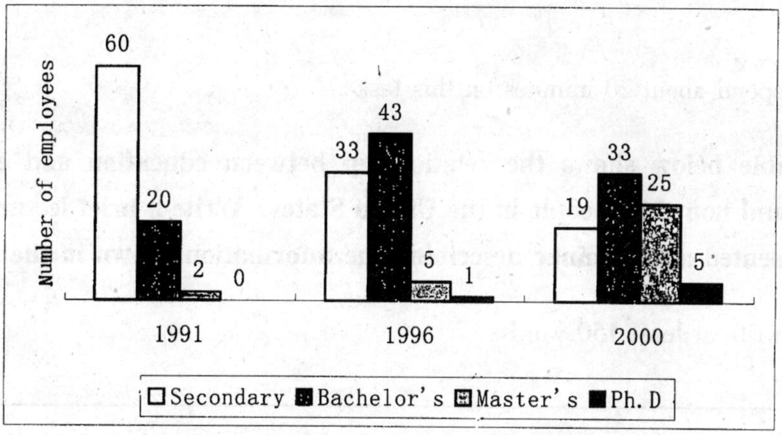

changes of employees' eclucation levels of the Alc company from 1991 to 2000

The diagram shows the changes in the last ten years of educational levels of staff members of the ALC Company. Staff members, according to the amount of education they had, are grouped into four categories. The first one is those who completed secondary education. The number of staff members in this group has been falling in the last ten years, from 60 in 1991 to 19 in 2000. The second group is those with a bachelor's degree only. Their number increased during the first half of the decade and then the trend reversed. Group three is those who have a master's degree. Their number grew all the way in the ten year period and it can be seen that the increase accelerated in the second half of the decade. People with Ph. D degrees are the last group. At the beginning of the ten year period, there was no one in the company who had a doctorate degree. Now there are five.
(161 words)

简评:

尽量避免使用已用过的单词。作文题中用了 educational backgrounds 和 employees,作文中用的是 educational levels 和 staff members。其他的例子有:category / group, ten year period / decade, Ph. D degree / doctorate degree。表示增减的词用了 fall, increase, the trend reversed, grew, the increase accelerated。写够 150 词不难,不必分析员工学历变化的原因,因为柱形图上根本未显示原因,亦不必指出员工学历的变化是否对公司有利。

为了方便读者练习,以下是十余个 A 类 Task 1 的题目。所有的题均由作者自编,没有所谓"真题"。题中涉及的数字均为杜撰,不是所涉及的公司或国家的真实数字。

Topic 1

You should spend about 20 minutes on this task.

The table below shows the relationship between education and earnings of white and nonwhite people in the United States. Write a brief lecture report to be presented at a seminar describing the information shown in the table.

You should write at least 150 words.

	Expected Lifetime Earnigs		
School years completed	White	Nonwhite	Nonwhite as percentage of white
Less than 8	$ 157,000	$ 95,000	61
8	191,000	123,000	64
9 to 11	221,000	132,000	60
12	253,000	151,000	60
13 to 15	301,000	162,000	54
16	395,000	185,000	47
17 or more	466,000	246,000	53

Relationship of education to white and nonwhite earnings

Topic 2

You should spend about 20 minutes on this task.

The table below shows the relationship between the amount of education of women with children and the number of births they gave. Write a brief lecture report to be presented at a seminar describing the information shown in the table.

You should write at least 150 words.

Education of women	Children ever born per ever-married woman
No education	4.7
Elementary	
1 – 4 years	4.5
5 – 7 years	3.9
8 years	3.3
High school	
1 – 3 years	3.1
4 years	2.8
College	
1 – 3 years	2.8
4 years	2.7
5^{+} years	2.5

Education of ever-married women, aged 35 – 39 compared to number of children ever born

Topic 3

You should spend about 20 minutes on this task.

The table below shows the relationship between the levels of education achieved by men and women and their income levels. Write a brief lecture report to be presented at a seminar describing the information shown in the table.

You should write at least 150 words.

Median Annual Income by Sex and Years of Schooling *

Schooling	Men	Women
Graduate school	$ 49,304(2.8)	$ 33,705(2.8)
College graduate	39,238(2.3)	28,017(2.3)
1 – 3 years college	31,734(1.8)	22,227(1.8)
High school graduate	26,635(1.5)	18,319(1.5)
9 – 12 years	20,602(1.2)	14,429(1.2)
8 years or less	17,394(1.0)	12,251(1.0)

* Persons age 25 years and over, working full time, 1990

Source: U.S. Bureau of the Census

<u>Topic 4</u>

You should spend about 20 minutes on this task.

The table below shows the enrollments of public and private institutions in the United States from 1955 to 1995. Write a brief lecture report to be presented at a seminar describing the information shown in the table.

You should write at least 150 words.

College Enrollment in the US, 1955 – 1995 (enrollments in thousands)

Year	Public institution	Private institution	Total enrollment
1995	1,484	1,117	2,601
1965	3,907	1,951	5,858
1975	8,835	2,350	11,185
1985	9,479	2,768	12,247
1995	11,695	3,251	14,946

Topic 5

You should spend about 20 minutes on this task.

The table below shows the estimated number of years for some countries to catch up with the current United States' GNP per capita. Write a brief lecture report to be presented at a seminar describing the information shown in the table.

You should write at least 150 words.

Country	1995 GNP Per capita (1995 US $)	Number of years needed to reach $ 7,200 per capita
Sweden	$ 4,994	11
France	3,848	18
United Kingdom	3,608	19
Japan	1,714	22
Israel	2,668	24
Australia	4,018	25
Thailand	252	98
Mexico	910	162
Colombia	554	358
Indonesia	198	593

Years needed to achieve current U.S. GNP per capita

Topic 6

You should spend about 20 minutes on this task.

The chart below shows the distribution of population in industrial and non-industrial societies. Write a brief lecture report to be presented at a seminar describing the information shown in the chart.

You should write at least 150 words.

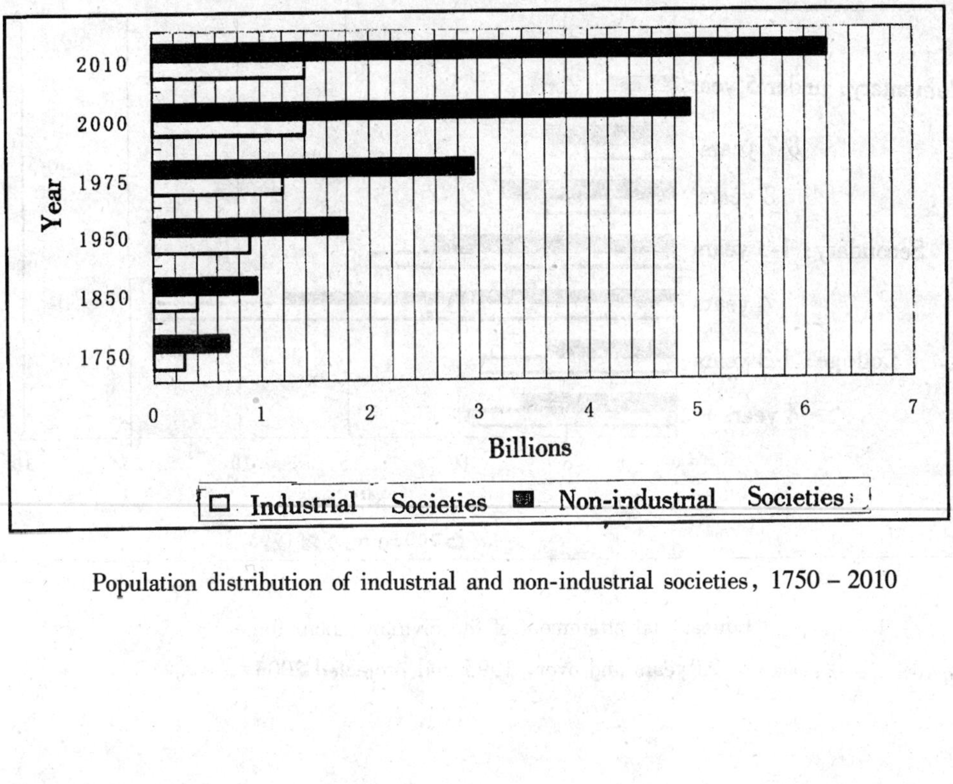

Population distribution of industrial and non-industrial societies, 1750 – 2010

Topic 7

You should spend about 20 minutes on this task.

The chart below shows the levels of education of people 25 years old and over. Write a brief lecture report to be presented at a seminar describing the information shown in the chart.

You should write at least 150 words.

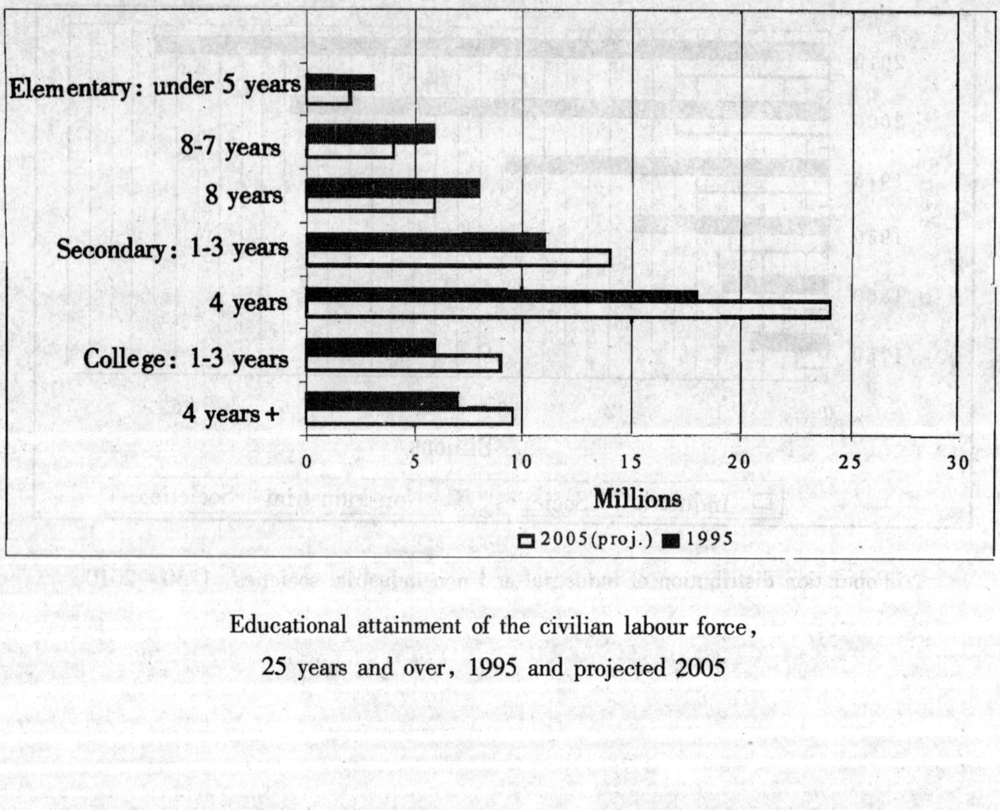

Educational attainment of the civilian labour force,
25 years and over, 1995 and projected 2005

Topic 8

You should spend about 20 minutes on this task.

> **The chart below shows the levels of power enjoyed by each department in three different companies and the average of 20 other companies. Write a brief report of the management of a company describing the information shown in the chart.**

You should write at least 150 words.

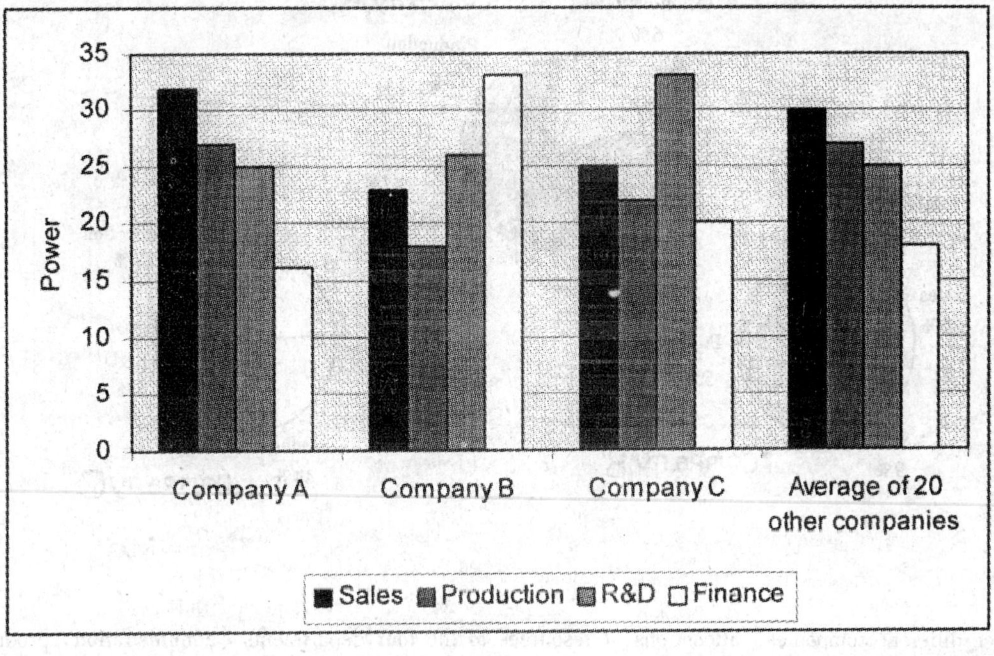

Topic 9

You should spend about 20 minutes on this task.

The chart below shows three different companies' allocations of resources to the four departments within each company. Write a report to the management of one of the companies describing the information shown in the chart.

You should write at least 150 words.

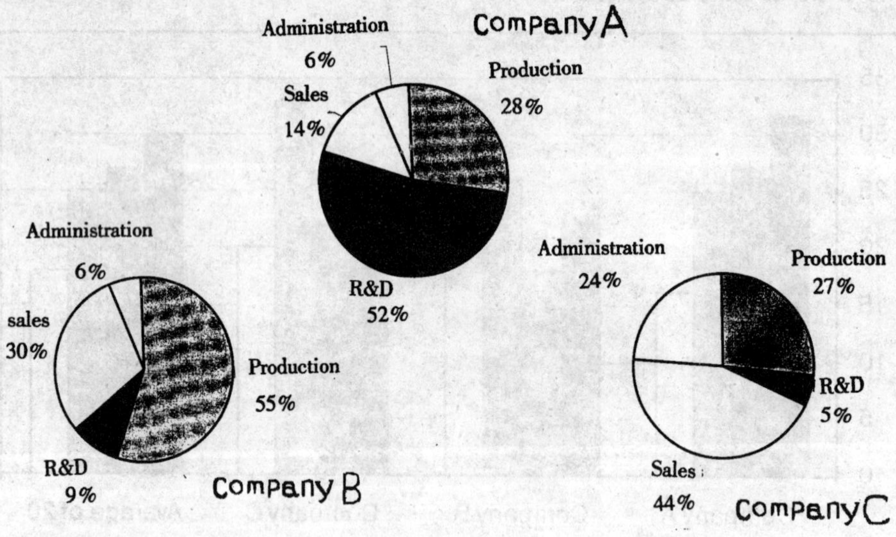

Three different companies' allocations of resources to the four departments (administration, production, research and development, sales)

Topic 10

You should spend about 20 minutes on this task.

The chart below shows the number of traffic accidents reported to the police of the city of Glasgow in the UK. Write a brief lecture report to be presented at a seminar describing the information shown in the chart.

You should write at least 150 words.

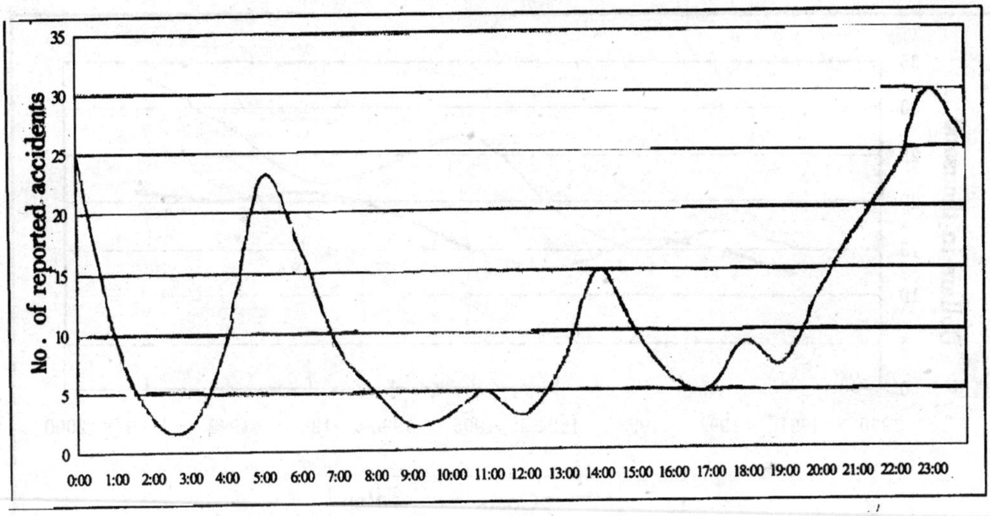

Average number of accidents reported to the Glasgow police in May 1999

Topic 11

You should spend about 20 minutes on this task.

The chart below shows the changes of costs and sales figures of a companey between 1991 and 1999. Write a report to the management of the company describing the information shown in the chart.

You should write at least 150 words.

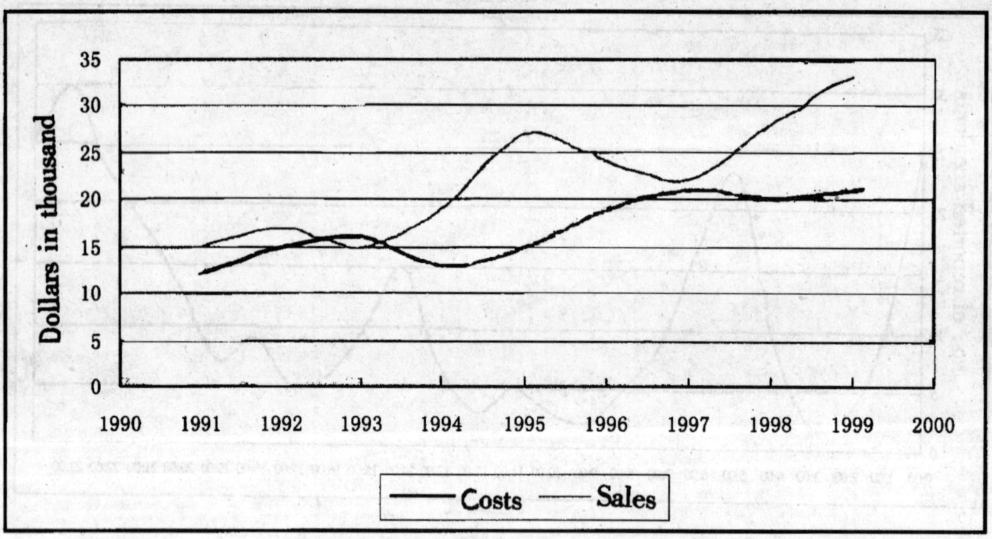

Changes of costs and sales figures between 1991 and 1999 of the T&T Company

二、G 类的 Task 1

考生应以解释、道歉、抱怨、祝贺、询问等为目的写一封信。

对许多考生来说，写信似乎比写论文容易。从比重上来看，也似乎应将重点放在 Task 2 上。但实际情况是，大多数考生虽然写过介绍自己的信，如求职、申请学校，但在表达道歉、抱怨等方面显得词不达意，很难用得体的词语来表达一些特殊的情感。解决这一问题的出路只能是多看范文，背一些较好的句型，然后多找一些相关的题目进行练习。

很多书信写作的教材中有很好的范例，但一般说来，写信人和收信人的地址完全没有必要写，但日期要写。要注意英文信函的日期的位置。如是给熟人写信，应以 first name 称呼，如 Dear Tom, Dear Kate 。如是给生人写信，则可用不同的称呼方式。

给报纸的"读者来信"栏目写信：Dear Editor:

给机构写信（询问、求职等）：Dear Sir / Madam:

给机构写信（抱怨、投诉等）：To Whom It May Concern 或 Dear Sir / Madam:

鉴于许多考生在一般的书信写作上均有一定的基础，本文不再赘述求职、自荐、询问等主题的写作模式，有需要者可在各类写作教材中找到大量的指导及范文。另外，考生不参考统一的模式，写出的作文有自己的特点，这也是笔者所希望看到的。在此仅对考生接触较少的一类信函 —— 投诉 —— 做一点介绍。

投诉信的一大特点是在信的开头以较强烈的口吻表达不满，在信的结尾表达对事件的圆满解决的期望。信的主体应以客观的态度描述事件的起因、过程、程度等。较常见的开始有：

Much to my regret, I write this letter to place a complaint against ...

I am writing to draw your attention to ...

I am sorry to point it out, but ...

I am afraid this is the most unsatisfactory ...

I feel something ought to be done about ...

I wish to complain in the strongest terms about...

常见的结尾有：

I look forward to a positive reply from you.

Please make sure that appropriate measures are taken to solve the problem.

I expect the courtesy of a prompt reply from you and the necessary remedial measures to be taken.

I expect to be informed of the development of the situation and would like to see a prompt settlement of the issue.

例 1:

WRITING TASK 1

You should spend about 20 minutes on this task.

At the airport of your traveling destination, you realized that your suitcase was broken and a few important items were missing. Write a letter to the airport authorities to complain the situation.

You should write at least 150 words.

July 21, 2000

Dear Sir / Madam:

I am writing this letter to complain the intolerable conduct of some of your staff. I traveled by TA508 from London to Emor on July 20, 2000, arriving at the Emor International Airport at 14:05. When I was waiting for my luggage, I was totally shocked to see my suitcase coming out on the belt — with the cover open!

It was a new suitcase with good locking mechanisms and reliable fastening belts. The following items were found missing:

1. *one bottle of Scotch whiskey*
2. *one pair of man's leather shoes*
3. *one compact Olympus camera*

These were new items that I bought a few days ago, with a total value of £230. Apparently, they were stolen at your airport, by your staff members!

I would like to see a timely investigation conducted and would like to be informed of the progress. Please e-mail me to charlier@fastmail.com. Meanwhile, please advise me of the compensation steps that I should take.

Charlie Robertson

(168 words)

简评:

先交代时间、地点、航班号等。目的地(Emor)是杜撰的,以免有诬告之嫌。考试时完全可以用一真实地名。衣箱质量可靠,有 good locking mechanisms and reliable fastening belts，如有破损，不应是货主的责任。所丢失的物品不应是珠宝、现金一类的东西，报价时不宜过高。结尾时留下联系方法，可以是电话号码或通讯地址。

例 2：

WRITING TASK 1

You should spend about 20 minutes on this task.

You are a student living in a dormitory building. Your next door neighbor frequently holds parties that last until very late and this disturbs you a lot. Write a letter to the management of the building to complain.

You should write at least 150 words.

July 21, 2000

Dear Sir / Madam:

I would like to complain to you about my noisy neighbor and hope you can do something about it.

I live in Room 221 and I have a habit of going to bed at about 11 pm. My next door neighbor, a student who lives in Room 223, frequently holds parties in the evening that sometimes last past midnight. He and his friends show no concern for others by playing wild music, talking loudly, and singing noisy songs. If this happened once or twice a month, I would try to be understanding and tolerant. However, these noisy parties are held at least twice a week, and not always at weekends.

I have spoken to my neighbor several times but he takes no notice of the complaints. I would like you to do something about it, and I am sure you agree that any student living in this building is entitled to peaceful evenings, at lease on weekdays. Or, give me a room on a different floor.

Sincerely

Michael Wang

(175) words

简评：

因邻居发出的噪音，晚上不能正常休息，这样的事例常见。关键是较细致地描述事件：parties past midnight, wild music, talking loudly, noisy songs。自己的态度及所采取的措施亦很重要：I would try to be understanding and tolerant. ... I have spoken to my neighbor several times.最后提出解决方法。

以下是一些供考生练习用的作文题，其中一部分是曾经使用过的真题。

1. Your friend is getting married. You have agreed to attend his/her wedding but now realize that you can't. Write a letter to your friend to explain.
2. You are going to attend a university course but now you are not able to start as planned. Write to the tutor to explain.
3. Arriving at an airport, you have found one of your bags missing. Write to the airline that you traveled by and ask the airline to find the bag.
4. Write a letter to a TV station to express your dislike for a program recently shown.
5. You have seen an attractive advertisement for a package tour. Write to the travel agency to ask for further details.
6. You've seen an advertisement for a sales position in an office furniture company. Write a letter to the company to express your interest in the job.
7. Your friend had a traffic accident. Though not badly injured, he/she is very upset emotionally. Write a letter to comfort him/her.
8. You bought a pair of shoes. When you arrived home, you found the shoes in the box were not the pair you selected in the shop. Write a letter to the shop.
9. You saw a customer being unreasonably rude to a shop assistant. Write to the shop to describe what you saw.
10. You just finished a word-processing course. You found it useful and write to your friend to recommend the course.
11. You returned home from a tour organized by a travel agency. You didn't like the tour and write to a newspaper to complain.
12. You prepared to be interviewed for a teaching position in a school. Now you are not able to be at the interview as agreed. Write to the school to ask to be interviewed at a different time.
13. You bought a CD player but found its quality poor. Write a letter to the shop where you bought it to express your wish to return it.
14. You are a tenant and have unintentionally damaged something that is the property of the owner. Write a letter to explain how it happened and apologize.

15. Write to a newspaper to express thanks for the reporters whose coverage of an important event was accurate and timely.

三、Task 2

一般来说,A类和G类的考生都应写一篇论说文。在每次考试中,这两类考生的作文题虽然不同,但在题材上没有本质的区别。如果一定要找出两类的差异,那就是A类考生的题目更偏重于“学术”,离老百姓的生活稍远,而G类考生的作文题则离日常生活更近一些。本章内所列出的所有Task 2作文题均为真题,但实在没有必要去追究哪些题是A类的,哪些题是G类的。

在写论说文时,考生一般会面对两个问题。一个是语言问题。这不是一日之功,要靠多年的英语学习逐步克服语法、词汇、习惯表达法、篇章的连惯表达等多方面的困难。这个问题还很自然地受到知识面、汉语修养等因素的影响。另一个问题是思维方式、表达方式的问题。这里重点讨论此问题。

一些专家认为,思维方式和表达方式具有文化特性。以英语写作为例,即使英语的语法、词汇等水平较高,也未必能按照英语是母语的人的思维去组织文章,将论点和论据用英美的模式呈现出来。美国的若干所大学曾做过一项研究,目的是了解文化背景对写作的影响。这项研究发现了东方式、斯拉夫式、阿拉伯式、西方式等写作模式。与我们有关的是西方式和东方式,因为我们是东方人,在用西方的语言写作,所写的文章又要由西方人评判。因此,我们要根据西方的“套路”来写。根据上述美国大学所做的研究,东、西方模式最突出地表现在以下三个方面:

1. 东方式的开头是 indirect,即间接、迂徊,而西方式的开头是 linear,即线性、直接。以“修地铁是中国大城市解决交通阻塞的惟一有效方法”为例,也许一个中国人会从邓小平南巡、改革进一步深化、人民生活水平提高、私车数量剧增这样一个形式做开场白。这种中国人的写作习惯,没有可以指责的地方,但用此法写一篇英文文章则有明显的兜圈子的色彩。而西方人的文章可能会以“Major cities all over the world face a common problem—traffic jams” 开头。这种写法开门见山,直扣主题。

2. 对于主题思想,东方模式给予充分的议论,以“修地铁”为例,用较多的篇幅讨论修地铁的意义,在西方人看来,这些讨论不直接与结论挂钩。西方模式会用较充分的论据、例子来说明主题思想。

3. 东方模式的结论缺乏实质内容,甚至可能用“让我们团结起来,为解决城市交通问题而共同努力”这样空洞的口号来结束全文。西方的模式可能会指出除修地铁以外的其他措施,并根据可行性、费用等情况具体推荐某种方法,如给公共汽车优先使用道路的权力。

笔者在此并无诽谤东方模式的意图，只是想提醒考生，不要简单地把英文创作变成汉译英，不要因为需凑够250词就胡乱加些空洞内容。上述“修地铁”的例子虽然有些夸张，但在我们的写作中有时仍可见到假大空的痕迹，因此应特别注意向所谓西方模式靠拢，以获得更好的成绩。

以下是其他一些应注意的事项。

1. 观点不要偏激

Task 2 的作文题常常是一个给正、反方都有争论余地的论点，如：

Computer games are harmful to children's development.

The use of monitors in places like banks and hotels violates people's right to privacy.

Convenience and comfortableness are the most important things to consider when selecting clothes. Fashions should be ignored.

The life styles in developed countries are responsible for the damages that have been done to the environment.

It is a waste to spend billions of dollars on space programs.

Young people now should enjoy life instead of saving money.

Most of the top positions in governments and enterprises are held by men. More positions should be reserved for women.

Leisure activities should be educational. Otherwise they are a waste of time.

Contrary to people's belief, international tourism does not promote understanding between people from different cultures.

Computers are becoming more important in education and will one day replace human teachers.

International sports events promote patriotism and enhance national pride.

在就这些论点发表议论时，不应表达偏激的思想，因为这样的思想可能会冒犯某些人。虽然大多数情况下阅卷者仅评判作文的语言，而不是作者的思想，但他们在评判语言时难免受到作者思想的影响，这种影响有时会影响到他们对作文的语言评判。记得我们曾参加过一次全国性的作文评判，作文题是“优秀运动员因获奥运会金牌而获巨额奖赏是否应该”。大多数作文表达了“应该，但希望政府能为提高全民素质给予更多的投入”等思想，但也有考生认为“不应该”、“大错特错”、“国家出钱培养他们，他们已领取了工资”、“许多为国家做出贡献的科学家、教师每月仅挣几百元，而他们就靠一跑一跳就挣了几百万”等等。这就是“偏激”的例子，总会有个别阅卷者很不欣赏这种思想，这样的作文也很可能由于思想偏激而少得几分。

2. 八股形式

据说英国人从古代中国学习了两件事。英国的公务员制度源自中国的科举制度;英国写作模式源自中国的八股文。此说法的准确程度不必去探讨,但这种“八股”形式的确在英文写作中有体现,其形式不外乎是“首先,其次,再者,最后……”。如何巧妙地运用这些表达顺序、层次的表示方法很重要,最重要的一条就是避免重复。在陈述论据时不应简单地用 first, second, third, ..., 还可选用 first, another, furthermore, finally。这当然不是惟一的方法,原则就是要用不同的词性、句中不同的位置等来表达并列或递进等关系。下文论述了继续教育的八个目的,请认真比较作者在表示顺序时所使用的不同方法(注意文中的黑体内容)。

The Purposes Of Continuing Education

What are the purposes of continuing career education? Some people think about the matter very simplistically, but most people realize that several goals must be sought simultaneously and that the process of doing this is difficult. We may identify at least eight purposes of continuing professional education.

The first of these is to keep up with the new knowledge required to perform responsibly in the chosen career. Just think, for example, how much has happened in the various professions in ten years. At the start of the decade, we had just learned how to keep a man in orbit around the earth; at its end, we had sent many men to the moon. At the same time, physicians and surgeons learned to save the lives of people who in previous times would have died. Patterns of resource allocation applied by public administrators are changing as a result of new doctrines. And pharmacists — perhaps more than the members of any other profession — have had to keep up with a changing scene, as new products and new therapies succeeded one another or enlarged the range of treatments available.

Practical careers rest upon theoretical bodies of knowledge. The health professions, including pharmacy, depend upon anatomy, physiology, pathology and biochemistry; agriculture is based upon soil chemistry, meteorology and plant pathology; and social work finds its roots in sociology, psychiatry and political science. The professional does not need to become expert in these underlying bodies of knowledge, but he or she does need to learn about developments in these fields. **Keeping up with changes in the relevant basic disciplines, therefore, constitutes the next aim.**

The third aim is to master new ideas about the nature of the profession itself. A recent study of dentistry noted that 25 or 30 years ago, dental practice was limited to relieving pain. Today it is concerned with the overall management of oral, facial and speech defects, and with the structures and tissues of the mouth as they relate to the total health of the individual. In other occupations, an equally profound change has occurred and the modern practitioner who does not understand that fact is obsolete.

The fourth purpose of career-oriented continuing education is to prepare the individual for changes in his or her career. A person may move in one of many directions, such as from generalist to specialist, from one speciality to another, upward in a hierarchy from a lesser to a more responsible job of the same sort, or into a completely new career.

In every kind of career, people go stale after a while. Consequently, maintaining freshness of outlook on one's work so that detail is not neglected, is also important. **This forms the next aim.** Perhaps education is not the only way to achieve this, but it can at least be aided by educational means, for example, by supervisory training, by self-appraisal and by peer review. It can also be achieved by putting oneself in a new work or study situation which demands attention to detail.

Continuing to grow as a well-rounded person is essential as well. The mind should never be fully engaged in the practice of work, to the exclusion of all other matters. One needs to withdraw from that practice occasionally so that one can be stimulated by contemplating theory or by seeking understanding and skill in different aspects of life. Otherwise, one becomes dogmatic, not only about a single speciality but about all aspects of life. **This, then, is another aim of continuing professional education.**

The seventh objective is to retain the power to learn. This objective is an important adjunct to all the others. The skills of mastering knowledge are like other skills: they are learned by practice, they are lost if they are not used regularly, and they can later be regained only with difficulty.

Finally, it is essential to ensure that the individual performs effectively the role imposed by membership in a profession. The professional must learn how to take collective responsibility, to make right choices on issues, to improve and extend the delivery of service, to collaborate with other professions, and to help monitor the actions of fellow professionals.

These eight purposes suggest that a fully fledged program of continuing professional education cannot be developed either easily or rapidly.

3. 关于写作文的"ideas"

前文说到,Task 2 的作为题常常是一个给正、反方都有争论余地的论点。这一类题通常是先陈述一种观点,然后问:To what extent do you agree? 这个问题实际上是在问：How much do you agree?

还有一些题要求考生从伦理、法学、社会等方面去阐述自己对某一现象或事物的看法，如：

What shall we do about young children who have committed serious crimes?

If a house owner shots dead a burglar who breaks into his house at night, is his act within legal range?

对于这样的作文题，考生一般能举出一些具体、生动的事例作为论据。由于社会、文化、科技发展等方面的不同，考生可能会遇到在西方已经过广泛议论，但对中国人来说是比较生疏的题目，这时我们会感到缺乏足够的论据来议论这个题目。例如：

Technological and scientific development will inevitably lead to a conflict between technology and traditional values.

大多数考生，不论是 A 类还是 G 类，都受过多年教育，又在为出国做准备，可谓见多识广。但由于这种文化或科技上的差异，不少考生会感到在论据的组织方面手足无措，根本的原因就是缺乏 ideas，十年前就有考生因碰到与电脑有关的作文题但自己从未接触过电脑而不能充分地发挥。上述关于传统价值与科技发展的冲突的问题，如不针对生物、遗传等研究所带来的伦理问题展开议论，很难写好这篇作文。面对“缺乏 ideas”的问题，考生除了要有较好的英文水平，能做到“能言善辩”以外，还应有宽广的知识面，做到“见多识广”。后者是前者得以发挥的基础，但知识面的问题不是英语课上所能解决的问题。

以下是在雅思考试中出现过的一些其他作文题：

What changes has electricity brought to your life?

What would our life be like in the year 2100?

Should parents pay for their children's education or should it be free?

What are the advantages and disadvantages of co-education (男女同校)?

What are the advantages and disadvantages of "equal job, equal pay"?

How are population, poverty and pollution interrelated?

What can we do to make our cities cleaner and safer?

A businessman has donated a huge amount of money to a school. Write a proposal to the school authorities about how to use this money.

Write a letter to the headmaster of a school to persuade him to buy more computers.

例 1:

WRITING TASK 2

You should spend about 40 minutes on this task.

> **The life styles in developed countries are responsible for the damages that have been done to the environment. To what extent do you agree with the statement?**

You should write at least 250 words.

Since the industrial revolution in 1760s, the economies in industrialised countries have been based on the burning of fossil fuels which releases carbon dioxide into the atmosphere. One of the environmental problems is the global warming caused by this. The use of CFCs also adds to the warming problem. It also depletes the ozone layer which protects us from damaging UV rays. Therefore it is safe to say that most of the environmental problems in the world have been caused by industrialised countries. Take America for instance. It is consuming disproportionately large amount of resources and adding comparable amounts of waste to the environment.

However, in the last one hundred years or so, Western people's awareness of environmental problems has been growing. So have science and technology to overcome environmental problems. London is not a foggy city anymore, and the river Danube is cleaner than before.

Developing countries, on the other hand, are catching up, both in life styles and in their shares of environmental damages. These countries typically have larger populations and lower level of conservation consciousness. When industries develop, it has substantial effect on the world's environment. There have been bad cases of poisoning of people and extinction of animal species because of pollution.

Though developing countries are causing more and more world's environmental problems, their wish for a better life and their measures for fulfilling the wish should not be inhibited. They should be given allowances to grow their awareness of environmental issues and their abilities to make a cleaner environment. (254 words)

简评：

首先指出发达国家在工业化进程中在二氧化碳和 CFCs(chlorofluorocarbons)的排放,原则上同意 the statement。但马上指出发达国家在环保意识和技术方面的进步以及成就。这种说法既客观,又不会冒犯考官。考官们对发展中国家的环境情况有切身的了解,因此不应只谴责别人,不做自我批评。文章的第3段指出发展中国家人口多,环保意识差,又迫切需要发展,并举例说明环保问题。最后指出,要给发展中国家时间,让其意识及环保措施得到发展。

此文的段落清晰,没有用"八股"手法表明层次。

例2:

WRITING TASK 2

You should spend about 40 minutes on this task.

Contrary to people's belief, international tourism does not promote understanding between people from different cultures. To what extent do you agree?

You should write at least 250 words.

Every year, hundreds of millions of people move around to see a different part of the world. It is natural to assume that tourists who have seen other countries have a better knowledge of the people. That assumption also leads to the conclusion that international tourism promotes understanding between nations. How true is this? Let us examine what tourists do in a different country.

First, before going abroad, tourists are often told by their travel agents of the possible hazards which sometimes include local people. They are given examples of extreme cases where victims are always the travelers. Then, when they arrive, they are immediately taken to their hotels in big coaches. They flood places where local people don't go. Their shopping, meals, entertainment all take place in secluded areas. They wear a bubble all the way. Apart from speaking to the guide and a few shop assistants, tourists rarely talk to the local people. To make it even worse, they meet pickpockets, they are ripped off by dishonest traders. Furthermore, very few local people bother to talk to them out of a genuine interest in the guests' country, people and culture. Therefore, when asked how much they know about the local people, their answer is "very little".

If someone really wants to understand a different culture, he has to learn its language, stay there for at least a few month without wearing a bubble, learn how to curse and swear, bargain with a vegetable vender and then he can say that he understands the people.(261 words)

简评:

这是一个已在西方得到广泛讨论的题目,普遍被接受的答案是旅游起不到促进民族、文化之间的交流与理解的作用。

不同文化所推崇的东西也不同,这里有一个 political correctness 的问题。要注意西方的时尚,如裘皮大衣、红木家具就不为青年人所推崇,参加旅游团也是退休的老头、老太太们的事。我们所追求的内容,如私人轿车、(旅行团式的)出国旅游在一些西方人看来有点"傻"。一些雅思考官就是这样的人。他们理应只评判我们的语言,但内容上使他们感到可以接受,至少不难接受岂不更好?

注意第 2 段中 first, then, to make it even worse, furthermore 的用法。

四、其他注意事项

1. 分清主次

从时间上看,Task 1 占三分之一,评分时的比重也自然不及 Task 2。一定要遵守时间,做到在 20 分钟内完成,否则就是拣芝麻,丢西瓜。这一点意义重大,但许多人做不到。常常有考生在 Task 1 上花了近 30 分钟。克服这一困难的另一办法是先写 Task 2,在 40 分钟左右时将其完成,再写 Task 1 。如决定这样做,应先进行一番演练,最好不要在考试时突然改变自己习惯了的方式。

2. 找"高手"评判

作文写得怎样,最好找个有较强写作能力的人评判。重要的不是某篇作文能得多少分,而是文章中有哪些不足,应如何改进。很多考生身边也许没有这样的高手,那只好自力更生,按实战要求去写,然后通过看范文找出不足,在下一篇作文中克服这些不足。除此之外没有更好的办法。最忌讳的就是背整篇的范文,然后根据实际作文题背写出一篇作文。曾出现过十余名考生写作成绩都是零分,原因是他们的作文如出一辙,考官认为他们作弊。

3. 要抄写作文题吗?

许多考生问是否要将作文题抄写在卷面上。不用。由于考生对此事的关注,我们曾与一位考官认真地交流过这个问题。他的回答是:1)阅卷的考官完全清楚每一批作文的题目,作文是否有标题丝毫不影响作文质量;2)没有作文题也就不会跑题(这一点是相对而言,不写作文题完全不等于可以文不对题。这里所说的不跑题是指有更广阔的发挥空间);3)将作文题原封不动地抄在卷面只能被认为是在凑字数;4)试卷上规定的作文题只是一个思想,而不是一个标题,例如:Some people think computers will eventually replace human teachers. To what extent do you agree or disagree? 前面的陈述可以作为文章的开场白,但不能作为标题,而后面的问题则更不能出现在标题中;5)要想有一个标题就得花时间去措词,这会浪费时间。

4. 信的格式

写信时是否要严格遵守英文的书信格式,即在信的正文上方写上写信人和收信人的姓名、地址、日期等。一般来说,写信人和收信人的地址完全不必写,但应有日期。要注意日期的位置和格式(见范文)。结尾处应有签名。

5. 钢笔还是铅笔?

在做听力和阅读试题时应用铅笔,写作文时可选择铅笔或钢笔。但为了便于修改,建议使用铅笔。大可不必怕用铅笔会被人看成 childish。

6. 是否有时间打草稿?

没有。在作文题旁边的空白处可以大概地勾划作文的框架,但没有时间,也没有地方(考试时不发稿纸,也不许带稿纸)打草稿。只能根据在作文题旁构划的框架一气呵成。

附录

1. IELTS 考试报名表

IELSTS Application Form

Please return to:

Centre stamp

Candidate's photo

1 Preferred Date of Test

____/ ____/ ____
(*day / month / year*)

Second Choice

____/ ____/ ____
(*day / month / year*)

For Office Use Only

Scheme:

Test Date ____/ ____/ ____
(*day / month / year*)

Date of Payment ____/ ____/ ____ Receipt Number
(*day / month / year*)

ID Checked/Absent Administrator's initials
(*circle as appropriate*)

2 Family Name ______________________ 3 Dr Mr Mrs Miss Ms
(*circle as appropriate*)

4 Other name(s) ______________________
(*These names must be the same as the names on your national identity document*)

5 Address for correspondence ______________________

____

____

6 Tel.No ____________ 7 Date of Birth ____/ ____/ ____ 8 Sex F / M
(*day / month / year*) (*circle as appropriate*)

9 ID Type: Passport / ID Card ID Document Numer ____________
(*circle as appropriate*) (*This document must be brought to the test*)

For questions 10 – 13 please enter codes. Codes will be found at the end of the IELTS Handlook.

10 Nationality ________ ☐☐☐ 11 First Language ________ ☐☐☐

12 Occupation (Sector)____________(Level)____________________ ☐☐☐

13 Why are you taking this test? ☐

14 Which country are you applying / intending to go to? (*circle as appropriate*)

Australia / Canada / New Zealand / Republic of Ireland / United Kingdom / United States of Ammerica / Other

15 Which IELTS Module are you taking? Academic General Training (*circle as appropriate*)

16 **HAVE YOU TAKEN IELTS BEFORE**? Yes No (*circle as appropriate*)

(*You are not allowed to repeat the test within* 3 *months at any centre*)

17 Most recent test details: Centre Name ____________ Date ____ / ____ / ____

Centre Number ☐ (*day / month / year*)

18 What level of education have you completed? (*circle as appropriate*)

Secondary up to 16 years/ Secondary 16 – 19 year/ Degree or equivalent/ Post-graduate

19 How many years have you been studying English? (*circle as appropriate*)

Less than 1	1	2	3	4	5	6	7	8	9 or more

20 Please give details below where you would like your results sent to (*if known*)

Name of Person / Department ____________________

Name of College / University / Institution ____________________

Address ____________________

____

IELTS entry requirement (Band, *if known*) ☐

Name of Person / Department ____________________

Name of College / University / Institution ____________________

Address ____________________

____

IELTS entry requirement (Band, *if known*) ☐

21 Do you have any special needs? ____________________

I certify that the information on this form is complete and accurate to the best of my knowledge.

I understand that I must not attempt to re-take IELTS at any centre within 3 months.

Signature ____________________ Date ____ / ____ / ____

(*day / month / year*)

2. IELTS 考点

北京:北京语言文化大学国外考试中心
北京市海淀区学院路 15 号　100083

上海:华东师范大学国外考试中心
上海市中山北路 3663 号文科楼 5 楼　200062

广州:仲恺农业技术学院 IELTS 考试中心
广州市河南纺织路东沙街 24 号　510225

成都:四川大学出国人员培训部考试办公室
成都市一环路南一段 24 号四川大学(西区)　610065

南京:南京东南大学外语系
南京市四牌楼 2 号　210018

西安:西安出国人员部考试办公室
西安外国语学院　710061

杭州:浙江新通出国留学服务中心
杭州市朝晖六区上塘路 238－1 号　310014

武汉:湖北省教育国际交流协会
武汉市武昌洪山路 8 号　430071

沈阳:辽宁教育国际交流服务中心
辽宁省沈阳市皇姑崇山东路 46－1 号　110032

福州:福建省教育国际交流中心
福州市鼓屏路台后 8 号左海花园　350003

深圳:深圳赛格人才培训中心
深圳市华强北路经济大厦 7 楼东　518031

香港:英国文化委员会
香港金钟法院道 3 号

实验考点:
天津:美通外国语培训中心天津市津沽进修学院
天津市和平区鞍山道 129 号　300070

济南:山东工业大学学术交流中心
山东济南市千佛山路 6 号　250014